More praise for *Israel in Afri...*

'This captivating book tells the ... misunderstood, story of Israel's i... ...rica over the last decades. From defence and ...tractive industries to migration, as well as the way in which the diplomatic jostling over Palestine and the ubiquitous rivalry with Iran play out on the continent, *Israel in Africa*'s insights deserve a broad readership.'
Ricardo Soares de Oliveira, University of Oxford

'The story of Israel's new alliances on the African continent is largely untold. Gidron does us a service by making them the subject of his book. *Israel in Africa* takes its place in a new wave of indispensable scholarship appraising the fast-changing place of African states in international relations.'
Jonny Steinberg, Oxford University

African Arguments

Written by experts with an unrivalled knowledge of the continent, African Arguments is a series of concise, engaging books that address the key issues currently facing Africa. Topical and thought-provoking, accessible but in-depth, they provide essential reading for anyone interested in getting to the heart of both why contemporary Africa is the way it is and how it is changing.

African Arguments Online

African Arguments Online is a website managed by the Royal African Society, which hosts debates on the African Arguments series and other topical issues that affect Africa: http://africanarguments.org

Series editors

Adam Branch, University of Cambridge

Alex de Waal, World Peace Foundation

Richard Dowden, journalist and author

Alcinda Honwana, Open University

Ebenezer Obadare, University of Kansas

Carlos Oya, SOAS, University of London

Managing editor

Stephanie Kitchen, International African Institute

Published by Zed Books and the IAI with the support of the following organisations:

The principal aim of the **International African Institute** is to promote scholarly understanding of Africa, notably its changing societies, cultures and languages. Founded in 1926 and based in London, it supports a range of seminars and publications including the journal Africa.
www.internationalafricaninstitute.org

The **Royal African Society** is a membership organisation that provides opportunities for people to connect, celebrate and engage critically with a wide range of topics and ideas about Africa today. Through events, publications and digital channels it shares insight, instigates debate and facilitates mutual understanding between the UK and Africa. The society amplifies African voices and interest in academia, business, politics, the arts and education, reaching a network of more than one million people globally.
www.royalafricansociety.org

The **World Peace Foundation**, founded in 1910, is located at the Fletcher School, Tufts University. The Foundation's mission is to promote innovative research and teaching, believing that these are critical to the challenges of making peace around the world, and should go hand in hand with advocacy and practical engagement with the toughest issues. Its central theme is 'reinventing peace' for the twenty-first century.
www.worldpeacefoundation.org

About the author

Yotam Gidron is a researcher whose writing focuses on migration, state-society relations and popular culture in Africa and Israel/Palestine. He has worked with human rights organisations in Israel and in East Africa, and is currently pursuing a PhD in African History at Durham University.

ISRAEL IN AFRICA

SECURITY, MIGRATION, INTERSTATE POLITICS

YOTAM GIDRON

In association with
International African Institute
Royal African Society
World Peace Foundation

ZED

Israel in Africa was first published in 2020 by Zed Books Ltd, The Foundry, 17 Oval Way, London SE11 5RR, UK.

www.zedbooks.net

Typeset in Haarlemmer by seagulls.net
Index by Rohan Bolton
Cover design by Jonathan Pelham
Cover photo © Robin Hammond, Panos Pictures

Printed and bound by CPI Group (UK) Ltd, Croydon, CR0 4YY

A catalogue record for this book is available from the British Library

ISBN 978-1-78699-503-2 hb
ISBN 978-1-78699-502-5 pb
ISBN 978-1-78699-504-9 pdf
ISBN 978-1-78699-505-6. epub
ISBN 978-1-78699-506-3 mobi

[A]ll of us are determined to remain outside world conflicts which do not concern us; singly we are too weak to avoid being used by those whose help we need, but together we shall be able to accept aid and investment without endangering our national integrity and independence. It is in this spirit that we are working towards African Unity. We have no desire to isolate our continent from the rest of the world, nor to build an aggressive, hostile continent.

Julius Nyerere to David Ben-Gurion, 22 June 1963[1]

CONTENTS

TABLES AND FIGURES

LIST OF ABBREVIATIONS

AIPAC	American Israel Public Affairs Committee
ANC	African National Congress (South Africa)
AU	African Union
BADEA	Arab Bank for Economic Development in Africa
BDS	Boycott, Divestment and Sanctions
BIR	Rapid Intervention Battalion (Cameroon)
CAR	Central African Republic
CUFI	Christians United for Israel
DEISI	Defend Embrace Invest Support Israel
DRC	Democratic Republic of the Congo
ECOWAS	Economic Community of West African States
ELF	Eritrean Liberation Front
ICEJ	International Christian Embassy in Jerusalem
IDF	Israel Defense Forces
IEC	Israel Electric Corporation
IMF	International Monetary Fund
IRRI	International Refugee Rights Initiative
IWI	Israel Weapon Industries
MASHAV	Israel's Agency for International Development Cooperation
MPLA	People's Movement for the Liberation of Angola
NGO	nongovernmental organisation
OAU	Organisation of African Unity
ODA	Official Development Assistance
OECD	Organisation for Economic Co-operation and Development

PFLP	Popular Front for the Liberation of Palestine
PLO	Palestine Liberation Organization
REG	Rwanda Energy Group
RSD	Refugee Status Determination
SAFI	South African Friends of Israel
SAZF	South African Zionist Federation
SIBAT	International Defense Cooperation Directorate (Israel)
SPLA	Sudan People's Liberation Army
UAE	United Arab Emirates
UNESCO	United Nations Educational, Scientific and Cultural Organization
UNGA	United Nations General Assembly
UNHCR	United Nations High Commissioner for Refugees
UNITA	National Union for the Total Independence of Angola
ZCC	Zion Christian Church

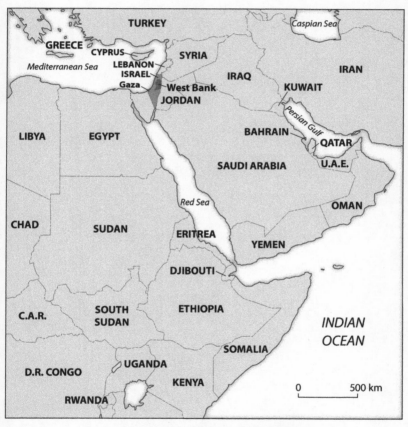

Israel, north-eastern Africa and the Middle East

ACKNOWLEDGEMENTS

Although while writing this book I spent many long days alone in libraries and in front of my laptop in the UK, Israel and Ethiopia, it draws on experiences and insights gained over close to a decade of working, studying, researching and interacting with a great number of people in these countries and others. Any mistakes, intellectual flaws and inaccuracies the following pages include are solely my own, but this book would never have been written if not for the guidance and support of many other individuals.

Among my mentors, colleagues and friends in Israel, I must mention Rami Gudovitch and Orit Marom, who first worked with me and guided me as an activist before and during the expulsion of the South Sudanese community from Israel in 2012, Inbal Ben-Yehuda and Yael Even-Or, who encouraged me to start writing on African and Israeli–African issues, in Hebrew, around that time as well, and Adi Drori-Avraham, who later helped remotely when I was researching Israel's transfer schemes with Rwanda and Uganda. I am especially grateful for the multiple opportunities I had to learn from and work with the lawyers of the Refugee Rights Clinic at Tel Aviv University – Anat Ben-Dor, Aelad Cahana and Yuval Livnat – before, during and after my time as a student in this institution.

Parts of this book draw on data gathered from 2015 as part of my work with the International Refugee Rights Initiative (IRRI) in Uganda. Olivia Bueno, Lucy Hovil, David Kigozi, Andie Lambe, Thijs Van-Laer and Tigranna Zakaryan all supported, in different ways and at different times, my research on Israel's refugee transfer schemes, as well as on several other issues not immediately linked to this book. Lucy has repeatedly encouraged me to take on projects that I myself did not initially know were within my capacity, and I owe her many thanks for that. Her guidance and advice have been instrumental in shaping my academic and professional path in recent years. Tigranna helped with investigating Israel's transfer schemes in 2017–18, as part of a joint monitoring project carried out by IRRI, the Hotline for Refugees and Migrants (Israel) and ASSAF (Aid Organization for Refugees and Asylum Seekers in Israel).

The book also draws on my research on Israel's involvement in Sudan's first civil war, conducted while I was a student in the African Studies Centre at the University of Oxford and supervised by Sebabatso Manoeli. This research drew me into writing about Israeli–African engagements in an academic environment despite my initial inclination to avoid this field, which, after several turbulent years of working with refugee rights organisations, felt too personal and controversial for further interrogation. The research was based on archival sources from Israel, the UK and Italy and interviews with former Mossad officials, and was published as an article in 2018 in *Journal of Eastern African Studies* (12 (3): 428–53). Although this book only deals with this topic briefly, this research informed my views and analysis on some of the wider issues discussed here.

Ken Barlow, then of Zed Books, first suggested writing a book on Israel's relationships with African countries following a short text I published on the African Arguments blog (africanarguments. org). I thank him for instigating this project. Cherry Leonardi and Jacob Wiebel helped me navigate between this project and my other academic obligations as a student in Durham University's Department of History. Stephanie Kitchen of the International African Institute guided me throughout the proposal and writing process and read the manuscript at several stages as I amended and revised it. François-Xavier Ada Affana, Arshmeena Durrani, Jacob Wiebel, Justin Willis and three anonymous reviewers also read earlier drafts of the manuscript or parts of it. I thank them all for their enlightening criticism and constructive comments.

Although this book does not explore their experiences and circumstances in great detail, I am indebted to the South Sudanese families who opened their lives and houses to me, first in Israel and, after leaving the country in 2012, in South Sudan, Uganda and Ethiopia. For reasons of privacy, I decided not to list their names here, but they have taught me a great deal about both Israel and Africa, and unknowingly set me off on a journey I could never have predicted. I am similarly grateful to the many other Sudanese and Eritreans who shared with me their life histories, experiences and dilemmas in recent years, as well those serving or former Israeli officials, not all of whom wished to be named and quoted here, who took the time to talk to me while I was working on this book. Unless mentioned otherwise, interviews referenced here were conducted in Hebrew. Quotes were translated by me.

My sisters, Moran, Inbar, Tehila and Naama, provided invaluable encouragement during the writing of this book, even when we were on different continents. They also often sent me materials from libraries in Israel when I was away. My parents, Adi and Rafi, taught me to ask questions, and then encouraged me to follow my curiosity even when it took me to unexpected places. This book is for them.

INTRODUCTION

On 28 November 2017, Israeli Prime Minister Binyamin Netanyahu embarked on a one-day visit to Nairobi. This was – Netanyahu
made sure to mention multiple times – his 'third visit to Africa' in
less than two years. The formal justification for the hasty trip was
attending Uhuru Kenyatta's swearing in ceremony for a second
term, after he won a contentious election boycotted by the opposition. The main aim, however, seemed to be publicity – perhaps
an improvised substitute for the widely celebrated Africa–Israel
summit that was planned to take place in Lomé a month earlier and
was 'postponed' amidst a political crisis in Togo and rumours that
it was being undermined by pressure from Arab countries and calls
for boycott. Netanyahu's formal announcement upon his departure
revealed little – merely that it was part of Israel's efforts to 'deepen
ties with Africa'.[1]

For security reasons, the Israeli prime minister did not partici-
pate in the main inauguration ceremony in Kasarani Stadium, where
tens of thousands of Kenyans gathered, but he did attend the exclusive luncheon, where he also had the opportunity to give a short
speech. Standing in front of several African leaders and hundreds
of high-level government officials and diplomats, Netanyahu duly
began by congratulating Kenyatta for his electoral success, but
quickly moved on to singing the praises of Israel's cooperation with
African countries and his aspiration to enhance it. 'We believe in
Africa, we believe in Kenya', he reassured the audience. 'We love
Africa.' He also called on the present leaders to support Israel's

bid for observer status at the African Union (AU) and stressed the importance of cooperation in the face of terrorism. 'There is a savage disease', he passionately warned. 'It rampages so many countries. Boko Haram, al-Shabaab … if we work together, we'll defeat the barbarians!'[2]

That same evening, Yohanes was sitting in the small Eritrean restaurant in Kampala where he worked as a cook and a waiter.[3] He was watching the news, and he was not impressed by Netanyahu's statements. In fact, he was irritated – so much so that when I met him and some of his friends a few days later in that same restaurant, he brought up Netanyahu's Kenyan speech without me even asking about it. 'Here he says he loves Africa but there he treats us as if we are not human beings', he protested, as if he was trying to make sure that I, the Israeli visitor, was fully aware of his resentment. His friends – all Eritreans who had previously sought asylum in Israel – seemed less preoccupied with Netanyahu. They were similarly relieved that they no longer had to live under the burden of Israel's asylum and visa bureaucracies but were more ambivalent with regard to other experiences they had in the Jewish state. As we were talking, a playlist that one of them set up was playing in the background, alternating between reggae and popular Israeli *Mizrahi* music.[4]

Yohanes migrated to Israel in 2010, travelling from Eritrea, via Sudan and Egypt. He spent five years working as a cleaner in malls and wedding venues, renewing his temporary visa every few months, before being ordered to relocate to an 'open residency facility' for 'infiltrators' in the middle of the Negev desert in southern Israel. After six months in the desert and thanks to the effective persuasion efforts of Israeli officials, like many other Eritreans, he decided to accept the Israeli government's offer and leave for Uganda. He had never been there before and had no clear idea what he would do once he arrived, but he was willing to take a chance. Life in Israel seemed to have reached a dead end. A free one-way ticket and a departure grant of $3,500 were provided by the Israeli authorities as an additional incentive. Soon, he was living undocumented in the Ugandan capital – one of hundreds, if not thousands, of men, women and children in that city who had travelled through a similar route.

Reconsidering Israel in Africa

While the media has certainly taken note of Israel's renewed interest in Africa in recent years, particularly after Netanyahu's widely promoted visits to the continent during 2016–17, the issue is yet to attract any scholarly attention. In fact, there has hardly been any academic engagement with Israel's foreign strategy in Africa since the end of the Cold War. A combination of factors can be said to account for this neglect. From the perspective of Israeli scholars, think tanks and the media, Africa is usually perceived as an uneventful sideshow to the politics of the Middle East. African Studies, once a popular discipline in some of Israel's leading universities, is now a marginal field in Israeli academia, rendering critical knowledge production on Israeli activities in Africa or African issues in general rare. Israel's own siege mentality and its tense relationships with its Arab neighbours mean that most Israelis view their country primarily as part of the Western world and experience Africa as much more distant than it really is.

Meanwhile, from the African perspective, Israel's scope of involvement and impact are understandably viewed as marginal when compared to those of powers like China, the US or even European countries. Language barriers, overt secrecy and the fact that Israel has no articulated and publicly available 'Africa policy' or a coherent international development agenda are some other factors that render engagement with the topic challenging. Thus, with Israeli scholars and students of the Middle East detached from contemporary African debates and concerns or simply viewing them as entirely inconsequential, and with a preponderance of Africanists reluctant to deal with the messy politics of the Middle

East and Israel/Palestine or simply unfamiliar with them,[5] Israeli–African relationships seem to be no one's focus. Structurally, as in the case of other cross-regional engagements, this neglect is also a consequence of the division between the Area Studies of the Middle East and Africa in academic institutions and the popular perception of these regions as largely separated from one another.[6]

But this neat division is uncomfortably artificial. Israel shares a land border with Africa: a line in the sand which was first negotiated between Britain and the Ottoman Empire over a century ago. It has a port on the Red Sea. It has been the destination of several significant waves of migration from Africa throughout its history. Perhaps more crucially, it has often sought to project its influence into the continent – far beyond its immediate neighbours – in order to safeguard its interests and undermine its adversaries. While it is true that Africa was never as central in Israel's international strategy as were its relationships with Western states or with other Middle Eastern countries, the neighbouring continent in general, and its north-eastern countries in particular, have repeatedly featured in Jerusalem's foreign policy calculations.

And this interest was not one-sided, or uninfluential, or limited to a small group of political or military elites. From imperial and later socialist Ethiopia, through post-independence Uganda and Sudan, apartheid South Africa, Zaire and later the Democratic Republic of the Congo (DRC), and all the way to contemporary Togo, South Sudan, Angola, Rwanda and Equatorial Guinea, African actors sought Israel's support and Israel's involvement has been highly significant. In some cases, it played a critical role in determining the trajectories of conflicts and the survival or rise to power of leaders. In recent years, Israeli–African (often clandestine) collaboration on migration management has impacted on the lives of tens of thousands of people. Support for Israel is an increasingly important theme in many evangelical churches in Africa, while the Palestinian cause remains a central concern for the Arab world and human rights groups.

There is a considerable body of literature that deals with the more distant history of Israel in Africa. Several studies have been written on Israel's involvement in Africa from the late 1950s and until the mid-1970s, focusing primarily on its technical assistance programmes and on the decision of most African countries to break ties with Israel during the Israeli–Arab war of 1973.[7] A few Israelis who worked in Africa during the 1960s also wrote illuminating memoirs.[8] Israel's alliance with apartheid South Africa and the slow restoration of ties with some African countries during the 1980s also attracted attention, but as Israel's interests in the continent declined after the end of the Cold War, so did the scholarly interest in what Israel and Israelis do in Africa.[9] In recent years, Israeli involvement in Africa during the 1960s has attracted some renewed academic attention, primarily from Israeli scholars.[10] This resulted in several studies that are more critical and evidence-based than much of the older literature on the same period, but which unavoidably also further entrenched the notion that Israeli–African partnerships are largely a thing of the past.

This book seeks to contribute to the existing debates and literature in two ways. First, by presenting a new history of the interplay between conflicts, violence and processes of state formation in Israel/Palestine and in the African continent. Second, by critically examining Israel's growing interest in and engagement with African countries over the past decade. The following chapters therefore aim to answer a set of interlinked questions: Why and how did Israel attempt to project its influence into Africa? What is behind the new Israeli 'love' for the continent? What developments in Africa and the Middle East brought about this new phase in the history of Israel in Africa, and what may the engagement between Israel and African countries mean for both the Middle East and Africa? How does Israel's longer history of involvement in Africa inform and influence its current rhetoric and activities? And finally, how did African leaders respond to Israel's forays, and why?

Securitisation, privatisation and states

From its independence in 1948, Israel was engaged in protracted conflicts and constantly saw itself – rightly or not – as facing existential threats.[11] As historian Avi Shlaim shows, all Israeli governments since the country's independence were guided by the conviction that Jewish sovereignty in the Middle East can only be guaranteed through force and deterrence, by making Israel so powerful that its adversaries will view it as unbreakable and, once sufficiently repressed and overpowered, give up their resistance to it.[12] Shlaim calls this strategy 'The Iron Wall' – a reference to a hawkish doctrine first formulated by Zionist leader Ze'ev Jabotinsky in the 1920s and subsequently followed by generations of Israeli leaders regardless of their political leanings. One central argument advanced in this book is that Israel's relationship with Africa should be understood as driven by the same rationale: in Africa, Israel repeatedly sought political and military alliances or influence that can be leveraged to pressure, weaken, undermine and deter its rivals in the Middle East.

Israel's forays into Africa therefore consistently reflected its conflicts in the Middle East. From the late 1950s, the continent was the site of intense political and military competition between Israel and the Arab world (primarily Egypt). Israel largely lost this battle during the 1973 Israeli–Arab war, when most African countries severed diplomatic relations with it. After Israel and Egypt signed a peace agreement in 1979, the urgency of guaranteeing African support declined, and the Israeli–Egyptian rivalry in Africa was slowly replaced with the much less militarised Israeli–Palestinian one. After Israel began to negotiate with the Palestinians, and following the Israeli–Jordanian peace agreement in the 1990s, Africa lost much of its strategic importance from the Israeli perspective. However, following the collapse of the Israeli–Palestinian peace process in the early 2000s and as Israel's international isolation grew again, it slowly began to 'return' to the continent, once again seeking alliances that would weaken its rivals in the Middle

East. If previous rounds of Israeli–Arab/Palestinian competition in Africa were intertwined in global Cold War dynamics, today the battle takes place within the context of the 'war on terror', the growing popularity of born-again Christian and reformist Islamic movements, and the renewed geostrategic interest of both Gulf and Asian powers in Africa.

Securitised international objectives also influenced the evolution and workings of Israeli state institutions. Since Israel's international strategy was always considered and presented as a matter of state or regime survival, the security sector came to dominate it and civilian institutions or bureaucracies, including the Ministry of Foreign Affairs, were regularly bypassed or obstructed. The military was always the most influential and respected institution in the Israeli polity, and Israeli society was always obsessed with security and defence. As the country grew older, however, and particularly since the wars of 1967 and 1973, the distinction between its military elite and civilian leadership became increasingly blurred, as former security personnel and generals began to occupy a growing number of senior positions in the government, state institutions, parastatals, the arms industry and, more recently, the closely linked high-tech industry. Ultimately, they formed what Sheffer and Barak called a 'security network' – a powerful group of like-minded security-oriented people that transcends formal institutions and shapes Israel's international strategy and national priorities.[13]

From an early stage, the security sector was deeply involved in Israel's Africa diplomacy, often dealing with issues that are not directly related to defence, such as propaganda or migration management. This matters not only because it indicates what Israel's priorities in Africa are and the extent to which its foreign strategy is shaped by its defence interests, but also because it determines which Israeli institutions interact with African states and peoples and how they operate. As opposed to civilian institutions, security agencies not only tend to seek military solutions to political problems but have great freedom to act in secrecy, based on the discretion of their members, and at the margins of the law or entirely outside of its realms. While civilian bureaucracies take pride in their rule-bound nature and emphasise consistency, security and intelligence agencies glorify the creative circumvention of rules and rely on opaqueness, informality and unpredictability. As the following chapters demonstrate, the resort to 'clandestine diplomacies', covert action and special 'operations' has been a salient feature of Israel's interaction with African states.[14]

Equally important, and closely linked to the securitisation and informalisation of Israel's presence in Africa and the opaqueness surrounding it, is its privatised nature. In the early 1960s, Israel's engagement with African countries was both state-led and underpinned by a distinctly 'statist' vision of modernisation and state-building. But in the following decades, private actors became increasingly dominant players. Some of Israel's largest security firms are technically private enterprises, though they are led and staffed by former members of Israel's security apparatuses and work closely with Israeli armed forces and intelligence agencies. Some of the most dominant Israeli civilian firms in Africa (operating in the construction and extractives industries) maintain close ties with Israeli officials to advance the business, defence and political interests of elites in both Israel and Africa. Politicians and private actors often work hand in hand in the process of profit-making. The distinction between national interests and private ones can be unclear.

Over the years, some Israeli civil servants, diplomats and politicians protested against these processes of securitisation and privatisation and the lack of transparency surrounding Israel's operations in Africa, claiming that they undermine Israel's political objectives, the integrity of its state institutions and its human rights obligations. Israeli Africanist, human rights activist and former member of Knesset (Israel's parliament) Naomi Chazan wrote in 2006 that behind Israel's Africa strategy was always 'an overt struggle between the diplomats and African aficionados on the one hand and the defense establishment and private interests on the other', which ultimately 'has been won by the latter'.[15] The rise and current operations of Israeli private actors and security firms in Africa is further explored in the following chapters. But while these actors certainly gained the upper hand, it is also important to acknowledge that their domination has not been uncontested. Beneath the surface of Israel's engagement with Africa always lay an internal Israeli debate about the Israeli state, its institutions and its priorities.

However, it was not only Israeli interests and initiatives that drove Israeli–African engagements or determined their trajectory. Students of Africa's international relations will be familiar with debates around the agency and leverage of African actors within the international system and vis-à-vis Western or BRICS countries, Brazil, Russia, India, China and South Africa. They will also be familiar with the argument – put forward by Christopher Clapham in the 1990s – that despite their economic and military marginality in the international sphere, African states are not passive victims of the whims of much richer external actors.[16] Rather, they are often able to take advantage of the geostrategic needs of more powerful states, offering them assets such as political loyalty or military access to strategically important territories in return for resources and support which can subsequently be used to advance local African agendas.

This book naturally focuses on Israel more than it does on any specific African state. However, the following chapters also aim to show that just as much as the history of Israel in Africa is a story about Israeli leaders seeking influence in the continent in order to curb their regional adversaries, it is also a story about African leaders utilising the rivalries of the Middle East and North Africa in order to draw Israeli material and political support for their own local ends. As we shall see, what Israel and Israelis did in Africa was determined by the changing economic and political circum-stances in specific African states just as much as it was determined by the conditions in Israel/Palestine. As strategies of governance transformed, as flows of resources shifted and as the tools for their accumulation and distribution changed in Africa, so did the ways in which different Israeli actors were seeking to establish their influence on the continent.

Structure, scope and sources

The first two chapters of the book deal with the history of Israel's engagement with Africa. The evolution of bilateral relations in the *longue durée* is crucial for understanding their current trajectory and dynamics. Political narratives, like institutional knowledge and capacities (or lack thereof), do not emerge out of nowhere. It is impossible to understand Israel's contemporary strategic interest and the rhetoric Israelis deploy on the continent without considering Israel's relationships with African countries in the early post-independence period, from the late 1950s and until the mid-1960s. Israeli foreign minister at the time, Golda Meir, referred to this period as Israel's 'African adventure'.[17] It was characterised by extensive Israeli civilian and military assistance to African countries as part of a geopolitical competition between Israel and the Arab world, underlined by Israel's attempt to establish itself as a legitimate member of the international community in general and the postcolonial 'Third World' in particular. This period is the focus of the first chapter.

The second chapter explores the transformation of Israel's engagement with African countries from the 1967 war, during which Israel occupied territories in Egypt, Jordan and Syria, through the Israeli–Arab war of 1973, during which most African countries severed ties with Israel, and until the early 2000s. This period saw a gradual process of militarisation, securitisation and privatisation of Israel's presence and diplomacy in Africa – a process that was influenced by the political and economic realities in both Israel/Palestine and Africa. One of the most enduring legacies of this period is the deep involvement of the Israeli business sector and arms industry in Israel's activities in Africa. As noted above, after the end of the Cold War Israeli geostrategic interest in Africa declined and Israel's presence on the continent was dominated by private actors, many of whom were former security personnel or military men with close links to both Israeli and African financial and political elites.

Chapters 3 to 5 all deal with more recent developments in Israel's relationship with African countries. The third chapter discusses Israel's attempts to 'return' to Africa over the last decade and their causes. It examines the emergence of Israel's new geopolitical interests in Africa: curbing Iranian influence and undermining Palestinian diplomatic efforts to pressure Israel to end the occupation. It also considers the new rhetoric surrounding Israel's African 'comeback', which focuses on counterterrorism and insecurity to consolidate and justify alliances, and, as was the case in the 1960s, seeks to position Israel as a developmental model for African countries. Finally, the chapter deals with Israel's attempts to promote the involvement of Israeli or Jewish private sector actors and civil society organisations in Africa in order to project its influence into the continent, and the role of Israel's development aid in this context.

The fourth chapter highlights the extent to which Israel's involvement in Africa has been shaped by the various interests of its local partners and explores the loose and diverse networks of actors that advance these interests. It does so by presenting four interlinked patterns of interactions that characterise Israel's contemporary engagements with African countries and shape its image and leverage on the continent. The first relates to security: the deployment of Israeli defence expertise by African leaders for propping up their regimes. The second relates to Israel's position as a link to Washington and therefore to American material and political support. The third relates to the growing influence of Africa's Pentecostal churches and other evangelical movements on Israel's bilateral relations and standing on the continent; and the fourth concerns the deployment of Israeli expertise and investments for infrastructure development and state-building.

The fifth chapter investigates Israel's efforts to control the movement of people between Israel and Africa. It describes, first, the debates around who should and who should not be allowed to cross this frontier and, second, the ways in which such movements have been managed by Israeli state institutions. The recent arrival of tens of thousands of Eritreans and Sudanese in Israel and Israel's attempts to remove them from the country attracted considerable attention from human rights organisations and academics. These were primarily concerned with the (il)legality of Israel's asylum policies and with the ways in which asylum-seekers were received by Israeli authorities. This book takes a different approach in analysing Israel's treatment of these populations by situating the recent attempts to stop migration from the Horn of Africa within the context of Israel's longer history of managing the migrations of populations from Africa, including of Jewish communities.

While this book deals with a wide range of themes, geographical regions and historical periods, I have limited myself here to the links and dynamics that shape the relationship between Israel and African leaders, states and peoples. This complex web of vectors is necessarily shaped by much wider flows of ideas and resources between Israel/Palestine, the Middle East and the African continent, but not all of these are discussed in detail here. Perhaps most significantly, the activities and efforts of Israel's adversaries in Africa are only explored here to the extent that they influence Israel's own operations and strategy. Those looking for a detailed account of Islamist politics in Africa vis-à-vis Israel/Palestine or a history of the Palestinian engagement with African countries and liberation movements – topics that certainly merit greater critical attention from scholars – will be disappointed. This is both a fair warning and a call for follow-up research that will investigate those fields that this book inevitably leaves uncharted.

The sources I draw on are as diverse as the themes explored. The historical parts make considerable use of secondary literature, though I also draw on some archival materials from the Israel State

Archives and my research on Israeli–southern Sudanese relations during Sudan's first civil war. More contemporary parts draw on various publicly available sources – newspapers and news websites, reports of UN agencies and nongovernmental organisations (NGOs), industry newsletters, government statistics and press releases, cables released by WikiLeaks, court cases, social media posts – as well as on a small number of interviews I conducted with former or serving Israeli officials. The sections on Eritrean, South Sudanese and Sudanese refugees mainly draw on my work with human rights organisations in Israel and Uganda since 2010, including dozens of interviews (conducted in 2015 and late 2017) with Sudanese and Eritreans who left Israel for Uganda and Rwanda. The sections on evangelical movements and Messianic Judaism in Africa are informed by research conducted in Ethiopia among members of such groups during 2018–19.

As all of the above suggests, however, my main objective in this book is to connect the dots between different actors, trends and ideas into a wide and historically informed map of Israeli–African interstate politics, and not to present a thorough investigation of any specific event, policy or bilateral relationship. Some of the issues discussed here – Israel's technical assistance programmes in Africa in the 1960s, the impact of the Israeli–Arab war of 1973 on Israel's position in Africa, Israel's relationship with apartheid South Africa, or the history and immigration to Israel of the Jews of Ethiopia – have been the subjects of significant bodies of literature. Readers who are interested in these topics will find useful references for further reading in the notes. I do not claim to be breaking new ground when discussing these topics here, but seek to fit them into the larger puzzle, primarily based on the very valuable work done by other scholars.

Other issues – Israel's propaganda and public relations efforts in Africa in the past and present, the impact of the rise of born-again Christianity on its standing on the continent, the role of the private sector in shaping the political economy of Israeli–African engagements, or the spread and impact of Messianic Jewish doctrines – have attracted much less attention from academics. For obvious reasons, I could only explore some of these issues by drawing on my own research and experience, and hence the evident reliance in some parts of the book on various 'para-scholarly' sources and journalistic accounts. I hope that this book will inspire further inquiries into these underexplored topics and into other layers of Middle Eastern–African engagements. There is much we can learn from such inquiries, I believe, not only about the relationship between the two regions but also about the nature of contemporary politics in each of them.

Chapter 1

AN AFRICAN ADVENTURE

Within four days at the end of April 1948, more than 1,100 Palestinian refugees arrived by sea at the Egyptian city of Port Said. Many of them were women and children, travelling on 'small steamers, fishing smacks, rowing boats and caiques'.[1] Coming from the coastal towns of Haifa and Jaffa, they were fleeing the violence that had erupted between Zionist and Palestinian armed groups after the UN General Assembly in November 1947 voted in favour of dividing Palestine into two independent states: one Jewish and one Arab. Most of the Palestinians who fled to Egypt were hosted in designated camps, but some of those who arrived early were able to settle in urban areas. On 16 May 1948, Hala Sakakini, the daughter of the Palestinian writer Khalil Sakakini who fled Jerusalem with her family, wrote in her diary that Cairo's neighbourhood of Heliopolis 'has become a Palestinian colony. Every other house is occupied by a Palestinian family'.[2]

By the time the Israeli–Arab war was over, more than 700,000 Palestinians were forcibly displaced or expelled, primarily to the West Bank, the Gaza Strip, Syria, Lebanon and Jordan, rather than to Egypt. For them, these events marked 'the catastrophe', or in Arabic, *al-Nakba*. Israelis, however, remember 1948 as their 'War of Independence', as it marked the establishment of the Jewish state. For them, the return of Palestinian refugees was, and remains to this day, unacceptable. When the war ended, there were some 156,000 Arabs and 716,000 Jews in Israel.[3] Allowing 700,000 Palestinian refugees to return to their homes would have threatened the Jewish demographic majority. A moment of liberation for the Jewish people and a disaster for the Palestinians, the violence of 1948 resulted in one of the world's greatest and most protracted refugee crises and led to one of its most persistent and politicised conflicts – both of which are yet to be resolved. It established a set of facts that continue to shape Israel's domestic and international politics today and have been a defining factor in the history of its engagement with Africa as well.

It did not take long for the impact of Israel's independence and the 1948 war to be felt in Africa beyond Egypt. The Arab League – comprising at the time Egypt, Iraq, Jordan, Lebanon, Saudi Arabia and Syria – refused to recognise the new Jewish state and boycotted it. Egypt argued that it had the right to ban Sudan, then under a joint Anglo-Egyptian government, from trading with Israel as well. Israel, however, saw in trade with colonial Sudan an opportunity to undermine the Arab boycott. Some Israeli officials even entertained the idea of seeking ties with the country, but this was never seriously pursued.[4] With its independence in January 1956, Sudan joined the Arab League. Over the next two years Israel tried to appeal to Washington and Paris to extend their political and financial support to Khartoum in order to keep it out of Egypt's sphere of influence, but its efforts did not bear fruit.[5] To find allies in Africa, Israel had to look further afield.

Israel turns to Africa

Histories of Israel's engagement with Africa most commonly begin a few years after 1948, with the resounding diplomatic shock of the Bandung Conference. In 1955 Israel was excluded from the first Asian–African Conference, which was held in Bandung, Indonesia, and brought together 29 young nations to discuss issues of mutual concern and political and cultural cooperation. From the African continent, Libya, Egypt, Ethiopia, Liberia, Gold Coast (now Ghana) and Sudan all participated. Israel was not only left out of this forum, but the participants formally expressed their support 'of the rights of the Arab people of Palestine and called for the implementation of the United Nations Resolutions on Palestine and the achievement of the peaceful settlement of the Palestine question'.[6] Similarly excluded from the conference was white-ruled South Africa – hardly a country Israel wanted to be associated with at the time.

A united Afro-Asian 'Third World' appeared to be emerging as a promising new force in the international sphere, and Israel was being branded as its enemy. The country's foreign policy strategy, it became clear in Jerusalem, had to be reconsidered. Since independence in 1948, Israel primarily focused on strengthening its relationships with Western countries, with the view that strong ties with North America, Europe and the Soviet Union would guarantee its existence and support its economy.[7] Otherwise, Israel's diplomatic efforts in Asia in the early 1950s were limited, and largely unsuccessful. Israel had a friendly relationship with Burma, one of the organisers of the conference in Bandung, but failed to establish close ties with any of the region's key powers, which all sided with the Palestinians. By the second half of the 1950s covert ties were also established with Turkey and Iran, the most significant aspect of which was a trilateral mechanism for intelligence sharing.[8]

'I used to look around me at the United Nations in 1957 and 1958 and think to myself: "We have no family here"', Golda Meir, Israel's foreign minister at the time, recalled.[9] Born in Russia in 1898 and educated in the US, in 1921 Meir migrated to British Mandate Palestine, where she joined the Histadrut, the Jewish General Federation of Labour in Palestine, and later Mapai, the Israeli Labour Party, which dominated the Israeli political landscape in the country's first decades of independence. In 1956, Ben-Gurion appointed her as foreign minister, a position she would hold for almost a decade. She had never visited Africa before and her knowledge of the continent was basic at best when she first stepped into her new office in the Ministry of Foreign Affairs in June 1956.[10] Little did she know that by the time she left the ministry, she would have become the politician most strongly associated with Africa in Israel's history.

Besides exclusion from the rising club of young postcolonial non-aligned states, another reason that Israeli attention turned to Africa in the late 1950s was the opening of the Red Sea for Israeli shipping. The right of Israeli ships to travel freely to and from Eilat, Israel's sole port on the Red Sea, through the Gulf of Aqaba and the Straits of Tiran, has been a matter of dispute between Israel and Egypt. In late October 1956, Israel invaded Egypt's Sinai Peninsula, supported by Britain and France. This quickly led to a political crisis, and both the US and the Soviets demanded that Israel withdraw from the Egyptian territories. The Soviets threatened Israel with a military intervention, and the US with cutting aid. Israel withdrew, but was able to pressure Egypt to open the Straits of Tiran for Israeli shipping in return.[11] A military invasion into a neighbouring Arab country in cooperation with two colonial powers certainly did not help Israel's reputation among young Afro-Asian states, but it did guarantee its access to the Red Sea and therefore to Ethiopia (then united with today's Eritrea), the East African Coast and southern Africa.

Formally, Israel had low-key diplomatic ties with both Liberia and Ethiopia by the mid-1950s,[12] but it was its relationship with Ghana that marked the beginning of its extensive diplomatic efforts in Africa. A consulate in Accra was established in 1956, prior to Ghana's independence, and was upgraded to an embassy upon independence in 1957. Ehud Avriel, Israel's first ambassador to Ghana, recounted that at independence Kwame Nkrumah presented the Israeli delegation with 'the same list of urgent requirements he expected from other older states', and within a year 'every single requirement on Nkrumah's list had become a subject for intensive cooperation between Ghana and Israel'.[13] As Levey writes, 'Avriel's objective was to turn Ghana into a showcase of Israel's aid in Africa's development'. He had three key aims:

First, the ambassador worked to gain both Prime Minister Nkrumah's confidence and influence over him. Second, he broadened
the scope of Israel's economic ties with Ghana. Third, he initiated a defense connection with Ghana that created a precedent
for Israel's military ties with other African states.[14]

A series of bilateral initiatives were soon developed. The Israeli
water planning authority (Tahal) assisted with water infrastructure
development, the Israeli Histadrut's construction firm Solel Boneh
helped establish the Ghana National Construction Company, and
a Ghanaian–Israeli shipping company was established – the Black
Star Shipping Line – 60% of which was owned by the government
of Ghana and 40% by the Israeli shipping company Zim. Israel sold
light arms and provided training to the Ghanaian army, and in 1958
the two countries signed a trade agreement and Israel extended
Ghana a $20 million loan.[15] Israelis, including military officers, also
assisted with the establishment of the Ghanaian Nautical College
and the Flying Training School, which trained pilots for the Ghana
Air Force and Ghana Airways.[16] One Israeli expert even assisted
with the establishment of the National Symphony Orchestra.[17]
Ambassador Avriel became a close confidant of Nkrumah, who was
able to facilitate contact with other African leaders.[18]

Following the experience in Ghana, a decision was taken in Jerusalem to pursue ties with other African nations before they gained
independence, in order to curb Arab influence as early as possible.[19]
Israel began sending envoys to African countries to court those local
leaders who were expected to lead their nations after independence, promising technical assistance and military training. These
initiatives had to be negotiated with Paris and London but were
not always pursued with their approval. Both France and Britain
were often concerned that allowing the establishment of official
Israeli representations would lead to similar Arab demands. For
this reason, for example, France opposed the opening of an Israeli
consulate general in Dakar,[20] and Britain refused to allow Israel to

open a consular office in Lagos.[21] When the British similarly refused to let Israel send a consul to Dar es Salaam, Israel went ahead and sent a delegate without informing the British about the political nature of his mission. The British later threatened to deport him.[22] Similar threats were made in Kenya, after the Israeli representative Asher Naim – who also travelled to Kenya after the British objected to the appointment of an Israeli consul general – met Jomo Kenyatta while the latter was under house arrest.[23]

As far as establishing diplomatic ties was concerned, the Israeli strategy proved successful. The growth in Israeli presence on the continent during the years of African independence was extraordinary, especially given the fact that Israel was a small, young country, whose ties in Africa did not build on any existing diplomatic networks from the colonial period. By 1963, Israel had 22 embassies in Africa, and by the late 1960s, it had established ties with 33 countries (34 if South Africa is included).[24] While some countries clearly had greater geostrategic importance than others, Israel was still unconstrained by an alliance with either side of the Cold War in the early 1960s. It tried to reach out to as many African countries as possible. The only two countries that achieved independence at the time south of the Sahara and did not establish ties with Israel were Mauritania and Somalia.

Official visits of high-level Israeli politicians to Africa and African leaders to Israel became common. Golda Meir first travelled to Africa in 1958, visiting Ghana, Liberia, Nigeria, Côte d'Ivoire and Senegal, and returned to the continent four more times by 1964, for extensive visits. Israeli President Yitzhak Ben-Zvi travelled to West Africa in 1962 and Prime Minister Levi Eshkol in 1966.[25] African heads of states and government officials also visited Israel frequently, where they were regularly presented with the country's development achievements. Africa quickly occupied an important place in Israel's international strategy. Israel succeeded in showing the world – and primarily its Arab neighbours – that it was not ostracised or isolated but rather recognised and warmly welcomed by a considerable number of young post-colonial nations. Despite its size, limited economic capacity and young age, in Africa Israel became well-known for its military support and technical assistance programmes.

Seeking allies in the Horn

Across Africa, Israeli initiatives sought to consolidate political alliances and curb Arab influence. But while in West Africa Israeli interests were primarily diplomatic, the dynamics of East Africa and the Horn of Africa were viewed as part of the Middle Eastern conflict and Israeli military and intelligence objectives in these regions played an important role. The war of 1948, after all, did not end with peace but rather with a series of armistice agreements, and Israeli leaders were preparing for what some of them viewed as an inevitable 'second round'. To counter its rivals and as part of a strategy that came to be known as the 'periphery doctrine' or the 'alliance of the periphery', Israel attempted to establish ties with the countries that surrounded its hostile Arab neighbours – to encircle its enemies with a ring of powerful, non-Arab, friends.[26] Iran, Turkey and Ethiopia all fell squarely within the scope of this strategy and became Israel's satellite allies to its east, north and south. The Mossad was the main institution in charge of cultivating these 'periphery' alliances and was therefore deeply involved in Israel's diplomacy in East Africa.

In the early years of Israeli engagement with Africa, some saw a potential fully-fledged military ally in Ethiopia. It was not only located in a strategic spot, but also possessed one of the largest militaries in Africa and sought to contain Arab influence in the region. The fact that most of the waters of the Nile – Egypt's economic life-blood – flow from the Ethiopian highlands only increased the Israeli urge to gain a foothold in the country. When in 1963, Shimon Peres, then deputy minister of defence, together with Yitzhak Rabin, then deputy chief of staff, visited Ethiopia, they met with Emperor Haile

Selassie, Prime Minister (and acting foreign minister) Aklilu Habta-Wold and military commanders, and were taken by their hosts on a small private tour to inspect the Blue Nile. 'It is our goal to reach an alliance with Ethiopia – cultural, economic, and military. We must spare no effort and resources in working toward this aim', Peres wrote following the visit.[27]

In fact, by 1963 there were already more than 30 Israeli experts working in Ethiopia, including university lecturers, doctors and engineers, as well as policemen who were advising and training the national police forces.[28] The latter were also armed with Israeli Uzi submachine guns.[29] A similar number of Israelis were attached as advisors to the Ethiopian army, working with each of its four divisions, the high command, the intelligence, the navy and the air force. As a memorandum prepared by the Israel Defense Forces (IDF) for the Israeli Ministry of Foreign Affairs in 1963 explained, military assistance had to 'be distributed widely and to the "depth" of the apparatus with a maximal emphasis on our role in the training of the senior command personnel'.[30] Israeli intelligence agencies were working closely with their Ethiopian counterparts, training them, and using Ethiopia as a base for operations in other countries.[31] The Israeli community in Ethiopia at the time already numbered more than 400 people.[32]

While much of Israel's military assistance in the early 1960s was focused on the Ogaden region in southern Ethiopia, where the imperial government was facing a Somali nationalist rebellion, Middle East politics were most influential along the coasts of the Red Sea, in the context of the struggle over Eritrea. In 1950, the UN General Assembly – under US pressure – adopted a resolution federating Eritrea, which was previously an Italian colony, with Ethiopia. By 1960, this led to the emergence of the Eritrean Liberation Front (ELF), a predominantly Muslim armed group that was first formed by Eritrean exiles in Cairo and, inspired by Nasser's pan-Arab ideologies of the time, opposed Haile Selassie's hegemonic aspirations in the region.[33] Arab countries, primarily Syria, supported the ELF, while Israel viewed the possibility of an independent Eritrean state as a threat to its access to the Red Sea and backed Ethiopia, providing training to the elite units that fought the rebels.[34]

Ethiopia's strategic importance also rendered Uganda, Tanganyika (later Tanzania) and Kenya a priority, though the first two were of greater concern for Israel because of their susceptibility to Arab and Soviet influence. Uganda also assumed strategic importance because of the White Nile, which flows through the country on its way to Sudan and Egypt. Following Uganda's independence, President Milton Obote turned to Israel for military training and arms. Israelis were deeply involved in training the Ugandan army, and some Ugandans travelled to Israel for training as well. By 1967, it was estimated that Uganda purchased more than $12 million worth of arms from Israel, including a number of light planes, transport aircrafts and a dozen tanks, all second-hand.[35] Meanwhile, in Tanzania, Israel trained hundreds of military officers, police maritime forces as well as a unit of 'police paratroopers' – a short-lived vanity project that apparently ended once it became evident that Tanzania did not possess any suitable planes to parachute the trained policemen.[36]

Israel as a developmental model

In Israel, as in most African states, the first decades of independence were characterised by an intensive process of state formation and state-led development. Being more than a decade older than most African countries, Israel positioned itself as a model: a young country that made the desert bloom, forged capable state institutions, and succeeded, within a short period of time, in creating a sense of national unity among its diverse population. The image of Zionist nation- and state-building that Israel projected in its early years had a lustre that spoke directly to African visions and aspirations of modernisation at the time. Drawing comparisons between the Jewish and young African states quickly became a central feature in Israeli–African engagements, with leaders highlighting Jewish and African histories of oppression and liberation and the supposedly similar challenges their countries faced. Both Israel and Tanganyika, Julius Nyerere wrote, faced 'two major tasks: building the nation and changing the face of the land, physically and economically'.[37]

A distinct characteristic of the Zionist state formation experience was its salient reliance on the military. The seemingly successful deployment of the Israeli army for uniting the nation, reconfiguring the country's social and physical landscape, making the state present in people's lives and pursuing civilian tasks such as infrastructure development was seen as an inspiration for young African countries.[38] Particularly appealing were the Israeli programmes of the Fighting Pioneer Youth (Nahal) and Youth Battalions (Gadna) which mobilised youths for paramilitary training, and, in the case of the Nahal, agricultural education and the development of new Jewish settlements. 'In Israel I have seen youths trained so that they are a source of pride to the nation, and they are readily available for all sorts of national work programmes', Tom Mboya, who visited Israel for the first time in 1962, later recounted. 'We must plan this way.'[39]

Israel was not in a position to offer African countries financial support comparable to that provided by the US, the Soviets or even European states.[40] The most celebrated aspects of its support were technical cooperation and training programmes. A section for technical cooperation was established in the Israeli Ministry of Foreign Affairs in 1958, which was transformed into an independent department and came to be known as Israel's Agency for International Development Cooperation (or MASHAV, the acronym of its Hebrew name).[41] Between 1958 and 1970 almost 2,500 Israeli experts were sent to Africa to provide training or support local development projects, and by 1972 more than 9,000 Africans had travelled to Israel for courses and training.[42] These commonly focused on agriculture, rural settlement projects and youth organisations, but covered numerous other areas, from health, through education, taxation, law and administration, engineering, communication, social work, poultry framing, construction and architecture.[43] And as much as the aim of Israel's aid projects was to transfer knowledge from Israel to African countries, they often also represented an opportunity for Israelis to gain valuable experience and expertise.[44]

Government-led joint ventures in the fields of trade, farming and infrastructure development were another popular modus operandi. These initiatives were conventionally co-owned by Israeli companies (often but not always owned by the government or the Histadrut) and African governments and combined training of local African staff with what were supposed to be economically sound investments. The Ghanaian–Israeli Black Star Shipping Line mentioned above is one example of such a collaboration. Israelis initially occupied the main administrative and technical positions, but these were slowly transferred to local African staff, as African governments also assumed full ownership of the enterprise.[45] Many of these collaborations left their mark on the urban landscapes of African capitals in the form of Israeli planned or constructed residential complexes, universities, hotels, government buildings and airports, some of which still stand and are in use today.

But as exported development models often are, many of the Israeli initiatives were wasteful and unrealistic. Israel and African countries had much less in common than political rhetoric suggested or than politicians or diplomats were willing to admit. While Israel was indeed a young country, the Jews in Israel were primarily settlers, immigrants and refugees, dominated by an educated European elite. The geographical and institutional conditions in Israel and in the African countries were also vastly different: Israelis inherited a far more developed state from the British than any African nation had.[46] Moreover, the post-independence process of state-building in Israel took place against the background of ongoing violence along the country's frontiers – a phenomenon that few African countries, if any, experienced.[47] While in Israel the army fought external threats, in Africa it was utilised to distribute resources and consolidate state power or capture it from those who failed to managed it wisely.

The initiative that came to epitomise the naivety of Israel's aspiration to transfer its nation-building experience to Africa was its aspiration to establish paramilitary youth organisations, which were loosely based on the Israeli *Nahal* and *Gadna* schemes. Israel assisted with the establishment of such youth programmes in more than 20 African countries,[48] seeking to promote national consciousness, unity and discipline, 'foster the spirit of national responsibility and pioneering among the youth and ... educate them for good citizenship'.[49] Assistance in the establishment of youth organisations was among Israel's most popular and sought-after forms of support in Africa. But while in Israel these programmes were mythologised as the ultimate representation of Zionist state-building and pioneership, in Africa they achieved few if any of their imagined developmental goals and proved too expensive to sustain. Ethnic tensions, high desertion rates and the fact that fresh graduates moved to urban areas in search of jobs in the civil service (after participating in the programmes and acquiring agricultural skills) often rendered the initiatives rather futile.[50]

Propaganda, aid and their limits

Israel's main objective in Africa was mobilising support for its position in the Israeli–Arab conflict. Along with direct assistance, therefore, the Israeli Ministry of Foreign Affairs and the Mossad invested a great amount of energy and resources in public diplomacy, propaganda and international reputation campaigns – *hasbara* (literally: 'explanation'), as these activities are collectively known in Hebrew. Israeli officials and diplomats closely monitored media coverage of the Israeli–Arab conflict and meticulously collected newspaper articles and foreign propaganda publications they came across. They also regularly reached out to local media outlets in order to promote stories that served Israeli interests and showed Arabs in a bad light (as anti-African, racist or sources of destabilisation and violence), share materials they wanted published and 'brief' editors and journalists about the situation in the Middle East. Their adversaries, of course, were doing more or less the same.

The Israeli–Arab competition over influence was therefore, from its very beginning, also an aggressive war of propaganda: a battle over the international narrative about Israeli–Arab–African relations and about the events unfolding in the Middle East, fought with brochures, newspapers, images, films, exhibitions, lectures and cultural events. Even technical assistance programmes, it was discreetly acknowledged, facilitated 'the dissemination of positive propaganda', not least because they projected an admirable image of Israel as a generous and peace-loving young nation, thereby countering the Arab propaganda that portrayed Israel as a cruel and violent agent of Western imperialism and equated Zionism with colonialism.[51] The fact that the Mossad was discreetly involved in Israel's image management efforts is a testament to the strategic importance Israel accorded to this issue.

At an early stage, Israel also tried to compete with Egypt over East Africa's airwaves and radio listeners. In late 1960, the Israeli public radio service *Kol Yisrael* ('Voice of Israel') began broadcasting a daily half-hour programme in Swahili. The initiative came as a response to the activities of Radio Cairo, which had broadcast Swahili programmes several hours a day since the mid-1950s, spreading anti-colonial and anti-Western ideas. Radio Cairo was particularly popular among Muslims in Zanzibar and along the Swahili Coast.[52] The Israeli broadcasts were managed from Jerusalem by two Tanganyikan students who translated texts that Israeli officials wrote for them, but the initiative was discontinued rather quickly, as the radio signal proved to be too weak to allow decent reception in East Africa.[53]

In the African postcolonial political order dominated by strongmen and centralised power, however, propaganda and public opinion had their limits. To begin with, the political sphere was small and hardly extended beyond urban areas, while political influence was concentrated in the hands of the few. Public displays of friendship and support were always important for Israeli diplomats, but for their efforts in Africa to be effective they also had to be close to the centres of power and to keep those who held power happy. Political support only mattered if given by the ruling elites of each country, and therefore these were the individuals with whom ties had to be cultivated. Rafael Ruppin, Israel's first ambassador to Tanganyika, recalled:

> As my familiarity with Tanganyika's elite deepened, it became apparent to me, that as far as foreign policy is concerned (and the position of the government of Tanganyika on the Israeli–Arab conflict is included in this area) 'public opinion' in Tanganyika narrowed down to no more than 300 to 400 people. The millions of citizens did not have an opinion on the matter, the issue was of no interest to them, and they had no tools to express their views or to influence policy makers. In an audience of this size one can deal with 'personal *hasbara*'.[54]

It is therefore not surprising that in every country assistance was channelled through key individuals who were supposed to be convinced to support the Israeli position on the Israeli–Arab conflict. More than an official or stated policy, this was a natural reaction to the conditions on the ground and to the fact that Israel had limited resources and very specific political objectives. Having witnessed several African coups, by the second half of the 1960s Israeli officials also came to understand the vulnerability of diplomacy that is based on personal deals with leaders and realised that they needed to identify and befriend high-profile military officers as well, as they might end up in power at some point.[55]

Over time, however, Israel could not sustain its investments in aid and publicity in the race for influence in Africa. Like all foreign aid in the postcolonial period, Israeli support was easily used by African leaders to advance their local objectives. Youth training programmes suffered from local attempts to 'transform them into personal political and patronage machines', for example, while African students sent for training were often chosen based on their personal connections rather than merit.[56] More problematic for Israel was the fact that the Israeli–Arab rivalry for African support gave African leaders great leverage vis-à-vis both sides, as they were always able to increase the price of their friendship by threatening, more or less explicitly, to strengthen their cooperation with the other side. Since technical cooperation and development aid emerged primarily as a tool for increasing Israeli political and ideological influence, it was often promised out of the Israeli urge to gain a foothold anywhere that would otherwise be occupied by the Egyptians or the Soviets.

Israeli attempts to convince Western countries, and primarily the US, to fund its aid operations in Africa were largely unsuccessful, and its economic problems at home made it increasingly difficult for it to expand or even maintain its operations in Africa.[57] Meanwhile, the expectations Israel raised, the promises it made and the requests it received exceeded its capacity. By the mid-1960s it became clear that Israeli developmental models were not going to magically transform Africa any time soon, and the volume of Israel's technical assistance began to decline. Many programmes had to be frozen, and Israel had to be more selective with its assistance and avoid expensive and wasteful initiatives such as the establishment of paramilitary youth organisations.[58]

The battle for diplomatic support

The challenges Israel faced in outmanoeuvring its Arab adversaries in the fields of propaganda and development aid were ultimately reflected in the Israeli struggle to secure African diplomatic support in multilateral fora. While the 1960s are often portrayed and remembered as a period of flourishing Israeli–African relations, Israel's ability to leverage its warm relationship with individual African states into political support was limited. That new African states consistently recognised Israel and established relations with it was important in and of itself. But Israel also needed the public backing of these new countries in international fora to protect its interests at home, and this support was much more difficult to gain than it initially seemed.

Since Egypt, under the leadership of Gamal Abdel Nasser, turned to Africa at the time as well and sought to curb Israeli influence,[59] the Middle Eastern rivalry featured in all the pan-Africanist conferences leading up to the formation of the Organisation of African Unity (OAU). The First Conference of Independent African States, which was held in Accra in April 1958, adopted a rather neutral statement on the Israeli–Arab conflict, calling for a 'just solution of the Palestine question'.[60] At the first conference of the All-African Peoples Organisation, which convened in Accra in December the same year, the Israeli–Arab conflict was kept off the agenda, to Israel's relief. At this point, some argue, Israel still benefited from the 'rivalry for continental leadership' between Nasser and Nkrumah.[61] When the Second Conference of Independent African States was convened in Addis Ababa in June 1960, it merely expressed its 'concern' that the Bandung and Accra declarations and the UN resolutions on Palestine were not implemented.[62]

But it was not long before Israel was embroiled in continental power struggles that it initially wished to avoid. In January 1961, the leaders of Ghana, Mali, Guinea, Morocco and the United Arab Republic (comprising of Egypt and Syria) convened in Casablanca against the background of the political crisis in Congo. Israel already had formal relations with Ghana, Mali and Guinea at the time. At Egypt's behest, one of the topics discussed in Casablanca was the Israeli–Arab conflict, and the leaders adopted a resolution in which they denounced 'Israel an instrument in the service of imperialism and neo-colonialism not only in the Middle East but also in Africa and Asia'.[63]

As a response to the so-called 'Casablanca Group', Senegal, Nigeria and Togo sponsored a conference in Monrovia in which

20 African states participated. The 'Monrovia states' were not necessarily more pro-Israel (among them were Somalia, Libya and Mauritania, none of which had relations with Israel) but at the conference they avoided the Israeli–Arab issue altogether for the sake of African unity, a position that ultimately served Israel. Due to the opposition of the Monrovia group, the issue also remained largely off the agenda of the OAU – established in Addis Ababa in 1963 – in its early years.[64] By delicately avoiding the Israeli–Arab issue, non-Arab African leaders could maintain ties with both sides and often benefit from both sides' assistance.

Keeping the OAU unconcerned with the Middle East conflict was useful for Israel, but it was at the UN that its battle for legitimacy mattered the most. Israelis did not hide the fact that they needed African votes at the UN and that they expected African leaders to support them on the diplomatic Israeli–Arab battlefield. On this front, however, Israeli efforts in Africa had mixed results, and whether or not they can be seen as a success depends very much on how one defines success in this context. African countries as a unified bloc never fully backed Israel, and the support of many of Israel's friends in Africa usually did not extend beyond a polite abstention in votes on Israel-related resolutions. But the existence of a significant number of states that were not necessarily allied with the Arab side still strengthened Israel's position and allowed it to obstruct Arab initiatives and, in particular, to undermine Arab attempts to pressure it by promoting the right of return of Palestinian refugees.[65]

In many cases, however, Israel found that strong influence over leaders in Africa did not necessarily translate into diplomatic support from the representatives of these leaders in New York. African delegates at the UN were not necessarily acting under clear orders from the political leadership back home and often decided how to vote independently.[66] This did not serve Israel well, given the Israeli focus on fostering close ties with local elites in Africa. Moreover, support for Israel had to be balanced with support for

Arab states, some of which were also members of the OAU, and the assistance Israel offered African countries was never significant enough to convince them to abandon their commitments to these countries or to stand in direct opposition to them. Ultimately, even those countries that enjoyed the greatest amounts of Israeli support were reluctant to stand by Israel at the UN.

But just as African countries were balancing their support for Israel with support for the Arab world, so Israel was trying to balance its support for African countries with support for the West. Its voting record in the UN therefore often placed it in opposition to African interests and undermined its efforts on the continent. In November 1959, for instance, Ghana initiated a UN resolution requesting France to refrain from conducting nuclear tests in the Sahara. Israel was already developing its own nuclear programme at the time, and France was its main ally and arms supplier. It voted with France, and against several African nations.[67] During the political crisis in Congo in 1960, Israel again stood with the West, despite opposition from some Israeli diplomats in Africa who warned that this would have damaging consequences.[68] As Ali Mazrui observed, 'Israel, sometimes genuinely interested in identifying with the liberation forces in Africa, nevertheless found herself supporting those against whom African fighters were waging a struggle'.[69]

The main exception in this context was Israel's position on South Africa. During the 1960s Israel was vocal and consistent in its opposition to apartheid. Along with African governments, it repeatedly condemned Pretoria at the UN, and made sure that its position on the matter was known to its African allies. More discreetly, so as not to damage its relationships in the West, Israel also established ties with, and extended symbolic assistance to, African liberation movements from southern Africa and the Portuguese colonies, including the Pan Africanist Congress (PAC) of South Africa, the Zimbabwe African National Union (ZANU) and the Mozambique Liberation Front (FRELIMO).[70] While many Israeli politicians genuinely opposed apartheid and colonial rule on moral grounds and invoked the long Jewish history of marginalisation and discrimination as a justification for this position, Israel also hoped that its vocal opposition to South Africa's policies and low-key support for African liberation movements would convince African leaders that Jerusalem was, after all, on their side.

An African adventure

The decade of 1957 to 1966 has often been described as the 'honeymoon' or 'golden age' of African–Israeli relations. And the strategic and material interests that were the driving force behind this romance notwithstanding, one reason that this period was cherished in Israeli memory is that Israeli engagement with African countries was closely linked to the urge of the Zionist elites to reimagine their own identity vis-à-vis their surroundings and neighbours. On the one hand, Israeli rhetoric in Africa portrayed Israel as a postcolonial nation and Zionism as a liberation movement, associating Israel with other young nations of the 'Third World' and rejecting the comparison between Zionism and imperialism. On the other hand, as Yacobi and Bar-Yosef argue, Zionist perceptions of Africa were heavily influenced by late colonial ideas about progress and civilisation and consistently stressed the differences between Israel and African countries.[71] Israel's position as a 'donor' and a model not only highlighted the inequality between Israel and African countries in terms of development and wealth but also positioned Israel as part of the 'modern' world, in contrast to Africa.[72]

In terms of the Israeli institutions involved, a major role was played by the Ministry of Foreign Affairs, Israeli security agencies (the military and the Mossad) and companies that took part in joint ventures with African governments. Israeli engagement therefore not only focused on state-building and state-led development but was also of a highly formal and state-centric nature. By the second half of the 1960s, tensions and disagreements between Israeli civilian institutions, private entrepreneurs and security agencies emerged, as diplomats began to feel that the activities of the latter two groups of actors were getting out of control. 'With no objective justification, a security empire has been erected in Africa', an Israeli official protested in 1966 to Abba Eban, then Israel's new foreign minister. 'This interferes with work, foments turmoil, and creates great political risk.'[73] In the following years, however, events in the Middle East and Africa slowly shifted the balance of power much further away from the state's civilian institutions and into the hands of both formal and informal security and business entrepreneurs.

Chapter 2

A SECURITY EMPIRE

Among the many African leaders who heard about Israel's technical and military assistance in the early 1960s and sought to benefit from it was a group of exiled southern Sudanese politicians. Their plan was to fight for the independence of southern Sudan: to liberate it from the Arab government in Khartoum. Their main problem was that they had few resources at their disposal: meagre funds, even less political backing and hardly any weapons. As early as 1961, southern leaders began appealing for Israeli assistance, writing letters to Jerusalem and knocking on the doors of Israeli embassies across Africa.[1] Israeli officials, however, were reluctant to support them. They understood that the war in Sudan represented a golden opportunity for fuelling the tensions between Africans and Arabs, something that could only strengthen Israel in the international sphere. But the southern secessionist agenda was unpopular among African leaders, and Israel did not want to damage its diplomatic efforts on the continent by supporting the controversial cause of a non-state armed group.

It was Israel's expansion during the war of 1967 that eventually led its leaders to change their minds. Throughout the mid-1960s, tensions between Israel and Syria escalated, prompting mutual exchanges of threats between Israel and its neighbours that resulted in the situation in the entire region spiralling out of control. On 15 May 1967 Egyptian troops entered the Sinai Peninsula and Egypt expelled the UN forces that had been based there since the 1956 Suez campaign. On 22 May Nasser announced the closure of the

Straits of Tiran to Israeli shipping. Not before securing American approval, on 5 June Israel launched a surprise attack, starting a war that ended on 10 June in a major Israeli victory. Within these six days Israel occupied the Egyptian Sinai Peninsula and Gaza Strip, the Jordanian West Bank and the Syrian Golan Heights.[2]

Israel's new occupation of Arab territories complicated its diplomatic position in Africa and altered its security concerns, which now focused on preserving its grip over territories and populations far beyond its original boundaries.[3] These developments unavoidably also drew Sudan and the Horn of Africa more clearly into the Middle Eastern conflict. In the following years, a war of attrition unfolded between Israel and Egypt, whose troops were stationed on the eastern and western banks of the Suez Canal. Egypt received most of its military support from the Soviets, but Sudan also lent a hand. The Mossad calculated that increasing the capacity of the rebels in southern Sudan would keep the Sudanese military busy at home, and suggested Israel should act. Golda Meir, who became Israel's prime minister in March 1969, approved the initiative. During the following two years, the Mossad led a covert operation that involved airdropping arms and humanitarian aid inside the headquarters of the southern Sudanese rebel group Anya-Nya and training its members in guerrilla warfare.

All Israeli assistance was provided via one southern rebel officer, Joseph Lagu. Thanks to Israel's support, Lagu was able to consolidate his position as the leader of the southern struggle, much to the dismay of other politicians who saw themselves pushed aside. The weapons Israel sent to Sudan were mainly Syrian and Jordanian booty captured during the 1967 conflict: limited in scope and sophistication but nonetheless significant given that the rebels previously had hardly any weapons.[4] Small delegations of Israeli military advisors, doctors and communication experts travelled through Uganda into Sudan to train the rebels, while additional equipment was transferred through western Ethiopia. The entire operation was carried out with the consent of Ethiopia, Kenya and, above all, Uganda, whose territories Israeli advisors used to sneak into Sudan. To maximise the impact of the operation in the international sphere, the Mossad also embarked on a secret propaganda campaign and disseminated posters and leaflets on behalf of Anya-Nya across the world, publicising the atrocities Khartoum, the Egyptians and the Soviets were committing against Africans.[5]

If the involvement in Sudan was a Mossad-led clandestine operation, after the 1967 war Israeli security agencies were quietly dominating Israel's presence in neighbouring countries as well. In Ethiopia, Israel began to promote a new secret military alliance (codenamed 'coffee') that envisioned the establishment of a joint Israeli–Ethiopian base in Assab, on the Red Sea, though the plan did not materialise.[6] In Uganda, Israeli military advisors were working in close cooperation with the Ugandan chief of staff, Idi Amin, who also used Israel's assistance and advice to take power in a military coup in January 1971. In exchange for Israeli support – and, according to some accounts, bribes – Amin advanced Israel's strategic and economic interests in Uganda, which included free access to southern Sudan.[7]

Israel's fall from grace in Africa

For Israel, the occupation of Sinai was a strategic asset at home and a diplomatic headache in Africa. On the one hand, Israel occupied Egyptian – therefore African – territory, refused to withdraw from it and soon began establishing military bases and civilian settlements in it. This made it increasingly difficult for Israel to fend off Arab and Soviet allegations that it is a colonial power or for African states to continue to claim that the Israeli–Arab conflict is of no relevance to Africa and should be kept off the OAU's agenda. On the other hand, with Sinai under control, Israel secured an invaluable buffer zone that protected it from potential Egyptian attacks and regained free access through the Straits of Tiran – advantages it was not willing to give up easily.

In the months following the 1967 war, the future of the occupied territories seemed unclear, and African states remained divided on the matter. The only country to sever ties with Israel following the war was Guinea. When the UN General Assembly in July 1967 voted on two resolutions – one supported by the US and considered more Israel-friendly, and the other supported by the Soviet Union and considered more Arab-friendly – 17 African states that had diplomatic ties with Israel supported the US-backed resolution, and only 9 supported the Soviet-backed one.[8] At least in this case, Israel's Africa policy seemed to have paid off, even though neither of the resolutions achieved a sufficient number of votes to be adopted.

It was eventually the UN Security Council that set the tone for the post-1967 negotiations between Israel and its neighbours with Resolution 242, adopted unanimously in November 1967. In essence, the Resolution called for peace in exchange for Israel's withdrawal from the lands it had occupied during the war. A UN mediator, Dr Gunnar Jarring, was tasked with promoting the implementation of the Resolution, but the negotiations in the following years went nowhere. Israel insisted that it would only withdraw once a peace agreement was achieved following direct negotiations, while Egypt and Jordan insisted that first Israel had to withdraw from their territories.[9] Meanwhile, Israel consolidated its control over the lands it had occupied during the war. After its remarkable military victory in 1967, its leaders believed that time was on their side.

At the OAU, however, the consensus was gradually shifting against Israel. In September 1967 the OAU issued a somewhat neutral 'declaration' expressing its 'concern' about the 'grave situation' in Egypt.[10] A year later, a resolution was adopted calling for Israel's withdrawal from 'all Arab territories occupied' during the 1967 war, and appealing to 'all Member States of the OAU to use their influence to ensure a strict implementation of this Resolution'.[11] In the following years, the Israeli–Arab conflict featured regularly in OAU meetings, as members reiterated their call for the implementation of Resolution 242.[12] Behind the principled position on the territorial integrity of a fellow African state, there was another material reason for African concern with the issue. Following the 1967 war, the Suez Canal was shut down. For every year that it remained closed, East African nations were losing some $125 million: the prices of their imports increased and the revenues they earned from exports dropped, as ships had to travel all the way around the Cape of Good Hope. South Africa was therefore the one benefiting, and Israel's refusal to withdraw from Sinai was seen as the main obstacle to solving the matter.[13]

One of the more interesting developments in the African position towards the Middle East at the time was the OAU's ambitious yet ultimately failed attempt to mediate between Israel and Egypt in order to bring the politically uncomfortable and economically damaging stalemate to an end. In February 1971, in response to a proposal made by Jarring, Egypt agreed to enter peace negotiations with Israel. By then, Golda Meir had become Israel's prime minister, having replaced Levi Eshkol, who died earlier in 1969. Replying to Jarring's proposal, however, Meir's government refused to commit to withdrawing to the pre-war borders, thus undermining his initiative.[14] The OAU adopted a resolution deploring 'Israel's defiance to that initiative', and requesting the OAU chairperson, then Ould Daddah of Mauritania, to 'consult with the Heads of State and Government so that they use their influence to ensure the full implementation of this resolution'.[15]

A committee of ten African heads of state was formed. Its mandate was not clearly defined but it was decided that a group of four of these leaders – led by Léopold Senghor of Senegal – would travel to Israel and Egypt to obtain information and come up with recommendations. Israeli officials initially considered boycotting the initiative altogether, but eventually decided to cooperate, not least because they did not want to damage Israel's relationship with African states and hoped that this would be an opportunity to prove that the Arab side was to blame for the stalemate in the negotiations.[16] Indeed, Senghor was one of the African leaders most sympathetic to Israel and to Zionism at the time and his conciliatory approach towards Jerusalem drew criticism from Cairo.[17] But by the time the mission ended even Senghor was frustrated with Israel's intransigence, as Golda Meir still refused to announce that Israel was not interested in annexing any part of Sinai. 'I must say, quite objectively, that the Egyptians made all the concessions they could', Senghor said later. 'Being an African, I understand the Egyptian position. Africa ends at the Sinai Peninsula. Territorial integrity has become a myth in our continent and both we and the Semites live on myths.'[18]

The OAU committee's key recommendation was that Egypt and Israel should resume their negotiations under the auspices of Jarring. But when its proposal was brought before the UN General Assembly in December 1971, most African countries did not support it. The Assembly instead adopted a resolution that politely expressed its 'appreciation' of the African initiative, but explicitly called upon Israel to 'respond favourably' to Jarring's proposal from February that year.[19] The OAU summit in Rabat in June 1972 was the final nail in the coffin of the OAU mediation efforts and represented 'a landmark in the shift of the OAU policy in respect to the Middle East crisis'.[20] The OAU deplored Israel's 'refusal to respond favorably to the initiative of OAU', and called on Israel to 'withdraw immediately from all the occupied Arab territories'.[21]

Meanwhile, Muammar al-Gaddafi, who came to power in 1969, embarked on a calculated diplomatic offensive against Israel's involvement in Africa. He achieved his first victory when Idi Amin, shortly after coming to power, decided to switch sides and dump Israel in favour of Libyan patronage, which now appeared much more lucrative. Amin began by refusing to allow the Mossad to continue using Uganda as a base for its operations in southern Sudan, and in March 1972 officially severed diplomatic ties with Israel. The embassy was closed, and hundreds of Israelis left the country. Israel initially blamed the decision on Amin's erratic and unstable personality, highlighting the fact that before breaking off ties, the Ugandan president demanded unrealistic amounts of military support from Israel, which Israel could not and did not want to provide.[22] But in November and December 1972, Chad and Congo (Brazzaville) severed ties as well, and were followed by Niger, Mali and Burundi in early 1973.

When OAU members convened again in Addis Ababa in May 1973, they adopted another resolution on the Middle East conflict, this time condemning the 'negative attitude of Israel, its acts of terrorism and its obstruction of all efforts aimed at a just and equitable solution' to the conflict with Egypt and calling for its 'immediate and unconditional withdrawal ... from all occupied African and Arab territories'.[23] Hoping that a complete diplomatic collapse could still be averted Israel decided not to disengage from the continent,[24] but did not seem to possess a coherent strategy that would allow it to reverse the pro-Arab trend in Africa while also sticking to its position on the occupied Arab territories. In September, the Non-Aligned Conference convened in Algeria, adopting a resolution that equated Zionism with imperialism and called upon all non-aligned countries to support the Palestinians' 'struggle against Zionist racist and colonialist settlements for the recovery of their full national rights' and to 'boycott Israel diplomatically, economically, militarily and culturally'.[25] Togo severed relations with Israel less than two weeks later, followed, in early October, by Zaire.

The Yom Kippur War and its aftermath

On Saturday 6 October 1973, the Israeli calculation that its Arab neighbours would not start a war and that the status quo in the Middle East could be maintained proved wrong. The story is almost too familiar and dramatic to bear repeating: Egypt and Syria launched a surprise attack against Israel on Yom Kippur (the Day of Atonement) – the most sacred day in the Jewish calendar. Israel was caught unprepared. As the Egyptian military confidently crossed the Suez Canal and Syrian forces entered the Golan Heights, confused Israeli soldiers hurried to the fronts from their homes. The US was initially reluctant to send Israel military aid but was ultimately convinced. With its support Israel managed not only to recover but to take the offensive. By the time the war ended, Israeli forces crossed to the west bank of the Suez Canal and were threatening to continue to Cairo.

The war was the final straw in the deterioration of Israel's diplomatic status in Africa. Dahomey (from 1975, Benin) severed ties on 6 October, the day the war began, followed by Rwanda three days later. The following week, Israeli forces crossed the Suez Canal from the Sinai Peninsula into what is unequivocally African soil and the Arab members of the Organization of Petroleum Exporting Countries (OPEC) decided to raise the prices of oil and place an oil embargo on states supportive of Israel.[26] Both events only increased the pressure on African states to distance themselves from Israel, if not out of solidarity with Egypt then out of fear for their own economies. Within a month, another 18 African states severed relations with Israel. The only African countries that did not were Lesotho, Swaziland, Malawi and Mauritius. The reward from the Arab world came in the form of various commitments for financial aid and the establishment of the Arab Bank for Economic Development in Africa (BADEA), headquartered in Khartoum.[27]

As Israeli bureaucrats were exchanging accusations about who was to blame for Israel's diplomatic downfall in Africa,[28] a number of African leaders approached Israeli representations with conciliatory messages that indicated that in fact they did not perceive the break of diplomatic ties with the same gravity the Israelis did. Some even expressed their hope that Israel would continue supporting them with its technical cooperation programmes despite the lack of formal ties. The Israeli Ministry of Foreign Affairs found this inappropriate, if not offensive. Providing aid to countries that clearly and openly rejected Israel seemed untenable. Not all Israeli assistance programmes were immediately terminated, but in the following years the number of Israeli experts in Africa and African students in Israel dropped.[29]

Nonetheless, after overcoming the initial shock of the diplomatic crisis, the Ministry of Foreign Affairs did instruct its representatives in the US and Europe that if African states approached them and expressed interest 'in creating or solidifying a semi-official Israeli presence, we are open to discussion of the matter'.[30] Thus, while the active diplomatic network the Ministry of Foreign Affairs had established in Africa essentially vanished, Israeli–African security, intelligence and commercial networks did not. Embassies were shut down, but Israeli interest offices were maintained in Kenya, Ghana and Côte d'Ivoire. The Israeli national airline, EL-AL, continued to fly to Nairobi regularly, and trade between Israel and Africa not only continued but grew.[31] Israeli companies that began operating in the continent during the 1960s stayed when the diplomats left, and even expanded their operations.

In the following years, African votes at the UN clearly shifted towards the Arab position on issues concerning Israel and they overwhelmingly supported resolutions that reaffirmed the rights of the Palestinian people.[32] The only exceptions were those states that did not sever ties with Israel, which still occasionally abstained. When the UN General Assembly voted in 1975 on a controversial resolution that defined Zionism as 'a form of racism and racial discrimination', only 5 African countries opposed it and 11 abstained, while the rest supported it.[33] Meanwhile, the Palestine Liberation Organization (PLO), benefiting from the new momentum of Afro-Arab solidarity, slowly began to broaden its diplomatic efforts in Africa, opening missions in countries that severed ties with Israel and mobilising African support for its cause.[34]

The rise of covert military diplomacy

In Israel, turbulent days followed the 1973 war. A national commission of inquiry cleared Golda Meir and her Defence Minister Moshe

Dayan of responsibility for the failure to predict and prepare for the Arab attack. The public was enraged. On 10 April 1974, amidst mass demonstrations, Golda Meir resigned. Yitzhak Rabin, who was chief of staff during the Six Day War and later Israel's ambassador to the US, replaced her. For the first time, Israel had a former chief of staff as its prime minister. Shimon Peres, by then with almost two decades of experience in Israel's defence establishment, lost the battle for the prime minister's position to Rabin and became minister of defence. Yigal Allon, who served as an IDF general during the 1948 war and was Rabin's commander in pre-state Palmach militia, was Israel's new foreign minister.[35]

If military figures dominated Israel's government, the military industries began to dominate its international strategy and economy. After the 1973 war, Israel's deterrence had to be restored. This meant rebuilding its army and, equally important, ensuring that it was as self-sufficient as possible.[36] As the Israeli defence industry massively expanded in the following years, experimenting with new and increasingly sophisticated technologies, the scale of Israeli arms exports soared. In 1967 Israel's total arms exports were esti-mated at around $30 million, most of which was ammunition. By 1973, this number had more or less doubled. By the early 1980s, the figure was above $1 billion annually.[37] To guarantee that the expan-sion of the defence establishment remained viable, Israeli leaders were soon ready to sell arms to whomever agreed to buy them. And their customers were exactly those states ready to buy arms from anyone who agreed to sell them.

The most significant ramification of these processes – politi-cally and economically – was the emergence of an alliance between Israel and the one African state it had previously tried to publicly avoid. Until the early 1970s, Jerusalem had an ambivalent relation-ship with South Africa. The South African Jewish community was one of the most important financial donors to Israel, and since the war of 1948, young Jewish South Africans regularly trav-elled to Israel to volunteer in its military – a 'tradition of military pilgrimage' that has continued until today.[38] But Israel's opposition to apartheid kept the two states apart. Not only did Israel regularly vote against South Africa in the UN, but some of the most vocal anti-apartheid activists in South Africa were Jewish. As Israel was losing ground in Africa, however, the similarities between the Jewish state and apartheid South Africa – two besieged, exclusive communities that viewed themselves as outposts of the West in a hostile, Soviet-dominated environment – became increasingly apparent, the identification between their leaders and publics grew, and their interests began to converge.

After the events of October 1973 and under the leadership of Shimon Peres on the Israeli side and Defence Minister P. W. Botha on the South African side, negotiations began on a comprehensive and far-reaching defence cooperation.[39] In 1976, South African Prime Minister John Vorster travelled to Israel on an official visit, giving the emerging relationship a public facet. But, as Sasha Polakow-Suransky shows in his detailed study of this alliance, its true nature and scope remained confidential. Away from the public's eyes, the defence elites of both countries developed remarkably close ties as they were regularly shuttling between Tel Aviv and Johannesburg, sharing intelligence and experiences in counterinsurgency warfare and developing new military technologies. Covert arms trade and military cooperation flourished and continued well after the UN Security Council in November 1977 passed a mandatory arms embargo against Pretoria. By 1979, some 35% of Israeli military exports were heading to South Africa – Israel's largest arms client.[40] The cooperation probably reached its most extreme level of secrecy with the collaboration in the development of nuclear bombs and delivery systems. The two countries exchanged not only knowledge in this field but also nuclear materials and are widely believed to have conducted a nuclear test together in the South Atlantic Ocean in September 1979.[41]

Another country that maintained a similarly discreet and highly influential relationship with Israel after 1973 was Ethiopia. In 1974, a revolution led to the overthrow of Emperor Haile Selassie and the emergence of the socialist Derg regime, led by Mengistu Haile Mariam. So deep was Israeli involvement in Ethiopia until 1973 that Israeli Ethiopianist Haggai Erlich has argued that the inability of the imperial establishment to deal with the popular protests it faced in 1974 was partly the result of the expulsion of Israeli military advisors from the country.[42] Soon after Mengistu took power, he followed in the steps of the emperor he had deposed and turned to Israel, seeking both military support and assistance with convincing Washington to continue its support to Ethiopia despite the brutality of its new Marxist-inspired regime. The Derg saw as its ultimate objective the establishment of a united centralised nation state in Ethiopia and continued to fight secessionists in the northern part of the country. Like Israel, it had an interest in preventing an independent Eritrea.

In return for access to Ethiopian ports in the Red Sea, Israel trained the Ethiopian military and supplied it with ammunition and spare parts.[43] The Derg also allowed several members of the Beta Israel community – the Jews of Ethiopia – to leave the country for Israel.[44] Before Mengistu managed to secure Soviet support, Israel tried to advocate on his behalf in the US and to mobilise President Jimmy Carter's support for a strong Israeli–Ethiopian cooperation, but Carter was unconvinced and reportedly perplexed by the importance the Israelis attached to the issue.[45] The covert Israeli–Ethiopian relationship temporarily fell apart in early 1978, when Moshe Dayan, then Israel's foreign minister, accidentally (or not) exposed it in an interview. The Derg responded in anger but admitted that the relationship existed because Israel was the only country that agreed to sell arms to Ethiopia.[46] According to Mossad veteran Yossi Alpher, Siad Barre, the president of Somalia, discreetly approached Israel, presumably hoping to attract Israeli and American support after the Soviets switched sides and abandoned him for Mengistu, but he was rebuffed.[47]

Meanwhile, just across the border from Ethiopia and Somalia, cooperation between Israeli and Kenyan security and intelligence agencies was also maintained despite the lack of formal bilateral ties. This relationship was particularly close, allowing Israel to carry out in 1976 the famous 'Operation Entebbe'. In July that year Israel sent its commando units to Uganda to raid Entebbe airport and release Israeli hostages that were held there after their plane was hijacked by the Popular Front for the Liberation of Palestine (PFLP). Kenya quietly provided support and allowed Israeli planes to refuel in Nairobi on their way back to Israel. In fact, earlier that same year, Israeli intelligence secretly cooperated with Kenya to thwart another attack by the PFLP – an attempt to shoot down an Israeli aircraft departing from Nairobi. Jomo Kenyatta was promised absolute confidentiality with regard to his country's cooperation with Israel on the matter.[48]

The expansion of arms diplomacy

In March 1979, following months of negotiations mediated by American President Jimmy Carter, Egypt and Israel signed a peace treaty. Over the next year Israel started evacuating its military and civilians from the Sinai Peninsula, and in February 1980 diplomatic relations were established between Israel and Egypt and ambassadors were exchanged. This was a historic moment – the result of an effort that won President Anwar al-Sadat of Egypt and Israeli Prime Minister Menachem Begin the Nobel Peace Prize. By no means, however, was it uncontroversial. The West Bank, Gaza and the Golan Heights remained under Israeli occupation and Israel had little intention of withdrawing from them.[49] Egypt, accused of betraying the other Arab nations by independently reaching a separate deal with Israel, was expelled from the Arab League, and in 1981 President Sadat was assassinated by Islamic fundamentalists.[50]

Nonetheless, the withdrawal from Sinai removed what was in theory the main reason African countries broke ties with Israel in 1973, and an Israeli attempt to initiate an African comeback came shortly afterwards, with the appointment of David Kimche as the director general of the Ministry of Foreign Affairs. Kimche is another interesting example of the expanding influence of the Israeli security elite on civilian institutions. He was one of Mossad's founding fathers and most respected spymasters and, during the 1960s, one of the agency's most influential agents in Africa. Working with a unit in the Mossad in charge of clandestine diplomacy and communication with foreign intelligence agencies, he is said to have regularly travelled around the continent under false identities.[51] He went on to serve as Mossad's deputy director, before leaving the organisation and joining the Ministry of Foreign Affairs in 1981.

Meanwhile, in Africa, the days of state-led development were over, as many states went through a process of decay due to the economic crises of the 1970s. Public sector expenditure declined, and state institutions crumbled as leaders were pressured to liberalise their economies and adopt the austerity measures proposed by the World Bank and the International Monetary Fund (IMF). They therefore had to find new ways to guarantee their access to external support and the survival of their regimes.[52] In this context, the first to restore ties with Israel were those leaders who sought to improve their links with Israel's patron, the US, in order to guarantee its assistance, and hoped that Israeli security expertise would help them 'coup proof' their regimes by providing them with high-quality training, intelligence and equipment for their personal guards or newly established elite units.[53] No country in Africa came close to purchasing from Israel the amounts of arms South Africa did, but Israeli security expertise came to play an important role in guaranteeing the survival of several leaders.

In late 1981, Israeli Defence Minister Ariel Sharon, the general-turned-politician who earlier, in the 1970s, had masterminded Israel's expansion into the West Bank through the establishment of settlements, went on an African tour. Sharon sought not only strategic allies and arms customers but also avenues to strengthen Israel's cooperation with the US through curbing Soviet influence around the world. He visited Côte d'Ivoire, Liberia, Central

African Republic (CAR), Gabon and Zaire.[54] Of all the leaders he met, Sharon was apparently most impressed by Mobutu, who invited him for a kosher lunch on his yacht on the Congo River. 'I had the distinct impression that I was in the presence of a leader', he later wrote.[55] Within weeks, a group of Israeli military advisors was training and arming Mobutu's personal bodyguards – a covert project that became 'the worst-kept secret in Kinshasa'.[56]

Mobutu, presiding over a militarised, corrupt and bankrupt state, announced in May 1982 that his country would re-establish diplomatic relations with Israel.[57] The official reasoning provided for this decision was Israel's withdrawal from Sinai. In reality, Mobutu sought to achieve three things: Israeli security assistance, Israeli support in salvaging his deteriorating reputation in Washington (and, by implication, American support for his regime) and investment in Zaire by Jewish or Israeli businessmen.[58] Having already allied himself with the Western side of the Cold War and having fought on the same side as South Africa in the war in Angola, Mobutu was not particularly deterred by Israel's close relationship with Pretoria or concerned about a potential Soviet backlash. He nonetheless paid a price for his decision: several Arab nations downgraded or severed diplomatic relations with Zaire, and the BADEA suspended its support.[59]

Israel had to demonstrate that the gains from restoring relations with it were greater than the damage countries might suffer from losing Arab support. Several Israeli high-level visits to Zaire were arranged, including by Foreign Minister Yitzhak Shamir, Defence Minister Ariel Sharon and President Haim Hertzog. Israeli businessmen with useful contacts were also mobilised for the purpose and encouraged to invest in Zaire. Behind the scenes and at Mobutu's behest, Israel also encouraged US officials to pressure the IMF to treat Zaire favourably in order to prevent an 'anti-Western turn' in Kinshasa.[60] Mobutu himself came to Israel in 1985, where he was ceremoniously received with a 21-gun salute, a band and a flyover by fighter jets.[61] According to media reports, Israel gave him credit for arms purchases and promised to encourage investment by Israelis and the Jewish diaspora in Zaire.[62]

Despite these efforts, relations with Zaire did not immediately lead to the resumption of ties with other African countries. A month after Zaire and Israel re-established ties, Israel invaded Lebanon – another initiative promoted by Ariel Sharon. The official objectives were to clear southern Lebanon of PLO insurgents 'once and for all', and to help Lebanon's Christians seize power.[63] Assistance to Lebanon's Maronite minority was based on the same logic that motivated Israel's support for southern Sudanese rebels more than a decade earlier, namely, that it is in the country's interest to support minorities in the Middle East who fight its Arab enemies. David Kimche, during his time in the Mossad, was one of the main architects of Israel's relationship with the Maronites. The invasion eventually caused immense destruction, and Israel's idea of putting in power a Christian ally in Beirut did not materialise. The war also worsened Israel's economic situation and international image. Egypt recalled its ambassador from Israel, and Israel's African comeback inevitably slowed down.[64]

Underlying Israel's activities in Africa during the 1980s was the Israeli–American rivalry with Muammar Gaddafi, who was not only Soviet-allied but who also supported the PLO and, after playing a key role in its diplomatic downfall in the continent in 1973, tried to undermine Israel's renewed efforts to project its influence into Africa. Militarily, the epicentre of this competition was Libya's southern neighbour, Chad, which Gaddafi hoped to dominate and use as a springboard into Central Africa. In 1982, 'anti-Libyan' Hissène Habré took power in N'Djamena in a coup – with US assistance and, according to some accounts, using Soviet arms that were retained by Israel and delivered to him by the CIA.[65] Supported by Zaire and the US, Habré fought Libya-backed rebels in the country's north, and in a clandestine initiative that was publicly denied by all involved, Israel also sent a small group of military advisors via Zaire to Chad in 1983, to support his efforts.[66]

The rivalry with Libya projected onto the wider region. While Israel hoped to capitalise on the antagonism and fears that Gaddafi's aggressive diplomacy raised among Western-allied African leaders in order to isolate him, African leaders were able to use the Israeli–Libyan competition to attract and manipulate external support. One person who did that was Liberia's Samuel Doe, who in August 1983 became the second African leader to announce that his country would restore ties with Israel. After taking power in a brutal coup in 1980, Doe opted to ally with the US rather than Libya. He did this against the advice of some of his left-leaning brothers in arms, who were soon executed.[67] Paranoid about a potential backlash and allegedly at American behest, he restored ties with Israel. Israel in return agreed to provide him with intelligence on Libya and military equipment and advice.[68] In the following years, Israeli military advisors trained Doe's bodyguards and elite units. By 1990, he claimed to have survived almost 40 assassination or coup attempts.[69]

In early 1984, after surviving two coup attempts, Cameroon's Paul Biya also secretly turned to Israel and asked for assistance in training his security services and, more importantly, in reorganising, training and arming his own guards.[70] The go-between who facilitated Israel's clandestine negotiations with Biya was Meir Meyouhas – an Egypt-born Israeli who was first sent to Zaire by the Mossad in the early 1960s and later established himself in West Africa as a businessman and served as an advisor to Mobutu. With his local connections, Meyouhas served as an informal emissary for the Israeli Ministry of Defense and David Kimche.[71] After Félix Houphouët-Boigny of Côte d'Ivoire announced in early 1986 that his country would restore ties with Israel, Biya formally did the same. Israeli military advisors and security companies had already been operating in Cameroon for some two years by then.

It was not only Libya, however, that was undermining Israel's efforts in Africa. Despite the secrecy that surrounded it, the Israeli–South African friendship attracted growing attention internationally, and by the mid-1980s was becoming a major *hasbara* concern for

Israel. For the critics of the two countries, this relationship was obviously a goldmine for propaganda.[72] Israeli diplomats and supporters – many genuinely unaware of the full scale of Israel's covert military cooperation with South Africa and others blatantly lying – went to great lengths to downplay its scope in order to minimise the damage it was causing. Moreover, Israeli politicians often continued to maintain a public façade of opposition to apartheid while they were secretly arming Pretoria. In August 1986, Shimon Peres, by then Israel's prime minister, visited Cameroon on a widely covered trip during which he told reporters that 'A Jewish person could never support apartheid'.[73] In reality, the Israeli–South African military cooperation continued until the dying days of the regime.

As the end of the Cold War was drawing nearer, the strategic interests of the superpowers in Africa declined and with it their motivation to support African rulers. Four more countries renewed ties with Israel by the end of the 1980s, all due to similar defence interests and hopes that closer ties with Israel would improve their relationship with the US administration. In June 1987, Gnassingbé Eyadéma – Togo's president since 1967 who was facing growing popular dissent – announced that his country would restore ties with Israel, and asked Israel to train his presidential guards. Togo was followed by Kenya (which re-established relations in 1988), CAR (January 1989) and Ethiopia, which was eager not only to court the West before the Soviet Union's final collapse, but also to trade the Beta Israel population in exchange for Israeli arms. We return to this bargain in Chapter 5.

Diplomacy on the cheap

If in Africa the end of the Cold War brought with it a wave of democratisation, in Israel it led to two historic agreements between Israel and its Arab neighbours. The first was an Israeli–Jordanian peace agreement, signed by Prime Minister Yitzhak Rabin and King Hussein in October 1994. The second was the Israeli–PLO

Oslo Accords. Signed between 1993 and 1995, these agreements provided for the withdrawal of Israeli military forces from the main Palestinian urban areas in the West Bank and Gaza and for the establishment of a Palestinian council which attained limited control over those territories. The Accords only set out an interim arrangement but reflected an Israeli willingness to withdraw from occupied territories in return for peace, something an increasingly vocal sector of the Israeli public viewed as unacceptable. On 4 November 1995, Rabin was assassinated by a right-wing extremist at a peace rally in Tel Aviv, and the following year Binyamin Netanyahu, who unequivocally opposed the Oslo Accords, was elected prime minister for the first time.

The collapse of the Soviet Union – the main patron of Israel's adversaries – and the consequent peace initiatives, transformed Israel's international standing. Already in 1991, when the UN General Assembly voted on a resolution revoking the 1975 'Zionism is racism' resolution, 111 states supported it. In Africa, the impact was also evident by the number of countries that were willing to establish diplomatic relations with Israel after 1991. Between 1991 and 1997, 29 African states established ties with Israel, including newly independent countries such as Eritrea and Namibia and the former Portuguese colonies that achieved their independence in the 1970s. A particularly important achievement from the Israeli perspective was also the establishment of ties with Mauritania – an Islamic country and a member of the Arab League. Notably, neither Ethiopia nor South Africa, where unpopular regimes that Israel supported collapsed, severed ties after the transformation. By the late 1990s Israel had formal diplomatic relations with 42 African states,[74] and ties with Morocco and Tunisia also improved.[75]

While Israel maintained its interest in the Red Sea and the Horn, by the time it finally achieved its full diplomatic comeback in Africa, the continent had lost much of its political importance in the international system as well as in Israel's foreign policy strategy. In the early 1990s Israel normalised its relationships not only with

Jordan and to a certain extent with the PLO in the Middle East, but also upgraded its relations with Turkey, and established ties with India, China and several other countries in Asia and in the Pacific Ocean.[76] Overall, between 1988 and 1998, Israel established or renewed relations with 58 countries around the world.[77] It was no longer the isolated pariah that it had been only a few years earlier and Africa was no longer an important theatre for its diplomatic – and certainly not its military – battles. Moreover, with the establishment of ties with countries in Israel's immediate vicinity, the logic behind the 'periphery doctrine' lost its relevance.

The re-establishment of ties with many African countries therefore did not lead to a relationship that was in any way similar to that nourished during the 1960s. Israeli regional embassies were opened in key political and economic centres on the continent and based on strategic interest, not in every country as during the 1960s. Government development aid programmes continued, but MASHAV focused its attention on other parts of the world and its budget shrank.[78] Several scholars have observed that by the 1990s Israel's presence in Africa was largely 'privatised'.[79] With the Israeli government uninterested in investing in its Africa diplomacy, and with the accelerated economic liberalisation the continent witnessed throughout the 1990s, businessmen and private companies effectively became the main actors representing Israel in Africa. In many countries they had much closer ties with the local leadership than Israeli diplomats, who were often absent from the scene altogether. What the term 'privatisation' fails to grasp, however, is the thick informal ties between private actors and the Israeli formal security sector and political elite. Such ties rendered the distinction between private and public interests and institutions blurred.

Former security officials who continued to operate in a quasi-formal role under a private hat as arms merchants, military advisors and informal emissaries were an important part of this process. In Cameroon, for instance, former IDF officer Avi Sivan, who served as Israel's military attaché to the country, stayed in Yaoundé after his retirement, opening a shelter for endangered apes with his wife while also serving as a private security advisor to President Biya. Back in Israel Sivan was the commander of the military's Duvdevan Unit – an elite force leading special undercover operations in the West Bank. In Cameroon, Sivan's counterinsurgency experience was put to use when he trained the rapid intervention battalion (known by its French acronym, BIR) and the Presidential Guard – elite forces that report directly to President Biya.[80] With his contacts with Israel's and Cameroon's elites, Sivan became the main interlocutor for Israeli companies that wanted to sell equipment to the Cameroonian security apparatus: 'It was impossible to enter and work in Cameroon in the fields of national defence without cooperating with him.'[81]

And there were other variations to the blending of private and public interests and institutions. In Rwanda, a dominant emissary became Hezi Bezalel, a businessman who started working in Africa in the 1980s and later established himself in multiple fields, including infrastructure, banking and security, in numerous African countries. Maintaining close ties with both Paul Kagame and the upper echelons of the Israeli security, political and economic elite, he went on to serve as the honorary consul of Rwanda in Israel.[82] In Uganda, relations with Israel were re-established during the 1990s with the facilitation of President Yoweri Museveni's brother, General Salim Saleh.[83] Saleh worked with Bezalel and other Israeli businessmen, including arms merchants who supplied the Ugandan military with both Israeli and non-Israeli equipment and services.[84] Coordinating Museveni's visit to Israel in 2003 was Amos Golan – a former military general and an arms merchant who represented Israeli military industries in Uganda and later served as the country's honorary consul in Israel.[85] Meanwhile, Burundi's honorary consul in Israel was Gaby Peretz – a former IDF general who in the late 1980s established a company that traded, among other things, in military equipment, primarily from Eastern European countries, and was reportedly active in no fewer than 15 African countries.[86]

Israeli businessmen and arms merchants who were less closely linked, if at all, to the Israeli diplomatic network in Africa acquired a particularly bad reputation for their involvement in diamond mining, informal markets and armed conflicts in countries such as Sierra Leone, Liberia, Angola, Rwanda and the DRC.[87] Diamond polishing has long been a major industry in Israel, but it was traditionally dependent on the imports of rough diamonds by foreign companies. Throughout the 1990s, however, Israeli businessmen became increasingly involved in mining operations in Africa. While formally Israel tried to distance itself from the controversies associated with mining and the arms trade, the distinction between what appeared to be entirely private business enterprises and bilateral relationships that had at least some formal facet was often vague, because independent entrepreneurs had close ties with members of Israel's 'security network' and the Ministry of Defense, and merely by facilitating arms exports were understood to be advancing the latter's interests.[88]

Consider, for example, the case of Israeli involvement in the DRC. Israeli billionaire Dan Gertler – a young ultra-Orthodox man and the grandson of the former president of the Israeli Diamond Bourse – was accused of using his close ties with Laurent Kabila to secure a monopoly on diamonds in the early 2000s. According to a UN report, in return for the monopoly, Kabila was promised $20 million and military support from Israeli security advisors whom Gertler recruited. These, it was later revealed, included ex-IDF general Avigdor Ben-Gal as well as Meir Dagan, who later became director of Mossad.[89] What ultimately came out of these negotiations is disputed, but Gertler is said to have maintained a close relationship with Joseph Kabila as well following the assassination of his father. He became the DRC's honorary consul in Israel, and reportedly lobbied on Kabila's behalf in Washington. By 2017 he was placed on a US sanctions list for his ongoing involvement in 'opaque and corrupt mining and oil deals' in the DRC.[90]

A security empire

A combination of processes starting from 1967 led to the gradual securitisation, privatisation and informalisation of Israel's presence in, and relationship with, African countries and leaders. The growing fusion between Israeli political and military elites following the wars of 1967 and 1973, coupled with the rise of the Israeli arms industry, made security personnel increasingly influential in shaping Israel's foreign and defence priorities. Israel's diplomatic downfall in Africa meant that the influence of Israeli security agencies and private actors on the continent increased and that of civilian agencies and the Ministry of Foreign Affairs was diminished, a process that was further enhanced by Africa's economic crises, the growing importance of informal markets and the liberalisation of African economies. Thus, the 'statist' bilateral ties of the 1960s were transformed into relationships dominated by informal networks of businessmen and (former or serving) officials that straddle the public–private divide.

In 1973, Israel was expelled from Africa because of its conflict with Egypt. Arab countries were able to use their political and economic weight and the power of African solidarity – articulated and magnified through the OAU and other multilateral fora – to convince almost all African leaders to formally abandon Israel, including some who were reluctant to do so. Ironically, Israel was able to forge new relationships in Africa in the following decades not only *despite* its conflicts with its Arab neighbours but also *because* of these conflicts, as African leaders increasingly sought to draw on Israeli experience and expertise, particularly in counterinsurgency and asymmetric warfare, to pursue their local objectives. With its arms industry and exports, Israel was able to turn its ongoing involvement in conflicts from a burden into an economic and diplomatic opportunity.[91]

If the early 1960s provided Israel with memories of bilateral partnerships that its leaders today take pride in, Israel's alliances with apartheid South Africa, Mengistu, Mobutu or Doe are not historical episodes that are publicly celebrated, and nor is the involvement of Israeli businessmen or arms in atrocities and corruption scandals in multiple African conflict zones in the 1990s. In retrospect, partnerships with autocratic regimes were often justified by Israel as a geostrategic necessity and the involvement of Israeli actors in shady businesses were dismissed as private ventures – ones that have little to do with formal Israeli institutions. Publicly praised or not, however, the network of businessmen and former security personnel that came to define Israel in Africa remains a central thread in its history on the continent, and so is the system-atic utilisation of arms exports for cementing bilateral ties. These are not legacies that can be easily untangled, and Israel never had a serious incentive to untangle them. Beneath the public surface, they continue to shape Israel's presence in Africa today.

Chapter 3

OLD BATTLES, NEW WARS

The Israeli–Palestinian Oslo Accords of 1993 established a framework that at least some had hoped would pave the way for a two-state solution and peace in Israel/Palestine. By the beginning of the Second Intifada in late 2000, it was clear that the peace process envisioned in Oslo was not going anywhere. Over the following decade, public opinion among Israel's Jewish population consolidated around a grim consensus according to which Israel is surrounded by enemies and faces multiple existential threats.[1] Peace or any democratic transformation in Israel/Palestine came to be viewed by the majority of the Jewish population as dangerous and irrational, the expansion of Israeli settlements in the Occupied Palestinian Territories was further entrenched and for most Israelis the occupation became a normal state of affairs.

Still, there were turbulent international waters to navigate. The attacks of 9/11 and the ensuing American 'war on terror' certainly gave renewed legitimacy to Israel's counterterrorism measures in the Occupied Territories, particularly but not only in the eyes of the US. Yet since the Oslo Accords, the international community has maintained its nominal support of the two-state solution, which Israel has shown less and less interest in implementing. And in the absence of any meaningful steps being taken towards ending the occupation, international criticism of Israel's policies continued, and the country's international standing, which improved during the 1990s, was slowly deteriorating again during the 2000s.[2] Israel managed international pressure by continuing to strategically cooperate with American peace initiatives, but it repeatedly opted for stalemate instead of separation into two states.[3]

As the peace process stalled, another issue came to dominate Israel's international strategy: its regional power struggle with Iran. As discussed in the first chapter, in the decades following its independence, Iran and Turkey were Israel's most important regional allies. By the late 2000s this had changed dramatically. Relations with Iran had already soured after the 1979 Islamic revolution but developed into a full-fledged rivalry over regional domination after the end of the Cold War, with Iran supporting the Syrian government, Hamas (in Gaza) and Hizbullah (in southern Lebanon).[4] By the late 2000s, Ankara was also shifting towards Tehran: Israel's relationship with Turkey, which had improved significantly during the 1990s, deteriorated following the 2008 Israeli offensive in Gaza and unravelled after the Israeli military in May 2010 killed ten Turkish citizens when it intercepted a flotilla of boats that attempted to break the Israeli naval blockade off the coastline of the Gaza Strip.

Against the background of its rivalry with Iran and the unpopularity of the occupation, Israeli leaders slowly began pursuing what some have described as an updated version of Israel's old 'periphery' strategy, looking for new international partnerships that would guarantee that Israel can guard its interests in Israel/Palestine, counter its enemies and reverse its slow isolation.[5] Over the last decade, this campaign led Israel to strengthen relations not only with African countries but also with other potential allies across the globe: from Gulf states, through Azerbaijan, Greece and Cyprus as a direct counterweight to Ankara and Tehran, and all the way to India, China, Latin American countries, Singapore, Japan and Australia. Due to their geographical proximity and large number, however, African states became a central part of this global charm offensive.

Israel, Iran and the Gulf in Africa

When Netanyahu came (back) to power in March 2009, he promised Israelis a new age of determination and firmness in the war against terrorism. Israel was under international criticism for its conduct during the war in Gaza (titled 'Operation Cast Lead' by Israel) which ended two months earlier and claimed the lives of some 1,400 Palestinians and 13 Israelis. A UN fact-finding mission headed by South African judge Richard Goldstone was investigating allegations of war crimes committed during the conflict (and its report was later endorsed by the United Nations General Assembly (UNGA), see Table 3.1). Meanwhile, Iranian President Mahmoud Ahmadinejad was trying to promote his country's relations with African countries in an attempt to battle against his own international isolation and to mobilise support for Iran's controversial nuclear programme, which Israel was determined to stop. He had already visited the continent several times since coming to power in 2005, courting African leaders with promises of economic investment and security support. In early 2009, Mauritania recalled its ambassador to Israel in protest at Israel's offensive in Gaza, and the following year severed ties and switched sides to Iran.[6]

Table 3.1 African votes in UNGA Resolution 64/10, November 2009, calling for independent inquiries by Israel and the Palestinians into the war crime claims made in the UN Fact Finding Mission's report on the Gaza Conflict ('Goldstone Report')

Yes (37)	No (0)	Abstain (8)	Absent (8)
Algeria, Angola, Benin, Botswana, CAR, Chad, Comoros, Congo (Brazzaville), DRC, Djibouti, Egypt, Eritrea, Gabon, Gambia, Ghana, Guinea, Guinea-Bissau, Lesotho, Libya, Malawi, Mali, Mauritania, Mauritius, Morocco, Mozambique, Namibia, Niger, Nigeria, Senegal, Sierra Leone, Somalia, South Africa, Sudan, Tunisia, Tanzania, Zambia, Zimbabwe		Burkina Faso, Burundi, Cameroon, Ethiopia, Kenya, Liberia, Swaziland, Uganda	Cape Verde, Côte d'Ivoire, Equatorial Guinea, Madagascar, Rwanda, São Tomé and Príncipe, Seychelles, Togo

Already in July 2009, Israel's new foreign minister, Avigdor Liberman of the *Yisrael Beiteinu* ('Israel is our home') party, travelled to Latin America, and in September embarked on his first Africa tour, visiting Ethiopia, Kenya, Uganda, Ghana and Nigeria. 'For many years, Israeli leaders were absent from entire regions around the world', he said before the visit.[7] Liberman signed several bilateral cooperation agreements focusing on civilian fields such as agriculture, irrigation and fishery. One cooperation agreement was also signed with the Economic Community of West African States (ECOWAS) – a significant step given that three ECOWAS members (Guinea, Mali and Niger) did not have diplomatic relations with Israel at the time.[8] A decision was also taken to open an Israeli embassy in Ghana, and it materialised in 2011. Israeli intelligence agencies, it should be noted, had an interest in West Africa not only due to the growing Iranian influence in the region but also due to the involvement of members of the Lebanese diaspora in West Africa in financing Hizbullah, the Iran-allied Shi'a armed group based in southern Lebanon.

Developments in West Africa notwithstanding, Israel was more concerned with Iran's involvement in East Africa and the Horn of Africa. Sudan has been on the radar of Israeli intelligence agencies since the 1990s because of the close ties it cultivated with Iran and its central role in supporting members of various Islamist militant groups, including Hamas and Palestinian Islamic Jihad (PIJ). When Osama bin Laden was based in Khartoum between 1992 and 1996, he maintained links with Egyptian, Palestinian and Lebanese Islamists, and Israel's surveillance of these actors drew its attention to his activities as well.[9] While al-Qaeda's efforts in the Horn were mainly directed against American interests, in 2002 its operatives also bombed a beach resort in Kenya known for hosting large groups of Israeli tourists, killing ten Kenyans and three Israelis, and attempted, unsuccessfully, to shoot down an Israeli plane that took off from Moi International Airport in Mombasa.[10]

By the time of the 2002 attacks, not much was left of al-Qaeda in the Horn of Africa. Bin Laden had already been expelled from

Khartoum in 1996, and Sudan had begun to support Washington's interests in the region. It did, however, continue to serve as a hub for arms-smuggling from Iran, via the Red Sea, to Hamas in Gaza. Israel's quest in the late 2000s to isolate Hamas from its patrons and arms suppliers in Iran therefore led it to Sudan once again. In January 2009, Israel (allegedly) bombed a convoy of weapons that was making its way through Sudan, destined for Gaza, and it was also assumed to be behind the targeted assassination of a Hamas member in Port Sudan in April 2011 and the bombing of the Yarmouk Industrial Complex near Khartoum in October 2012.[11] Constructed in the mid-1990s, the complex was partly Iranian-owned and was run by the Sudanese National Intelligence and Security Service with Iranian support.[12]

The notion of a new Israeli East African 'periphery' – comprising, as it did in the 1960s, Kenya, Uganda, Ethiopia and newly independent South Sudan – seems to have emerged in 2011–12, not necessarily as a clearly articulated policy but as a broad attempt to counter Iran's growing influence in the Red Sea and East Africa. Another important factor behind Israel's new attempt to consolidate alliances in East Africa at the time was the Arab Spring, which reshuffled the Middle East's political landscape and generated uncertainty and concerns that actors viewed by Israel as enemies would gain influence across its immediate neighbourhood. In particular, the ousting of Hosni Mubarak and the consequent electoral victory of the Muslim Brotherhood in Egypt in 2012 was seen in Jerusalem as a troubling boost to Iran's influence in the region and the potential loss of an important regional ally.[13]

Crucially, geopolitical conditions in the Horn of Africa were also conducive to Israel's interests. The emergence of al-Shabaab in Somalia as a new local Islamist threat after the demise of al-Qaeda meant that by the late 2000s, Ethiopia, Uganda and Kenya were all entangled in the American 'war on terror' agenda and keen to attract Israeli counterterrorism and political support. Ethiopia invaded Somalia in 2006, Uganda contributed troops to the AU

Mission to Somalia (AMISOM) from 2007 and Kenya invaded southern Somalia in late 2011 and later joined AMISOM as well. While South Sudan was not involved in Somalia, it was on the brink of war with Sudan after its 2011 independence due to disputes over territories along their shared border, and Juba was supporting rebel groups inside Sudan. Both Ugandan President Yoweri Museveni and Kenyan Prime Minister Raila Odinga visited Israel in November 2011, immediately following Kenya's invasion of Somalia, and were followed by South Sudan's Salva Kiir in December.[14] Netanyahu even announced at the time that he planned to visit Kenya and Uganda, but later quietly cancelled the trip.

In the following years, Israeli efforts in Africa spread more widely, driven by additional diplomatic and economic objectives (further explored below) but also as regional threats and alliances in the Middle East and the Horn of Africa transformed. In 2013, the Muslim Brotherhood was overthrown, and Cairo returned to the American–Israeli fold. Meanwhile, the relationship with Juba slowly lost its centrality after civil war broke out in South Sudan and as Khartoum enhanced its cooperation with the US and appeared increasingly open to relations with Israel as well. Israel had lobbied on Sudan's behalf in Washington, urging the US to soften its stance towards Khartoum in order to further distance it from Tehran,[15] and by early 2016 careful conciliatory signs in the Israeli–Sudanese relationship began to emerge in public after Omar al-Bashir cut diplomatic ties with Iran under pressure from Riyadh. Further west, Chad, one of the few African countries that had not renewed ties with Israel since breaking them off in 1972, joined the trend: after years of quiet rapprochement, President Idriss Déby visited Jerusalem in November 2018 and in early 2019 Netanyahu travelled to Ndjamena and bilateral ties between Israel and Chad were formally restored.

As the Sudanese shift indicates, Israel's efforts to project its influence in Africa were affected by the attempts of Gulf countries to do the same, but with much more visibility and cash. Two events, neither immediately linked to Israel, led Gulf countries to compete aggressively for allies in the Horn of Africa in the years following the Arab Spring. The first was the war in Yemen (2015), in which Saudi Arabia and the UAE intervened in order to curb Huthi rebels associated with Iran. The second was the consequent Gulf Crisis (2017), which pitted the two countries (along with Egypt and Bahrain) against Qatar, due, among other things, to the latter's relations with Iran and support for the Muslim Brotherhood. The fact that Riyadh and Abu Dhabi had been united in their opposition to Tehran has served Israeli interests, as their growing military, political and economic involvement in the Horn of Africa displaced Iranian influence, mainly along the southern shores of the Red Sea. Most crucially, it led both Eritrea and Sudan, previously Iran's partners in the region, to upgrade their ties with Saudi Arabia and the UAE.

Although publicly they maintain a critical stance towards Israel's policies in the Occupied Territories, in recent years both Saudi Arabia and the UAE have shown a growing interest in developing economic and, much subtler and more secretive, political and security cooperation with Israel as part of a mutual Middle Eastern front against Iran. Together with Oman – which Netanyahu also visited in 2018 – they can be said to represent Israel's Gulf 'periphery' partners. The slow improvement in Israel's quiet relations with Arab countries on both sides of the Red Sea was quietly manifested by Sudan's and Saudi Arabia's decisions to allow commercial flights (of non-Israeli airlines) to regularly fly over their territories when travelling to Tel Aviv from New Delhi and Addis Ababa.[16] As long as the Saudi–Emirati bloc seemed to be gaining the upper hand in the Horn, therefore, Israel was satisfied. But it followed closely the efforts of Qatar (and, from outside the Gulf, Turkey) to counter this trend through investments in infrastructure, aid, trade, cultural cooperation and public diplomacy.

The US is another distant but important part of this regional geopolitical puzzle. It was no secret that President Barack Obama and Netanyahu did not see eye to eye on Iran. After the former left the White House in January 2017, however, Washington's position on the issue changed dramatically, as Donald Trump's Middle East strategy was being shaped by foreign policy hawks who readily endorsed the Israeli vision of a regional anti-Iran coalition, comprising of Saudi Arabia, the UAE and Israel. And this vision concerned not only Iran. Underlying Israel's evolving partnerships with Riyadh and Abu Dhabi was Jerusalem's apparent hope that the latter two would forgo the Palestinian issue for the sake of the economic and political benefits of a strategic alliance with Israel and the US. With Trump in the White House, therefore, Netanyahu's hope to bury the Palestinian issue by leaving the Palestinians with no support from the Arab world and forcing them to accept the status quo or a deal under Israel's terms – to 'sign onto apartheid', chief Palestinian negotiator Saeb Erekat complained – slowly appeared to be turning into reality.[17] Israel's objective in Africa has been to convince African leaders that it is in their best interests to abandon their pro-Palestinian stance as well and stand by Israel and its allies.

Israel and the Palestinians in Africa

Folded within the tectonic geopolitical rivalries of Middle Eastern powers in Africa is also a subtler legal–diplomatic battle over the future of Palestine. Since renewing ties with Israel in the 1990s, African countries largely maintained their pro-Palestinian voting record at multilateral fora. They usually continued to follow the formal position of the OAU, and later the AU, on this matter, and since Arab League members and the Palestinians had and continue to have considerable influence in these institutions, their position has consistently been one of solidarity with the Palestinians. Israel, well acquainted with the problematic effect the combination of Arab influence and pan-African solidarity can have on its status in Africa, has been eager to change this pattern by either convincing African countries not to cast their vote at other international fora according to the AU's position, or breaking the AU's support for the Palestinians.

In the past, Israel had slightly more room for lobbying in Africa since it had the status of an observer state at the OAU. 'We used to attend the summits', Avi Granot, who was Israel's ambassador to Ethiopia during the late 1990s and the head of the Africa Division at the Ministry of Foreign Affairs between 2011 and 2015, recalled. 'Our main work was in the corridors: to try to persuade foreign ministers and heads of state not to vote automatically in favour of the Palestinians with resolutions that were really malicious ... worded by the Palestinians.' However limited the effect of these diplomatic efforts was, after the OAU was disbanded in 2002, Israel was not granted observer status again at its successor, the AU. Gaddafi, who donated to the new institution and sought to use it to project his influence in Africa, fiercely opposed any Israeli presence, and is said to have blocked Israel from accessing the new institution. 'He became the owner of the house ... and from that moment onwards Israel could no longer be invited as an observer', Granot added. 'All the countries in the world and the international organisations are observers. Ninety nine percent of them don't show up, because they don't care. For us, it was very, very, very important.'[18]

During the new organisation's first years of activity it repeatedly expressed its support for the Palestinian leadership, called for the implementation of the two-state solution and the ending of the Israeli occupation, and condemned Israel's policies in the Occupied Territories. In July 2007, the AU Assembly also endorsed in a formal declaration the Arab Peace Initiative – a proposal by the Arab League's 22 members that calls for the normalisation of relations between Israel and the Arab world in return for Israel's withdrawal from the Occupied Territories and the establishment of an independent Palestinian state with East Jerusalem as its capital.[19] Israeli leaders have never shown sincere interest in accepting this proposal, apparently believing that, with time, normalisation with the Arab world will be achieved even without

Palestinian statehood. The pro-Palestinian stance of the AU irritated Israel, but hardly had any influence on the balance of power in the Middle East at the time.

More recently, things have changed. Around 2009, disillusioned with almost two decades of US-sponsored negotiations that led nowhere and only allowed Israel to maintain the occupation and continue building illegal settlements, the Palestinian leadership decided to turn to international bodies and unilaterally ask them to recognise Palestine as an independent state. In late 2011 Palestine was granted full membership at UNESCO, and its next objective was to be admitted as a non-member observer state to the UN.[20] Israel and the US opposed these efforts, arguing that they damage the prospect of meaningful direct negotiations for peace. Liberman accused Palestinian President Mahmoud Abbas of 'diplomatic terror'.[21] The Arab League and the Non-Aligned Movement supported the Palestinian Authority, as did the AU. At its eighteenth Ordinary Session in January 2012, the Assembly of the AU adopted a decision supporting the Palestinian efforts, holding Israel responsible 'for the faltering peace process and negotiations' and condemning the expansion of Israeli settlements in the West Bank and the blockade on the Gaza Strip.[22]

As opposed to full membership in the UN, which requires the approval of the Security Council, the status of a non-member observer state is in the hands of the General Assembly, where the US has no veto power and African states have a significant weight. When the matter was brought before the General Assembly in November 2012, an overwhelming majority of 138 countries supported granting Palestine non-member observer state status. In line with the AU position, no African country supported Israel, though eight of them abstained or did not vote at all (see Table 3.2). Some African states, when questioned about their position on the matter, stated that they supported Palestine due to the continental position on the issue. 'We work through regional groups', Ugandan State Minister for International Affairs Oryem-Okello explained,

Table 3.2 *African votes in UNGA Resolution 67/19, November 2012, upgrading Palestine to a non-member observer state in the United Nations*

Yes (46)	No (0)	Abstain (5)	Absent (3)
Algeria, Angola, Benin, Botswana, Burkina Faso, Burundi, Cape Verde, CAR, Chad, Comoros, Congo (Brazzaville), Côte d'Ivoire, Djibouti, Egypt, Eritrea, Ethiopia, Gabon, Gambia, Ghana, Guinea, Guinea-Bissau, Kenya, Lesotho, Libya, Mali, Mauritania, Mauritius, Morocco, Mozambique, Namibia, Niger, Nigeria, São Tomé and Príncipe, Senegal, Seychelles, Sierra Leone, Somalia, South Africa, South Sudan, Sudan, Swaziland, Tanzania, Tunisia, Uganda, Zambia, Zimbabwe		Cameroon, DRC, Malawi, Rwanda, Togo	Equatorial Guinea, Liberia, Madagascar

'and since the African Union and the Non-Aligned Movement unanimously agreed on Palestine to get Observer status, Uganda has conceded to vote by this position in spite of our close relationship with Israel'.[23]

By the time Israel's battle over Palestine's recognition by the UN was already lost, the Israeli Ministry of Foreign Affairs was hopeful that regaining observer status at the AU was possible, not least because Gaddafi had already been deposed and killed in 2011 and was no longer around to block its efforts. In early 2013, Israel went for elections. Netanyahu remained in power and Liberman retained his position as foreign minister. The following year, a 'Lobby for Strengthening the Relations between Israel and African Countries' was established in the Knesset as a platform to promote Israeli–African relations. At the Lobby's first session, Liberman announced that steps would be taken to make Israel an observer state at the AU within a year – a timeframe that proved naive in retrospect.[24] In June 2014, he returned to Africa. This time he visited Ethiopia, Rwanda, Côte d'Ivoire, Ghana and Kenya, and mobilising support for Israel's bid to become an observer state at the AU was one of the main issues on his agenda.

Meanwhile, Palestinian efforts to pressure Israel to end the occupation, which reached a dead end through US-sponsored negotiations, assumed a new momentum at the international level. The Palestinian turn to the UN and its success in gaining the status of a non-member observer state opened new avenues for the Palestinian leadership to try to leverage multilateral fora and international law in order to hold Israel accountable for its activities in the Occupied Territories and to advance Palestine's claims as an independent state. UN membership also allowed Palestine to join the International Criminal Court (ICC), something Mahmoud Abbas did in late 2014. The more the conflict in Israel/Palestine was internationalised and debated in international legal terms and in international fora – from UNESCO's executive board, through the UN Human Rights Council to the UN General Assembly – the more important diplomatic support became for both Israel and the Palestinians in advancing their interests.

In recent years, the AU Assembly has regularly adopted declarations on the situation in Israel/Palestine, calling for the release of Palestinian prisoners from Israeli jails, denouncing Israel's illegal settlements, urging member states to boycott goods that are produced in them, and demanding the lifting of the Gaza blockade.[25] Despite its intensive efforts, Israel was not granted observer status at the AU following Liberman's African tour in 2014, and the application which was submitted to the then chairperson of the AU Commission, Nkosazana Dlamini-Zuma, was not approved.[26] In late 2014, Netanyahu's government was dissolved, and Israel went for early elections, but Israeli officials did not relinquish their efforts to gain a foothold in the AU or to change the way African states vote at the UN with regard to Israel/Palestine. On the contrary: these efforts were only stepped up and, from 2016, assumed unprecedented visibility.

Rebranding Israel in Africa

Despite widespread predictions to the contrary, Netanyahu won the 2015 elections in a crushing victory. While he retained his position as prime minister, Netanyahu also became Israel's foreign minister – a move many interpreted as an attempt to circumvent the Ministry of Foreign Affairs rather than strengthen it. Avigdor Liberman later became minister of defence. Israel's engagement with African countries advanced significantly after 2009, during Liberman's term as foreign minister, but he never accorded publicity and image management the same importance as Netanyahu. During the 1980s, Netanyahu was the deputy chief of mission at the Israeli embassy in Washington and served as Israel's representative to the UN. He was a spokesperson – an international *hasbara* expert.[27] Doubling as foreign minister during his fourth term as prime minister, he deployed his public relations skills in Africa, making considerable efforts to cement a new narrative about Israel's relationship with the continent.

In early 2016, a new 'Knesset Lobby for Relations between Israel and African Countries' was launched (lobbies are dissolved before every election). African ambassadors to Israel were invited to attend the ceremonial opening session in Jerusalem, as Netanyahu gave a speech that was full of grand promises and included all the mantras that he was to repeat in the following years before African audiences. 'We have these two great things before us', he stated. 'Overcoming the dark forces of militant Islamic terrorism and seizing the opportunities of the future with technology and everything else we can bring to bear.' As part of the cooperation around these issues, he added, 'What I'd like to see is the closeness of our relationship reflected also in the voting pattern of the African Union'.[28] In other words, behind the rhetoric of shared security interests and mutually beneficial cooperation, as Naomi Chazan observed, Israel appeared to be 'reviving old notions of barter agreements with African states, based on economic and security support in exchange for African votes in international forums'.[29]

The same proposition – security and development in exchange for diplomatic support – became Israel's new terms of engagement with Africa, perpetuated in Israeli official rhetoric across institutions. Over the next three years, Netanyahu himself repeated the same message – and occasionally also the same anecdotes and jokes – time and again not only before the multiple African leaders that visited Jerusalem, but in four widely covered trips he made to the continent: a grand 'historic' (as the press and public were constantly reminded) African tour that took him to Uganda, Kenya, Rwanda and Ethiopia in July 2016, and three additional short visits to Monrovia (June 2017), to speak before the ECOWAS summit and hold meetings with West African leaders; Nairobi (November 2017), to attend Uhuru Kenyatta's inauguration; and N'Djamena (January 2019), to formally announce the restoration of ties with Chad. Four trips by a head of state to Africa within less than three years was a strong testament to Israel's renewed interest in the continent. They were also, however, a testament to Netanyahu's personal style and his belief in soft power and image management.

There are clear parallels between Israel's new rhetoric in Africa and its rhetoric in the 1960s. To begin with, Israeli official rhetoric presents Israel's current engagement with the African continent as part of a history of mutually beneficial cooperation that dates back to the early period of African independence. Nostalgic references to Israel's early work in Africa are common. More importantly, the invocation of history and the fusion of older memories of cooperation with the contemporary tropes of counterterrorism, securitised governance and high-tech positions Israel once again both as a friend of the continent and as a developmental model for African states: a hub of innovation, digital modernity, economic prosperity and stability that can supposedly help African countries develop in a similar direction. Israeli public relations and *hasbara* platforms go to great lengths to promote Israel's image as the 'Start-Up Nation' and a global leader in technology and security, and to perpetuate the notion that 'Israeli

solutions' can address 'African problems' and benefit the continent and its people.

And while Israel has made it clear that it expects African
states to support it politically as a manifestation of their 'friendship', its cooperation and assistance are otherwise not conditional
on human rights or democratic reforms. Israel looks for friends.
It does not mind how they govern their states. In fact, to justify
its pleas for diplomatic support, Israel has positioned itself as a
friend of Africa that is, supposedly like African states, being
unfairly criticised by a two-faced and hypocritical international
community. As one Israeli journalist observed, when Netanyahu
was touring East Africa he was 'back at his days as an ambassador
to the UN, with a small difference – now he was the ambassador
against the UN'.[30] Israeli officials regularly complain that Israel is
being misunderstood and singled out by the West or that there is
an anti-Israel bias at UN forums such as the General Assembly, the
Human Rights Council and UNESCO, and Netanyahu has repeatedly asked African leaders to support Israel in order to change
this situation.

The most conspicuous aspect of Israel's official rhetoric in
Africa, however, remains counterterrorism and security – Israel's
main agenda in the international sphere and the ultimate justification it invokes for all of its policies in Israel/Palestine and for the
continuation of the occupation. Terrorism has been mentioned by
Netanyahu in virtually every speech in Africa (and elsewhere) and
is the main rhetorical framework around which Israel's engagement with Africa is built, positioning Israeli and African leaders
as allies in the war against 'an axis of evil that stretches from the
Middle East to West and East Africa', to use Liberman's words.[31]
As part of Netanyahu's East African tour in 2016, for example, he
convened a 'Regional Summit on Counter-terrorism' in Entebbe
which was attended by Yoweri Museveni, Hailemariam Desalegn,
Uhuru Kenyatta, Paul Kagame, Salva Kiir and Edgar Lungu. The
participating leaders issued a symbolic 'joint declaration', stating

that 'terrorism continues to be a major threat to international peace and security and to the very survival of human civilization'.[32]

The appeal of Israel's new rhetoric in Africa – the emphasis on security, the carefully managed 'Start-Up Nation' brand, the unapologetic attacks on international organisations that represent the Western liberal agenda – can only be understood against the background of broader trends of 'democracy fatigue' that have affected the continent.[33] These trends include an apparent democratic recession in many countries, the securitisation of politics, and the growing appreciation of the advantages of illiberal developmentalism and hegemonic, authoritarian, state-building.[34] To be sure, Israel is far from the main driver behind these processes. But its recent efforts on the continent have nonetheless benefited from the fact that there were a growing number of governments championing illiberal and securitised development, and whose leaders were interested in the benefits associated with relations with Jerusalem and viewed Israel once again as a model – proof that the Western paradigm of human rights and liberal democracy can be successfully defied.

The role of the private sector

Accompanying Israel's geostrategic and diplomatic interests in Africa has been a search for economic opportunities. Despite Israel's geographical proximity to Africa, and the deep involvement of Israeli companies and entrepreneurs in several African economies (further explored in the next chapter), as of 2017 Israel's exports to the continent represented about 1.5% of its total exports. Trade between Israel and African countries has actually declined since 2011, though this can also be attributed to the parallel decline in commodity prices (Figures 3.1–3.3). Israeli policymakers and officials, however, influenced by the 'Africa rising' narrative, see in Africa opportunities for Israeli companies and service providers, and in recent years have been seeking ways to increase

Israel's economic engagement with African countries with renewed vigour. Israel's economic and political objectives in Africa therefore continue to mingle, with the assumption being that enhanced private economic engagement will not only benefit Israel economically but also improve its political standing and leverage in the continent.

Figure 3.1 Israel's trade with Africa, 2009–18 (US$ million)[35]

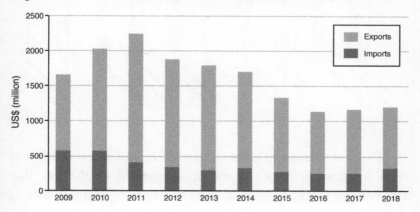

Figure 3.2 Israel's top ten trade partners in Africa, 2017 (US$ million)[36]

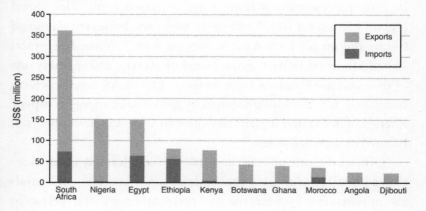

Figure 3.3 Top sectors of Israel's Africa trade, 2017 (US$ million)[37]

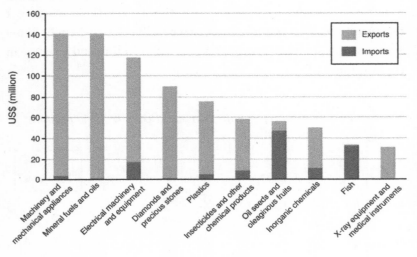

That politicians and businessmen rely on each other to advance their interests in Africa is well demonstrated by the fact that Israeli high-profile diplomatic visits to Africa regularly double as marketing and networking tours for Israeli civilian businesses and security firms. During his 2009 African trip, Avigdor Liberman was accompanied by a delegation of some 20 Israeli businessmen, including representatives from Israel's largest security firms.[38] In 2014, representatives from some 50 Israeli companies joined him on his second trip,[39] and some 80 Israeli businessmen joined Netanyahu on his East African tour in 2016.[40] When Netanyahu visited Monrovia in 2017, at the centre of his trip, and arguably one of the main justifications for it as far as ECOWAS members were concerned, was the announcement by Israeli solar energy company Energiya Global that it plans to deploy $1 billion in investments in ECOWAS member states.[41]

Official rhetoric on African markets, though rarely much more than a bricolage of slogans about Africa as the continent of boundless opportunities, reflects the very real sentiment that Israel has to 'catch up' with other global powers that have already 'discovered' Africa's economic potential, and that Israeli expertise in technology, agriculture, health and security has something to contribute to the continent and its people. The urge to seek economic opportunities in Africa has also increased in recent years in light of the fears that the international pro-Palestinian Boycott, Divestment and Sanctions (BDS) campaign will harm Israel's trade with its traditional partners in Europe.[42] In reality, the BDS campaign is yet to have any significant effect on Israel's economy, but its rise and salient influence on Israel's international image has nonetheless signalled to Israeli policymakers that just like its political alliances, Israel's trading partners should also be broadened and diversified.

If Israel's latest 'Africa strategy' was articulated in any formal policy document, it was in the government's resolution from June 2016 which allocated the modest sum of NIS 50 million ($13 million) for the purpose of 'strengthening economic ties and cooperation with African countries'.[43] The resolution, it should be noted, followed similar resolutions on Israel's economic ties with Latin American countries, China and Japan, which were adopted in 2014–15. And while it did not fundamentally change Israel's engagement with Africa, it did indicate how the government saw its future. Among other things, the resolution instructed the relevant institutions to open two new Israeli economic and trade missions in Africa (in Nairobi and Accra, in addition to an existing one in Johannesburg), to pursue bilateral agreements in order to increase African countries' access to Israeli products (by funding feasibility studies) and to establish new MASHAV 'Excellence Centres' in Africa which focus on training and capacity-building based on Israeli technologies in agriculture, water or health.

While MASHAV projects are part of Israel's development assistance (further discussed in the next section), and are run through the Ministry of Foreign Affairs , they also 'make Israel's technological abilities known to businesspeople and government officials in African countries and thereby assist in increasing Israeli exports to these countries'.[44] Otherwise, the main institution involved in strengthening Israeli trade with Africa is the Foreign Trade Administration at the Ministry of Economy and Industry. Among other things, it has been making efforts to encourage Israeli companies to take part in international development projects funded by multilateral development finance institutions such as the World Bank. The Israel Export and International Cooperation Institute – a semi-governmental organisation that supports foreign trade – is also involved, supporting businesses by organising delegations and other events and outreach initiatives to encourage Israeli trade with African countries.

Government financial support to private actors operating in Africa has long been limited but is likely to increase in the future. The government-owned Israel Foreign Trade Risks Insurance Corporation (ASHRA) promotes international trade by providing limited coverage to some export transactions, and it has reported a steady rise in Israeli contracts with African customers in recent years.[45] In 2018, however, the prime minister's office established a special committee tasked with planning a new international development strategy for Israel in order to 'maximise the political and economic potential that lies in this field'.[46] One of the key options advanced by the committee was to establish an Israeli development bank in order to make it easier for Israeli businesses to win contracts in developing countries and compete with companies from states that already support their private sector through national development finance institutions. 'The Chinese, for example, are entering developing countries with big money from government funds', said Netanyahu's chief of staff, Yoav Horowitz. 'Israel has a small window of opportunity to act, and we must act fast.'[47]

Behind the public emphasis on agriculture, innovation and clean energy, Israel's defence industry continues to play a major role. As opposed to general trade with Africa, which was in decline, defence exports have steadily increased in recent years. The platform that promotes and coordinates arms exports is the

Figure 3.4 Israel's defence exports to Africa, 2009–18 (US$ million, value of contracts signed)[48]

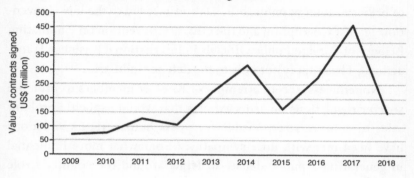

International Defense Cooperation Directorate (SIBAT) in the Ministry of Defense. According to its data, the value of new contracts for defence exports to Africa grew over the past decade, peaking in 2017 but declining again in 2018 (Figure 3.4). The precise destinations of weapons and types of equipment that is being sold are not publicly discussed. SIBAT publishes an annual aggregated sum of exports by continent but not by country, and while Israel usually submits data on exports of major arms to the UN Register of Conventional Arms, its reports do not include data on the export of small arms or intelligence systems – which are among its most popular commodities in Africa.[49]

After the involvement of Israeli arms merchants in human rights abuses and corruption scandals during the 1990s and early 2000s, some steps were taken to strengthen the supervision of arms exports. An Israeli Defense Export Controls Agency was established in 2006, and in 2007 the Defense Export Controls Act came into force, creating a loose regulatory framework that is supposed to prevent arms deals that violate Israel's international obligations or can damage its national interests. Given the secrecy surrounding the defence establishment, the strategic importance of arms exports for the Israeli military and economy, and the close informal ties between military and political elites and key figures in the arms industry, critics argue that the new regulations are not much more than window dressing.[50] In 2008 Israel also criminalised the payment of bribes to foreign public officials and acceded to the UN Convention against Corruption and the OECD Convention on Combating Bribery of Foreign Public Officials in International Business Transactions. These apply not only to the defence industries.[51]

Nonetheless, recent attempts of Knesset members to promote stricter regulations on arms exports that would explicitly prohibit sales to countries responsible for gross human rights violations have been met with little sympathy.[52] Somewhat more influential in generating a public debate in Israel around the country's role in arming autocratic regimes and enabling abuses has been the work of activists, lawyers and concerned citizens – including some from religious and conservative circles that are usually more reluctant to criticise the Israeli security sector.[53] While the efforts of these actors in the form of petitions and small protests may have enhanced public visibility of the issue, the Ministry of Defense still regularly succeeds in shielding itself from scrutiny by arguing that for security and strategic reasons, detailed information on defence exports cannot be revealed. Specific examples of the uses (and misuses) of Israeli arms in Africa are discussed in the next chapter.

Development aid and the role of civil society

Underlying MASHAV's work is the notion that Israel should focus in its development assistance on fields in which it has expertise, and on knowledge sharing rather than financial donations. This means that Israeli development initiatives are primarily focused on agriculture, rural development, education and public health. In line with the narrative of Israel as a developmental model for Africa, the focus is on 'transferring Israeli know-how, innovation, technologies, and expertise'. The most common modus operandi is short-capacity building courses that take place either in Africa or in Israel, although there are also several agricultural programmes that are carried out in Africa in cooperation with the Israeli Ministry of Agriculture and Rural Development, such as the Rwanda–Israel Centre of Excellence for Horticultural Development, inaugurated in 2014.[54] Another aspect of MASHAV's work is humanitarian aid, which usually consists of medical or food donations in cases of emergency, such as the assistance that was sent to Liberia and Sierra Leone in 2015 during the Ebola epidemic, or limited ad hoc donations to populations with specific needs or to medical institutions.

On a less pronounced level, Israel's focus on more technocratic and seemingly less political fields such as agriculture, education and emergency humanitarian aid fits with its approach of non-interference in issues of democracy or human rights. Selective endorsement of tropes that are politically uncontroversial in Israel and among Israel's African partners – women's rights, poverty reduction, access to healthcare, agricultural development – prevents Israeli officials feeling out of place among Western development circles while at the same time avoiding those aspects of the liberal development paradigm that come with a political price tag Israel is unwilling and unable to pay. The assumption also appears to be that if Israel publicly comments on the human rights record of other countries, its critics will accuse it of hypocrisy and reply by making similar accusations against Israel for its own human rights abuses, thus setting in motion *hasbara* crises Israel clearly prefers to avoid.[55]

The boundary between Israeli development assistance and *hasbara* is porous. Many of MASHAV's activities – educational trips, conferences, training, symbolic donations – are textbook examples of public diplomacy that are geared towards improving Israel's image in Africa and across the world. Humanitarian donations often come with abundant Israeli flags, T-shirts and other branded merchandise, and are regularly treated as photo-ops, documentation of which is disseminated by uncritical media channels and across government social media platforms in various languages (including Arabic) to praise Israel and counter criticism of its domestic policies. These ostensibly serve as proofs that – to use the title of one recent Israeli social media campaign – #IsraelCares. In the same vein, assistance is clearly used to cement bilateral ties, is often provided as a symbolic reward to 'loyal' friends and can be withdrawn from those who misbehave. When Senegal co-sponsored a UN Security Council resolution in December 2016 declaring Israeli settlements illegal, Israel immediately announced that aid programmes to the country were cancelled.[56]

Israel often highlights its development and humanitarian endeavours in Africa as a proof of its generosity and positive intentions, and diplomats appear to recognise the important role these play in fostering and maintaining bilateral ties. However, the resources Israel devotes to development aid remain slim to an extent that clearly limits MASHAV's capacity to pursue any coherent independent developmental agenda, even if a significant portion of its resources are indeed devoted to activities in Africa. In recent years, MASHAV's total annual budget was roughly $9 million. Following Israel joining the OECD in 2010, officials in the Ministry of Foreign Affairs advocated for an increase in the resources devoted to international development aid, but little has changed. MASHAV director Gil Haskel told the Knesset in late 2015 that Israeli investment in development aid is so marginal that he 'prefers not to publish [its scope] in international forums'.[57] Privately, some Israeli officials refer to it as a farce. As far as Israeli leaders are concerned, the future of Israel's involvement in international development lies with the private sector.

The scope of Israel's total official development assistance (ODA) is slightly higher. In 2016 it was $220 million, representing 0.07% of GNI. This figure, however, is inclusive of assistance to the West Bank and the Gaza Strip – which are effectively under Israeli control – as well as funding allocated to the absorption of new Jewish immigrants and the treatment of asylum-seekers in Israel (on which much more in Chapter 5).[58] Thus, the actual amount dedicated to assistance is much smaller. About 10% of Israel's ODA – $20 million in 2015 – is provided through multilateral organisations, primarily the UN and the World Bank.[59] In Africa, besides MASHAV's operations, as part of the 2016 government decision to strengthen ties with Africa the Ministry of Public Security was instructed to organise courses for African police forces, and the Ministry of Health was instructed to organise programmes with African governments in the fields of public health and emergency preparedness.

More influential and in many cases also more visible than Israel's official government assistance, however, has been the emergence in recent years of Israeli and other Jewish NGOs that are not funded by the Israeli government but are nonetheless commonly associated (and associate themselves) with Israel in several ways. First, these organisations often frame their work as based on Jewish notions of social justice and charity, invoking the concept of *tikkun olam* ('repair of the world') which is popularly understood as the Jewish obligation to better the world, or the biblical notion that the Jewish people should be a 'light unto the nations'. Second, they usually maintain strong links to the Jewish diaspora (particularly but not only in the US), which is the source of most of their funding. Third, they view their work, among other things, as a means of improving Israel's international image and reputation and by implication its diplomatic standing. For all of these reasons, they are endorsed by Israeli diplomats and government agencies who welcome them as unofficial 'ambassadors' of Israel in Africa, and therefore an inherent part of its national *hasbara* machinery.

Among the more celebrated of these NGOs, for example, is Innovation: Africa, an organisation which was originally called Jewish Heart for Africa and is dedicated to bringing 'Israeli innovation to African villages' by installing solar energy systems and basic agricultural technologies in villages, clinics, and schools in rural areas in a number of African countries. According to its founder Sivan Ya'ari its work is 'not only helping Africa but helping Israel by helping the Israeli economy and Israel's image'.[60] Indeed, Ya'ari herself regularly speaks about her NGO at pro-Israel conferences around the world, presenting it as an example of Israeli humanitarianism and benevolence in Africa – part of 'Golda Meir's legacy' that 'inspired generations of Israelis ... to look beyond our own borders'.[61] IsraAID is another notable example, though much more integrated into the mainstream aid industry. It provides humanitarian assistance in developing countries and in a number of locations in Africa. Despite its name and its logo (which features the Israeli flag), it is not a government agency. Save a Child's Heart is a well-known, and older, Israeli NGO that provides paediatric cardiac care for children from developing countries, regularly conducting heart surgery in Israel.

There are other Israeli NGOs that operate in Africa. Not all of them maintain the same level of cooperation with Israeli formal institutions or the Jewish diaspora, but as part of Israel's 'return' to Africa, efforts were made to promote their work and associate it with Israel. The Ministry of Foreign Affairs held special forums that brought together Israel's ambassadors to African countries and representatives of Israeli NGOs that are active in Africa. Recognising that these organisations 'make a huge contribution to the Israeli state and its positive image around the world', the intention of the forums was to promote the ministry's cooperation with them and facilitate their operations.[62] Supporting these initiatives was also the Israeli branch of the Society for International Development (SID). When Israeli President Reuven Rivlin visited Ethiopia in May 2018, he participated in a conference titled 'Impact for Good' which brought together Israeli and international Jewish private actors and civil society organisations with the objective of encouraging their involvement in Africa.[63]

'It is a development of the last decade', Gideon Behar, head of the Africa Bureau at the Ministry of Foreign Affairs, explained. 'When I was an ambassador in Senegal between 2006 and 2011, I hardly saw any [Israeli] civil society actors in my area in West Africa.' In recent years, however, this has changed, and along with government-to-government ties and private sector engagements, civil society organisations have become one of the main pillars sustaining Israel's relationships with African states. 'We are constantly checking the possibilities, how we can help them', Behar added, citing the positive impact of organisations like Innovation Africa and CultivAid, an Israeli NGO focusing on capacity-building in the fields of agricultural and water management. 'We are not assisting financially because we have no resources, but we help with contacts, facilitating meetings, getting to know the right people, opening doors. As we do with the private sector – precisely the same thing.'[64]

Old battles, new wars

While Netanyahu's widely covered African tours in 2016 attracted global attention, they were the culmination of a slow process that started unfolding from the late 2000s, when Israel's growing international isolation, its rivalry with Iran and its search for new trading partners led it to turn to Africa once again – to seek new allies and consolidate older relationships that Israeli politicians had previously neglected. Israel's efforts in Africa under Netanyahu certainly generated renewed attention to Israeli–African relations, but the enhanced publicity and demonstrations of affection did not necessarily come with a significant increase in the investment of resources or with an articulation of a new overarching strategy for Israel's operations in Africa. Promises of development were not accompanied by a significant increase in development aid, while statements about terrorism and insecurity were not accompanied by commitments for financial or military support to African countries or by Israeli political engagement with African peace and security architecture. Meanwhile, the Ministry of Foreign Affairs has been subject to budget cuts in recent years, with officials complaining that it is being deliberately and systematically weakened and undermined.[65]

While official rhetoric portrays Israel's 'return' to Africa as part of a long tradition of cooperation that goes back to Golda Meir, and once again represents Israel as a friend and a developmental model, Israeli–African relationships operate in a very different manner today than they did back in the 1960s. Underpinning the current Israeli approach is the expectation that Israeli and Jewish civil society organisations and private actors will step in to infuse the official rhetoric with content by increasing their engagement with African countries and by associating their work, more or less explicitly, with Israel. Security support is largely left to the arms industry, humanitarian aid to Israeli and Jewish NGOs, and development to Israeli start-ups and multinationals. Put slightly differently, while Israeli rhetoric goes back to the 1960s, the mechanics of contemporary Israeli–African partnerships build on everything that has happened since then, as Israeli political leaders try to reassert their authority over, and reap political benefits from, bilateral relations that since the end of the Cold War have been dominated by private actors and business interests.

Chapter 4

AFRICA'S ISRAELS

That Israel once again seeks African support and approval is one thing. That African leaders are interested in this partnership is another. The Israeli quest for influence in Africa has its roots in the local and regional politics of Israel/Palestine and the Middle East, but the shape and form it takes on the ground are inseparable from broader processes that have affected Africa's political landscape over the last two decades. The rise of the 'war on terror' in Africa turned the US into an important source of funds and support, and by implication increased Israel's leverage. It also created a demand for Israeli security equipment and 'know-how' as well as a political environment in which some view Israel's terrorism-focused rhetoric as appealing and potentially beneficial for their international standing. The growth of Pentecostal and other evangelical Christian movements slowly forges new constituencies that promote Israel's interests in Africa, while Africa's commodities boom and the emergence of African state-led capitalistic development have created new opportunities for Israeli private actors.

Any attempt to understand how these processes influence Israel's standing in Africa has to begin by piercing through official rhetoric and formal institutions. Israel's presence or strategy in Africa cannot be reduced to the operations or objectives of the prime minister's office, MASHAV, SIBAT or the Foreign Trade Administration. These are only some of the visible branches of wider, more influential, but much less coordinated, centralised or homogeneous networks of actors and interests that link leaders, financial elites and publics in Israel and in the African continent – materially, politically and spiritually. Given the rudimentary nature of Israel's formal presence in Africa and the diversity of the continent, its regimes, international alliances, peoples and religions, it is impossible to speak of a single dynamic that characterises Israeli–African engagements. Certain themes and patterns of interactions, however, do stand out and indicate how Israel has been able to mobilise support for its political objectives and why in some cases this remains a challenge.

The politics of (in)security

The increased securitisation of African politics since the emergence of the 'war on terror' created a renewed interest in Israeli defence products and expertise. The training and arming of special elite units – now often branded as counterterrorism forces – is still a central aspect of Israeli security involvement in Africa. The recent rise of Israel's high-tech industry, however, has also turned the country into a dominant player in the world of SIGINT (signals intelligence) and cybersecurity – fields that are becoming increasingly influential as the use of mobile phones and social media for political mobilisation grows. In an environment in which defence cooperation and arms exports are a central aspect of the activities of virtually all major foreign powers in Africa, two things give Israel a comparative advantage. The first is the quality of its products – all battle-proven, tried and tested. The second is its willingness to cooperate – whether by providing direct military support or, more commonly, by approving military sales by private Israeli firms – with relative flexibility and usually without raising human rights concerns.

The centrality of arms exports in Israel's efforts in Africa corresponds with its securitised political rhetoric and the notion that it understands the threats African countries face and their defence needs better than Western countries, which have less experience in counterinsurgency warfare and are sometimes more concerned with democracy and human rights. Cables released by Wikileaks show how in the late 2000s, when Ethiopian military leaders and Prime Minister Meles Zenawi were dissatisfied with the scope of US counterterrorism cooperation and frustrated with American criticism of Ethiopia's human rights record, they repeatedly protested before US officials that, as opposed to the US, Israel and China 'never promise much but always deliver on what little they do promise, and without human rights and other conditions'.[1] A similar attitude underpins Israel's partnership with the other frontline states in East Africa's 'war on terror' and regional security – Kenya, Uganda and Rwanda – all of which, like Israel, are allies of the West that have been irritated by criticism of their human rights records.

The material implications of these alliances should be put in perspective. In the global 'rentier market' of the 'war on terror',[2] Israel is an important ideological vanguard and an agenda-setter but not a major donor like the US or some Western countries. Its efforts in Africa focus on encouraging arms exports through SIBAT (introduced in Chapter 3), rather than on generous direct security support or the establishment of expensive military bases in foreign lands. Formal cooperation in intelligence gathering or counterterrorism are limited and overtly shrouded in secrecy. Collaborations that have at least some public facet are run through the IDF's International Cooperation Unit, which oversees Israel's military diplomacy. These, however, seem to be primarily geared towards consolidating political alliances rather than securing any immediate Israeli security needs and usually comprise workshops and 'study tours' in Israel and training by Israeli officers in Africa. In 2018, for example, Ghanaian elite units received a short counterterrorism course from Israeli officers and Rwandan officers travelled to Israel on a study tour, visiting IDF bases and arms manufacturers.[3] The counterterrorism instructors of the Israel Border Police also provided training to elite units in several African countries in recent years, with Rwanda being the only such country whose identity was revealed.[4]

Security firms, therefore, are the main means through which experience, knowledge and equipment is transferred from Israel/ Palestine to African countries. For a start, dozens of Israeli companies provide security services or equipment across the continent, guarding facilities such as airports, malls, ports, embassies, government buildings, sport venues, hotels and so on. Magal Security Systems, for example, a manufacturer of surveillance equipment that was involved in the construction of the separation wall in the West Bank and the fences around Gaza and along the Israeli–Egyptian border, provided services for the African Cup of Nations games in Gabon (in 2012 and 2017),[5] the ports in Mombasa and Cotonou,[6] and Nairobi's Jomo Kenyatta International Airport.[7] It was also reported that the company was in negotiations with the Kenyan government on an agreement to construct a fence along Kenya's border with Somalia, inspired by the fence Israel built around Gaza.[8] The Israeli government-owned Rafael Advanced Defense Systems was contracted in 2017 to protect Kenya's energy infrastructure and oil pipelines.[9]

In many countries Israeli equipment and expertise were deployed to carry out not only highly sensitive but also controversial tasks. In Uganda, the Joint Anti-Terrorism Task Force – which was established to coordinate the country's counterterrorism efforts but was accused of torturing and intimidating regime opponents – received much of its training in the late 2000s from Israeli private actors.[10] In Congo (Brazzaville), Israeli firms trained the presidential guard and supplied the government with surveillance equipment.[11] In Burundi, Amnesty International documented the use of Israeli-made armoured vehicles and tear gas grenades by the security forces during the protests against President Pierre Nkurunziza's decision to run for a third term in the 2015 elections.[12] A 2014 Al Jazeera investigation accused Kenyan counterterrorism troops that were trained by Israel of conducting targeted killings – a practice Israeli security apparatuses have long promoted as a method of fighting terrorists.[13] Israeli firms also provided counterterrorism training to elite troops of the Nigerian air force,[14] and reportedly trained some units of the Central Africa Armed Forces.[15] Intelligence and defence exports to Angola, Togo and Equatorial Guinea, further discussed in the following sections, have also been a central aspect of Israel's relationship with these countries. Chad, despite the lack of formal diplomatic ties until 2019, purchased Israeli rifles, armoured vehicles and, according to some reports, also intelligence and surveillance equipment, during and after the civil war (2005–10).[16]

In Cameroon, the Israeli-trained and -armed BIR (whose origins were discussed in Chapter 2) became 'an army within the army' – better equipped, trained and rewarded, and more trusted by the president than other security forces. While the military was neglected and weakened, the Israeli-trained special units that operate directly under the president were nurtured and rein-forced.[17] Even though Avi Sivan, who led Biya's special forces, died in a helicopter crash in 2010, he was reportedly replaced by another Israeli officer whose identity remains obscure,[18] and Cameroonian elite forces were spotted with Israeli rifles and other equipment on multiple occasions.[19] Though initially formed to protect the coun-try's borders, the forces went on to perform various other tasks, as the government adopted an increasingly repressive and militaristic approach to dealing with domestic dissent, from cracking down on protestors,[20] through fighting Boko Haram in the Far North Region, to violently repressing separatist groups in Cameroon's English-speaking South-west and North-west regions. In both the Far North Region and English-speaking regions, the forces were accused of human rights abuses.[21]

Recent security sales to South Sudan ended more disastrously. As noted earlier, for Israel, South Sudan's independence meant a new sovereign 'periphery' ally. With its wealthy oil-based economy, there also seemed to be attractive opportunities for investment, and due to Israel's support to southern rebels in the past and the two nations' shared sense of hostility with the Arab world, the rela-tionship was warm from the beginning. A popular South Sudanese song at the time of the country's independence praised the Sudan People's Liberation Army (SPLA), the rebel group which became South Sudan's national military, for being 'like the army of Israel … which does not leave a gun behind for the enemy'.[22] Appropriately, after independence, South Sudanese officials sought Israel's security support and purchased automatic rifles produced by the Israel Weapon Industries (IWI).[23] IWI assault rifles – Galil and Tavor – are popular across Africa among elite units and presidential guards.

In December 2013 war broke out in South Sudan. During its first days, a Dinka militia loyal to President Salva Kiir massacred thousands of Nuer citizens in Juba and, according to testimonies collected by a UN Panel of Experts, its members were using those rifles acquired from Israel a few months earlier.[24] Following the killings in Juba, the violence spread throughout the country and large sections of the SPLA defected and formed a rebel movement under the leadership of Vice-President Riek Machar. Uganda intervened in support of Kiir and, among other things, provided it with more Israeli rifles that it had bought a few years earlier. Israel later claimed that Uganda did not request permission to transfer the weapons to South Sudan, but this was not the first overt case of diversion of Israeli arms in Africa: just north of South Sudan, rifles sold to Chad in 2006, coincidentally or not, ended up in the hands of Justice and Equality Movement (JEM) rebels in Darfur.[25]

When the UN Panel of Experts exposed the involvement of Israeli arms in the violence in South Sudan, Israeli officials claimed that despite appeals for support from both sides of the conflict, from the beginning of the war Israel had prohibited the sale of arms to South Sudanese actors and only allowed the export of 'non-lethal' equipment.[26] These denials notwithstanding, one Israeli who has maintained a close relationship with South Sudanese elites and is said to have supplied arms to both the government and the opposition is retired IDF major general Israel Ziv. Since leaving the IDF in 2006, Ziv has been involved in several controversial security deals, primarily in Latin America but also in West Africa. In 2009, without the prior approval of the Israeli Ministry of Defense, his company Global CST reportedly won a contract to train the presidential guard of Guinean leader Moussa Dadis Camara, who took power in a military coup in late 2008.[27]

The operations of Ziv and his colleagues in South Sudan were ostensibly limited to agricultural projects that promote sustainable development and food security. They repeatedly denied any involvement in the security sector, though rumours persisted. In December 2018, the US imposed sanctions on the retired general, accusing him of selling Juba some $150 million worth of arms. 'While Ziv maintained the loyalty of senior Government of South Sudan officials through bribery and promises of security support', the US Department of the Treasury held, 'he has also reportedly planned to organize attacks by mercenaries on South Sudanese oil fields and infrastructure, in an effort to create a problem that only his company and affiliates could solve'.[28] The Israeli Ministry of Foreign Affairs, which in theory was supposed to be aware of any arms deals, said that it would examine the accusations. Ziv, predictably, denied them.[29]

The UN also claimed that Israeli companies provided Juba with surveillance equipment that facilitated the government's ability to 'identify and illegally apprehend' political opponents.[30] While the specific gear or companies involved in the South Sudanese case were not revealed by the UN, Israeli surveillance, SIGINT and cybersecurity firms seem to have gained great popularity in Africa (as in other parts of the world) in recent years. Again, though these are usually private enterprises, as with other security firms, they are commonly run and staffed by former military personnel and, in this case, members of the Israeli military intelligence and the well-known Unit 8200 – the largest and one of the most prestigious units in the Israeli military which is responsible for signal intelligence and interceptions. In Africa, these firms offer training and equipment to both governments and private businesses.

In 2015, for example, following the passing of new anti-terrorism legislation in Uganda that granted the state enhanced surveillance powers, the Israeli high-tech company NICE Systems (reportedly) won a contract to establish the national 'Monitoring Centre' for the interception of communications.[31] Facing growing popular criticism from young, urban constituencies, Museveni's government has been eager to curb expressions of political dissent on social media. Another Israeli company that is said to have worked with it is Cyberbit – a subsidiary of the renowned Elbit Systems.[32] In 2017, Cyberbit was accused of enabling the Ethiopian government to target political dissidents around the world using its PC Surveillance System – spyware that allows its users to access and monitor computers remotely.[33] As with any other security equipment, the line between legitimate use and abuse – fighting terrorists and silencing political opponents – is easily crossed.

The politics of US patronage

African leaders turn to Israel when they want to win favour with the US. As described in Chapter 2, this strategy was first clearly introduced by Mengistu and Mobutu. It has continued, in different variations, until today. For decades, Israel has managed to access unparalleled American political and financial support, not only because its existence and prowess is said to be advancing American geostrategic interests in the Middle East, but also because of the effective lobbying efforts and political influence of American pro-Israel groups, both Jewish and evangelical Christian.[34] It has an influential power base within the US, which African governments whose relationship with Washington is strained can benefit from. Much of the leverage Israel has in Africa, therefore, comes from Washington rather than Jerusalem, as Israel and various American pro-Israel groups serve as intermediaries that facilitate access to American support by trying to influence US foreign policy strategy.

Even without direct or formal Israeli or Jewish lobbying on behalf of any specific country, however, the US plays an explicit role as Israel's guardian in multilateral fora. The US Department of State, for instance, publishes an annual 'Voting Practices' report in which countries are ranked, among other things, according to the way they vote on Israel-related resolutions at the UN General Assembly. Of all African states, South Sudan, Cameroon, Togo, Rwanda and the DRC (in this order) achieved the 'best' results in this grading in 2017.[35] The allocation of US support is naturally affected by numerous factors, and it is difficult to measure the specific effect of voting patterns in the UN and the precise reasoning behind every vote, but it is also clear that featuring in a positive spot on such a list can be beneficial. Showing support for Israel means showing support for the US.

While all US administrations in recent decades have unequivocally supported Israel and followed, with more or less enthusiasm, the policy prescriptions of American pro-Israel lobby groups, the American commitment to bullying other countries into supporting Israel has been enhanced under the Trump administration, along with the determination to extend aid to 'America's friends' only. US ambassador to the UN, Nikki Haley, explicitly stated that the US expects 'acceptable return on our investment' and that the annual Voting Practices Report 'speaks for itself'.[36] In December 2017, before the vote on the UN resolution condemning the US decision to move its embassy in Israel from Tel Aviv to Jerusalem, Haley warned that the US will be 'taking names' of countries that vote against it.[37] Most African countries still supported the resolution, but 16 of them abstained or refrained from voting (Table 4.1). Togo was the only African country that voted with the US and Israel.

The extent to which Israel or pro-Israel groups in the US are capable of advancing the interests of African governments can be debated, but their influence on Israel's relations with African countries is salient. The Israeli–Rwandan alliance, for example, was promoted to a large extent by leading figures of the Jewish

Table 4.1 African votes in UNGA Resolution ES-10/L.22, December 2017, affirming that any action altering the status of Jerusalem is 'null and void'

Yes (37)	No (1)	Abstain (8)	Absent (8)
Algeria, Angola, Botswana, Burkina Faso, Burundi, Cape Verde, Chad, Comoros, Congo (Brazzaville), Côte d'Ivoire, Djibouti, Egypt, Eritrea, Ethiopia, Gabon, Gambia, Ghana, Guinea, Liberia, Libya, Madagascar, Mali, Mauritania, Mauritius, Morocco, Mozambique, Namibia, Niger, Nigeria, Senegal, Seychelles, Somalia, South Africa, Sudan, Tanzania, Tunisia, Zimbabwe	Togo	Benin, Cameroon, Equatorial Guinea, Lesotho, Malawi, Rwanda, South Sudan, Uganda	CAR, DRC, Guinea-Bissau, Kenya, São Tomé and Príncipe, Sierra Leone, Swaziland, Zambia

community in the US and Jewish philanthropists who were initially drawn to Rwanda by the similar histories of the Jews and the Tutsi as victims of genocide.[38] The most vocal of them, and Paul Kagame's key advocate among Jewish circles in the US in recent years, has been celebrity-Rabbi Shmuley Boteach – a fierce supporter of Netanyahu and a close confidant of American casino magnate, republican mega-donor and Netanyahu's patron, Sheldon Adelson. Adelson has long been using his fortune to influence electoral politics in both Israel and the US and is widely seen as the key influence behind Donald Trump's controversial decision to move the US embassy from Tel Aviv to Jerusalem. He even offered to pay for the relocation.[39]

Meanwhile, Boteach's voice in Rwanda's international advocacy efforts is difficult to ignore. Even though he originally made his fame as Michael Jackson's 'spiritual advisor' and as the author of several self-help books, he is now known primarily for his relentless pro-Israel advocacy. In recent years he has been using his high-profile media presence to promote Kagame's image as a brilliant statesman and battle Western criticism of Kigali's repressive policies, often tying his pro-Israel and pro-Rwanda advocacy efforts together, supposedly for the benefit of both countries.[40] In 2015, for example, he published a controversial full-page advertisement in the *New York Times* accusing US National Security Advisor

Susan Rice of turning a blind eye to the Rwandan genocide in 1994, after she criticised Netanyahu for his opposition to the nuclear talks with the 'genocidal Islamic republic' of Iran.[41] 'Susan Rice has a blind spot: Genocide', the advertisement read.

In appreciation of his 'stalwart support of the Jewish state', in 2017 Paul Kagame received the Sheldon Adelson Prize for Outstanding Friendship with the Jewish People – a prize that is awarded by none other than Boteach's organisation, the World Values Network. In an accompanying text published in the *Jerusalem Post*, Boteach praised Rwanda's pro-Israel voting record in the UN Security Council, UN General Assembly, UNESCO and the International Atomic Energy Agency (IAEA).[42] The same year, Kagame also became the first African leader to address the American Israel Public Affairs Committee (AIPAC) – the largest pro-Israel lobby group in the US and one of the most powerful and influential forces in Washington. In his speech, he stressed the bond between the two nations and their commitment to the security of their peoples: 'Together with friends like the United States, we must call for renewed global solidarity against the reckless efforts to deny genocide and to trivialize the victims.'[43]

Another African politician who participated in the 2017 AIPAC conference and highlighted his country's support for Israel was the foreign minister of Togo, Robert Dussey. Togo is an interesting case of African–Israeli cooperation. Unlike the case of Rwanda, where the experiences of genocide serve as a powerful uniting narrative, there are no dramatic historical events that Israeli and Togolese leaders can draw on. The two countries and their peoples hardly have anything in common. Nonetheless, Togo has been one of Israel's most enthusiastic supporters in Africa in recent years. Beneath the public surface of this relationship, a combination of business, security and political interests are at play: Israelis are still said to be providing security services to the Togolese presidency,[44] and Israeli 'advisors' and mining firms are deeply involved in Togo's highly strategic phosphates sector, which is tightly controlled by the president.[45] Visiting Israel in 2012, President Faure Gnassingbé met with producers of phosphates and fertilisers,[46] and in 2015 Israeli group Elenilto (in cooperation with Chinese group Wengfu) won a tender to develop a large phosphate mining and fertilisers plant in the country.[47]

Accompanying these economic and security interests, however, was Togo's concern with its international image. The Israeli–Togolese relationship flourished against the background of a protracted political crisis in Togo, ongoing popular calls for institutional and electoral reforms and several explosions of mass demonstrations against President Faure Gnassingbé, who came to power following the death of his father in 2005 and in 2015 ran for a controversial third term. Togolese activists seemed to have had little doubt that their government's enthusiastic support for Israel was part of a public relations campaign – which has also included hiring American lobbyists and contributing troops to peace operations – that was meant to delegitimise their protests and brand Gnassingbé as a source of stability and peace in the region and an important ally of the West, rather than an unpopular leader clinging to power. 'Americans love terrorism, so let us tell them that we have terrorism in Togo, and they will give us money', was how exiled Togolese political activist Farida Nabourema interpreted the government's strategy. 'Let us tell them that the reason why the protests started was because they don't like Israel, and we like Israel, so we voted for Israel, so, as a result, the Americans will support us.'[48]

The hallmark of Israel's 'return' to Africa was supposed to be a grand Israeli–African business summit, originally scheduled to take place in October 2017 in Lomé. The colourful brochure produced before the summit praised Togo as 'a loyal and historic friend of the State of Israel' and a 'beacon of political and economic stability' in West Africa.[49] Ironically, weeks before the event mass demonstrations broke out in Togo. The summit was postponed, and no new date was announced. Even though Israeli officials publicly insisted that the cancellation of the summit had nothing to do with political pressure,[50] Togo's decision to host the summit and its pro-Israel stance were not viewed favourably by Muslim-majority and Arab countries and by other members of the Organisation of Islamic Cooperation (OIC), some of whom worked to undermine the event and threatened to suspend aid to the West African country.[51]

There are other interesting variations to the dynamics between Israel, American pro-Israel groups, Washington and African leaders. Coincidently or not, for example, Chad's decision to renew diplomatic ties with Israel in early 2019 came shortly after the US Justice Department accused President Idriss Déby of receiving bribes for providing a Chinese company with oil rights in the country.[52] Two years earlier, Congolese President Joseph Kabila attracted considerable media attention when he tasked the Israeli security and telecommunication firm Mer Group with coordinating his government's lobbying efforts in Washington.[53] In 2008, Blaise Compaoré decided to attend Israel's Independence Day celebrations in Jerusalem in order to 'demonstrate his integrity' to the US prior to a visit to Washington.[54] While the actors involved and specific arrangements between them vary from case to case, the principal commodities traded in these relationships are similar: political support, assistance with image management and influence in Washington.

The politics of blessings

There is a long history of Western evangelical support for Zionism and Israel, particularly, since the 1970s, from Christian groups in the US. And while official Israeli rhetoric in Africa does not make overt references to Christianity, this support is becoming an increasingly dominant force in Israel's relationships with African leaders and peoples. Israeli diplomats and politicians have endorsed and featured as guests in evangelical pro-Israel conferences across Africa in recent years, and Israeli government officials warmly welcome high-profile African pastors when they visit Israel/Palestine on pilgrimage tours. The evangelical theological justifications for support for Israel mean little to Jewish Israelis, and diplomats also often stress the importance of establishing Israel's image in Africa as a modern, tech-savvy nation and not only as the ancient Holy Land many Africans know from the Bible. And yet the pro-Israel messages evangelicals promote, their suspicion of Islam, their urge to express unconditional support for Israeli policies and their expanding influence on public life in many parts of Africa render them invaluable allies of the Jewish state.

Support for Israel comes from various Christian movements in Africa, but the most dominant among them are the Pentecostal and neo-charismatic churches that have emerged in West Africa since the 1980s (primarily in Nigeria and Ghana, discussed below) and have gained immense popularity and influence across the continent ever since. Israel has long enjoyed a positive image among Christian populations because of its association with biblical narratives and the ancient people of Israel. In Ethiopia, for centuries the national myth positioned all leaders as descendants of the Queen of Sheba and King Solomon. But the rise of new large faith-based organisations and religious movements that consider actively supporting Israel to be an avenue for self-help and personal salvation has created new constituencies that are keen to promote the interests of the Jewish state. Unsurprisingly, Israel's public diplomacy efforts in several African countries have assumed a distinctly evangelical tone in recent years.

Some of the evangelical pro-Israel activities and pre-millennial dispensationalist teachings spreading in Africa in recent years are being promoted and supported by non-Israeli groups from outside the continent. The Africa–Israel Initiative, an organisation that seeks to create 'a highway of blessings from Israel to Africa and from Africa to Israel',[55] is one of them. Since its establishment in 2012 by Norwegian evangelists, it has been organising pilgrimage trips to Israel for Africans as well as mass prayers, conferences and pro-Israel events in numerous countries including Kenya (where it now maintains its headquarters), Ghana, Nigeria, Uganda, Zambia and South Africa.[56] Christians United for Israel (CUFI) – America's largest Christian pro-Israel group that boasts 4 million members in the US alone and extends great influence over American policy-makers – has similarly been organising activities in Africa in recent years, with different degrees of cooperation with Israeli embassies, including Israeli Independence Day celebrations and 'Nights to Honour Israel'.[57] The International Christian Embassy in Jerusalem (ICEJ) – an organisation that mobilises evangelicals around the world in support of Israel and runs humanitarian projects in the country – has representatives in several African countries as well.

Different movements offer different explanations for their position towards Israel and the Jewish people, and a detailed discussion of these political-theological visions is beyond the scope of this book. Among many evangelical groups, support for Israel is underpinned by the belief that God's covenant with Abraham is still valid and that therefore the Jews are still God's 'Chosen People' and have a unique right over the 'Promised Land'.[58] Unwavering support for Israel's policies is also commonly explained as based on Genesis 12:3, where God promises to Abraham to bless whoever blesses him. Evangelicals often view Israel's wealth, military prowess and developmental achievements as clear indications of blessings and righteousness, and its ongoing conflicts (with Islamic countries or peoples) as the fulfilment of biblical prophesies: struggles against the devil and an indication that the events of the end of times and Second Coming of Christ are fast approaching.[59] 'The problems that we are seeing between the Jews and the rest of the world, is because they are the favourites of God', Nigerian megapastor Enoch Adeboye of the Redeemed Christian Church of God explained in 2011 while visiting Israeli settlements in the Occupied Palestinian Territories. 'When you are special to God, then automatically the devil wouldn't like you either.'[60]

The notion that pro-Israel activism can have positive consequences also resonates with the Pentecostal emphasis on healing, entrepreneurship and prosperity. As Reverend Gilbert Apreala, the

Nigerian pastor who was the country director for the Africa–Israel Initiative in Ghana, explained: 'Every person who loves and prays for Israel is qualified to be a member [of the Africa–Israel Initiative], and the benefits are the blessings of God who makes rich and adds no sorrow.'[61] Crucially, this logic also applies to national policies: 'We want African countries to support Israel at the United Nations level, and for Africa to be blessed by the God of Israel for supporting Israel.'[62] Beyond the political support and obvious impact on Israel's image among Pentecostal constituencies, the imperative to bless Israel also results in an interesting reversal of the conventional status of Israel as a donor state, as Pentecostal elites often make symbolic humanitarian donations to Israeli institutions or NGOs. On his regular pilgrimage tours to Israel in recent years, for example, Pastor Enoch Adeboye donated several ambulances to the Israeli national emergency service and disaster recovery organisations.[63]

Based on the same rationale, anti-Israeli policies are viewed as having polluting and damaging consequences. Apostle Zilly Aggrey from Nigeria, visiting Israel in 2007 with a group of evangelical delegates from around the world who came to celebrate the fortieth anniversary of the 'reunification' of Jerusalem during the 1967 war, said that 'African Christians would love to kiss the ground in Israel. They would love to kiss the feet of a Jew'. In an event organised by the Knesset Christian Allies Caucus, he further explained that Nigeria's decision to cut ties with Israel in 1973 was the reason for the country's financial crisis: 'Any nation that does not serve you will perish', he told the Knesset. 'Our economy went down after we cut ties, and we became one of the poorest nations in the world. Since we have restored relations with Israel, our economy is back up.'[64]

Indeed, nowhere in Africa have the political implications of the rise of Pentecostalism in recent decades for Israel–Africa relations been as evident as in the case of Nigeria – the epicentre of Africa's 'Pentecostal revolution'. For a start, the country is the largest African source of pilgrims to Israel. In 2011 some 45,000 Nigerians visited Israel/Palestine, though numbers have declined since then.[65]

Members of Nigeria's Pentecostal elite, like Pastors Chris Oyakhilome, T. B. Joshua and Enoch Adeboye – all celebrity-preachers with a high-profile media presence, representing churches with branches across the world and influencing millions of believers – have visited the Holy Land in recent years. Some returned, multiple times, accompanied by hundreds of pilgrims, regularly sharing impressive footage from their trips on social media and their popular TV channels. Prophet T. B. Joshua even caused a small controversy in Nigeria when he announced his intention to relocate to Israel altogether after visiting in 2017.[66]

These men, as Ebenezer Obadare shows, are powerful actors in the country's political landscape.[67] President Goodluck Jonathan (2010–15), a Christian from the country's south-east, 'wore his supposed Christian and Pentecostalist credentials on his sleeve' and strategically courted the nation's most influential Pentecostal pastors and tapped into their powerful public influence.[68] Among other things, he repeatedly visited Israel on pilgrimage tours – once as vice-president in 2007 and then twice during his presidency – each time travelling with an entourage of high-profile officials and pastors. Jonathan's trip to Jerusalem in 2013 made him the first Nigerian head of state to visit Israel.[69] In 2014, months before the elections that he eventually lost, he visited Israel accompanied by Bishop David Oyedepo, the founder of one of Africa's largest congregations – the Living Faith World Outreach Ministry, aka Winners' Chapel.[70]

As part of Jonathan's branding of himself as Nigeria's *Pentecostal* president, pilgrimage tours doubled as friendly formal visits and relations with Israel improved. To Israel's benefit, Nigeria was a non-permanent member of the UN Security Council in 2014–15. In December 2014, when the Council voted on a resolution calling for Israel to withdraw from the Palestinian Territories, Nigeria (with Rwanda) abstained, though reportedly only after a last-minute personal phone call from Netanyahu to Jonathan.[71] Muhammadu Buhari, who came to power in 2015, had no similar incentives to support Israel. He distanced himself from Jerusalem and was even said to have blocked Netanyahu from participating in the ECOWAS summit in 2016.[72] Nonetheless, Israeli ties with Pentecostal churches and high-profile evangelicals in Nigeria remain firm and continue to serve Israeli business and political interests in the country.

A very similar manifestation of the politics of blessings can be identified in Ghana, where Pentecostal influence on public life has been just as pervasive. As in Nigeria, Israel found some of its most ardent advocates in the country among its evangelical and Pentecostal elites and has cultivated close ties with them. Though an Israeli embassy was only opened in Accra in 2011, ties between Israeli businesses and Ghanaian evangelicals had already developed earlier. Since its re-establishment, the Israeli embassy openly supported the activities of the local branch of the Africa–Israel Initiative, hosted its leaders at the ambassador's residency, participated in their religious conferences and in recent years even organised its own prayer events.[73] A regular attendee of the Israeli embassy's events is Archbishop Nicolas Duncan-Williams – the founder of the Christian Action Faith Ministries and one of the most influential religious figures in Africa.[74]

As faith-based organisations increasingly extend their spiritual and material influence into spheres that are commonly perceived as 'secular' – electoral politics, business, education, popular culture – their impact on Israel's standing is multi-layered. 'Our main objective as an embassy of the State of Israel is to strengthen the ties between Israel and Ghana. And we do this on three levels: … government-to-government … business-to-business … and people-to-people', Shani Cooper-Zubida, Israel's ambassador to Ghana, explained. 'These churches are integrated in all three fields.' Not only do they influence the media, public opinion and governments (regardless of the party in power), they are also important economic actors. 'That you are a man of God does not prevent you from being a very successful businessman', Cooper-Zubida noted. 'This world is full of trade and seeks business opportunities, and certainly we have opportunities there to advance Israel and our relationship.'[75] Indeed, Archbishop Duncan-Williams is also the 'Patron' of the Ghana–Israel Business Chamber, inaugurated in 2016.[76]

Even in countries where Israel has no formal diplomatic presence, however, local religious organisations have often willingly stepped in to serve as advocates for the Israeli state among both the masses and elites. Uganda, where Israel does not maintain an embassy, is one striking example. The first East African branch of the international group Christians for Israel was established in Uganda in 2009 by Drake Kanaabo,[77] a known evangelist from one of the most popular and oldest Pentecostal churches in Uganda, the Redeemed of the Lord Evangelistic Church. Like other pro-Israel Christian groups in Africa, the organisation runs pilgrimage tours to Israel and religious conferences for members of various churches in Uganda and other East African countries. For several years, however, it has also been hosting major Israeli Independence Day celebrations in Uganda, from exclusive cocktails in posh hotels to mass street parades, attended by both Israeli and Ugandan officials.

The organisation's offices are conveniently located in central Kampala close to the Ugandan parliament, and its members have been participating on a regular basis in 'prayer breakfasts' in this institution. In 2016, Christians for Israel even held a special 'Repentance Conference' for Ugandan military officers. During the event – which was attended by the Israeli deputy ambassador from the embassy in Nairobi and a visiting preacher from Europe – high-ranking military officers prayed and fasted for several days in order to repent, on behalf of the Ugandan military, for Uganda's mistreatment of Israel during the period of Idi Amin's rule. 'These people, when they knelt down to confess, all of them burst into tears', one volunteer of the organisation later described the event. 'It was historical!'[78] The following year, the Israeli embassy in Kenya donated equipment for a medical facility established by evangelist Drake Kanaabo, to mark Israel's Independence Day.[79]

South Africa is another country where Israeli diplomats have allied with Christian groups to advance their interests. The forces at play here are very different, however, both because there is a largely pro-Israel white Jewish community and because there is a strong sense of solidarity with the Palestinians among South African civil society and political leadership. With the exception of Arab countries, nowhere in Africa is criticism of Israel more prevalent, nowhere has the BDS movement gained comparable momentum and legitimacy, and nowhere is the comparison between Israel's policies and apartheid more widely agreed on. Prominent veterans of the anti-apartheid struggle like Desmond Tutu and Ahmed Kathrada have repeatedly stressed their support for the Palestinian struggle, expressions of support for Israel regularly cause public controversies and draw condemnations, and the African National Congress (ANC) remains largely consistent in its solidarity with the Palestinian people and its support for the two-state solution. That the Palestinian issue has been instrumentalised by local politicians for electoral gain is obvious. Nonetheless, one should not underestimate the extent to which the injustices perpetrated in Israel/Palestine resonate with those who were the victims of similar forms of oppression until not so long ago.

Against this backdrop, South Africa has become an important front for Israeli public diplomacy efforts. And Israel's most consistent local partners in this battle, beyond South Africa's Jewish community, are a host of evangelical organisations. Much of the pro-Israel advocacy in the country in recent years has been led by South African Friends of Israel (SAFI), the outreach arm of the South African Zionist Federation (SAZF). SAFI runs pro-Israel campaigns and events with the objective of 'educating' new audiences on the Middle East. Its partners include the local branch of the evangelical Africa–Israel Initiative, the Institute for Christian Leadership Development and Defend Embrace Invest Support Israel (DEISI) – an organisation that was founded by

Reverend Kenneth Meshoe, the leader of the African Christian Democratic Party and one of the most vocal supporters of Israel in South Africa.[80] DEISI (led by Meshoe's daughter) occasionally cooperates with CUFI, the large American evangelical organisation mentioned above.[81]

Here, too, the fusion of pro-Israel advocacy and religious rhetoric is conspicuous. SAFI's 2018 annual conference in Johannesburg, for example, was organised in cooperation with the Israeli Ministry of Strategic Affairs, which is in charge of public diplomacy and combatting the BDS movement internationally.[82] The Ministry, it should be noted, often runs its international anti-BDS activities through independent local groups in foreign countries, so as not to appear to be interfering in their domestic politics.[83] At SAFI's conference, Ben Swartz, co-chair of SAFI and chair of SAZF, addressed the several hundred Jews and Christians who gathered at Johannesburg City Hall. Denouncing the ANC's 'radical' pro-Palestinian stance and criticism of Israel, he made an explicit biblical reference by calling on those present to

> help us push back this scourge and this obsession that has captured the ruling party, for we do not wish to bring upon us the curse associated with these actions. We wish to bring upon South Africa the blessings that South Africa so rightfully deserves.[84]

Less vocal in the public sphere but nonetheless central to Israel's advocacy efforts in South Africa have also been the Zion Christian Church (ZCC) and its leader Bishop Barnabas Lekganyane. Despite their name, the Zionist churches in southern Africa, of which the ZCC is the largest, are not related to the Jewish Zionist national movement. Their name derives from the Zionist Christian movement that was founded in the US and spread in southern Africa in the early twentieth century.[85] The ZCC is estimated to have some 5 million members but has throughout its history distanced itself from mainstream politics. During the apartheid era its acceptance of, and tacit cooperation with, the regime drew criticism.[86] Today, the Church's supposedly apolitical stance makes it a useful partner for pro-Israel advocates. The Israeli embassy and the SAZF courted it for support, and in 2017 Bishop Lekganyane and the ZCC leadership travelled to Israel on a quasi-diplomatic 'Peace Mission' organised by SAFI and met with Israeli officials and President Reuven Rivlin.[87] At least according to SAFI, Lekganyane later asked President Cyril Ramaphosa, who assumed office in February 2018, to moderate the ANC's position on Israel.[88]

The business of state-building

At the foundations of Israel's relationship with several African countries remains a small but often well-connected business community. The experts that Israel sent to Africa in the hundreds and thousands during the 1960s – to help young states modernise their agriculture sectors or develop their infrastructure or government bureaucracies – have now been replaced by Israeli expatriates and entrepreneurs who sell Israeli expertise and technologies to whomever is willing to pay, including in countries that have no diplomatic relations with Israel. The scope of their involvement cannot be compared to that of Chinese, American or even some European actors, but the impact of their presence and skills is evident in a number of African countries. And the most influential cases of Israeli private sector involvement – in fields such as agriculture, housing, health, telecommunication and water management – have been in those countries that have witnessed accelerated economic growth since the early 2000s and in which older personal ties guaranteed direct Israeli access to the highest political echelons and thus also to lucrative business opportunities.

Angola is one such case. Several Israelis were deeply involved in the country's diamond sector and arms trade from the 1990s, during the civil war, and worked closely with Angolan elites.[89]

Some of them remain active in the local mining industry until today. The Israeli company LR Group, founded by three ex-fighter pilots, became José Eduardo dos Santos' main provider of military equipment at the time. From the early 1990s and as war against the National Union for the Total Independence of Angola (UNITA) raged, they acquired for the People's Movement for the Liberation of Angola (MPLA) – mostly but not only from Israeli arms manu- facturers – airport control towers, weapons and ammunition for the police forces and military, unmanned planes and intelligence equipment, a presidential plane (renovated in Israel) and, in the late 1990s, Sukhoi jets (from Uzbekistan).[90] Payment for some of these deals reportedly came in the form of oil, coffee and other goods.[91] Strengthening the MPLA's air power played a crucial role in bringing the war to an end through a military victory, and rumours about the role of Israeli intelligence and equipment in locating UNITA leader Jonas Savimbi in 2002 persist.[92]

After helping the government defeat UNITA in 2002 (a process that apparently earned them great wealth), the company's founders expanded into the civilian sphere, turning into partners of the MPLA in the reconstruction of the country. The transition came with the establishment for the Angolan government of the widely celebrated Aldeia Nova project, an agricultural settlement for ex-soldiers and farmers which was modelled after the coopera- tive villages established in Israel in the 1950s (*Moshav*).[93] Although a private enterprise on the Israeli side, Aldeia Nova shared much of its Zionist social engineering and modernist ambitions with the Israeli state-led initiatives of the 1960s and, like these earlier projects, implementation of the plan proved more problematic than expected: unfit for Angolan conditions and local capacities, it became dysfunctional and costly to run.[94] By 2011, three years after the Angolan government took over the project from the Israeli management, Israelis were brought back to salvage it: the project was handed to the Mitrelli Group, which split from the LR Group and was led by some of its founders.[95]

While LR shifted its focus to similar projects in other African countries, Mitrelli went on to execute projects for and in cooperation with the Angolan government in agriculture and farming, water management, housing, energy, education and vocational training, health and maritime security.[96] Vital Capital Fund – led by Eytan Stibbe, one of the founders of LR – has invested in various infrastructure projects in Angola (including several of Mitrelli's).[97] Angola's reconstruction allowed these Israeli actors to distance themselves from the notorious arms and mining businesses of the 1990s and, like the MPLA itself, assume the new role of developmentalists who highlight their commitment to social impact and philanthropy. Mitrelli and Vital Capital, for instance, also sponsor arts and culture projects in Angola and academic programmes in Israel, including the African Studies Centre at Ben-Gurion University of the Negev.[98] They are all, however, instrumental for the hegemonic agenda of the MPLA, which, as expert on Lusophone African politics Ricardo Soares de Oliveira noted, has relied on external expertise to 'advance reconstruction, but on its own terms'.[99]

Israeli private sector involvement in Equatorial Guinea – another oil-rich country with an even more predatory authoritarian regime – followed a very similar pattern. Here, too, personal connections are a central part of the story. Yardena Ovadia, arguably the most dominant but not the only Israeli entrepreneur operating in the country, first met President Teodoro Obiang Nguema Mbasogo at a dinner in Morocco in the early 2000s. At least so the story goes. Unlike Stibbe and his partners in Angola, Ovadia is not an ex-fighter with connections in the Israeli defence establishment but a Morocco-born merchant who grew up in a marginalised town in Israel's periphery. She remained close to Obiang, however, and in the following years was able to mediate deals with Israeli companies, including the purchasing of military equipment and patrol vessels reportedly worth up to $100 million.[100] Israeli firms are still said to be supporting the security arrangements of Obiang himself – Africa's longest serving head of state at the time of writing.

Ovadia's business success was directly linked to the wealth and needs of the Equatoguinean leadership. From the mid-1990s, Equatorial Guinea enjoyed a remarkable influx of cash from its newly discovered oilfields. Its leadership, facing repeated accusations of corruption, theft and human rights abuses, invested in conspicuous and costly infrastructure projects – white elephants that supposedly prove that funds are spent on the modernisation of the country.[101] While investment in social welfare was low on the government's agenda, it did invest in a few high-profile, exclusive hospitals in politically important locations.[102] These became the hallmark of Ovadia's career: a series of institutions that were designed by Israelis, equipped with Israeli products, staffed by dozens of Israeli and other foreign doctors and are managed from Israel through Ovadia's company, International Medical Services (IMS). The company states as its mission 'to take part in Africa's progression towards modernization'.[103]

The fact that Israel is a popular medical tourism destination for African elites perhaps explains some of the attraction in tasking Israelis with the establishment and management of these institutions. The hospitals boast state of the art infrastructure, equipment and services – enclaves of Israeli medical expertise within an otherwise dilapidated state and dysfunctional health sector. 'It's like taking a private hospital from Israel or the US and putting it in the middle of the African bush', says the Israeli manager of the hospital in Bata.[104] A former Israeli employee described it as a 'palace in the middle of jungle' – an image that seems to suit many of Obiang's eccentric infrastructure projects.[105] But even if these institutions operate as professionally as their employees claim, the extent to which they serve the Equatoguinean people or address their needs is highly questionable, to say the least. In a recent report, Human Rights Watch criticised the Equatoguinean government for spending funds on few high-profile hospitals 'that appear to be almost exclusively for the benefit of elites – rather than on primary healthcare that benefits most citizens'.[106]

A third example is that of Rwanda, which has mobilised Israel's high-tech experience to advance its developmental agenda. Rwanda's Vision 2020 – the government's strategy to make Rwanda a middle-income country by 2020 – focused on development through a private sector-led and knowledge-based economy. Since the early 2000s, high-tech entrepreneurship was actively encouraged by the government, which was set to make Rwanda the 'Singapore of Africa' and integrate it into the global economy as a reliable business hub.[107] This is where Israel's 'Start-Up Nation' reputation came in. Given the common comparisons between Rwandan and Israeli histories and political circumstances, the notion that Israel can serve as a model for the small East African nation came to underpin much of the Israeli business involvement in the country. As one Israeli entrepreneur put it, like besieged Israel, landlocked Rwanda has to practise 'innovation out of necessity'.[108]

Israeli private sector involvement in Rwanda is wide-ranging, facilitating the implementation of Kigali's hegemonic developmental and political vision in multiple spheres.[109] A key Israeli informal business–diplomatic emissary in Rwanda remains Hezi Bezalel, who was first mentioned in Chapter 2. Bezalel's company – Marathon Group – is known to have invested in Rwanda's telecommunication sector and partly owns one of Rwanda's leading cellular providers, Tigo.[110] In a more symbolic venture, Bezalel recently worked with another Israeli entrepreneur to establish 42Kura – an Israeli–Rwandan start-up incubator in Kigali. Their stated vision was to help Rwanda 'become the African Start-up Nation'.[111] In the health sector, the Israeli start-up PrePex – which developed a small device for non-surgical male circumcision – was deployed by the Rwandan government to pursue mass national voluntary medical male circumcision campaigns, as part of a strategy to reduce HIV prevalence.[112]

In the energy sector, the (Israeli–American-led) Dutch company Gigawatt Global with its Israeli affiliate Energiya Global and the support of United States Agency for International Development's (USAID) Power Africa and several European funders established an 8.5-megawatt grid-connected solar power plant in 2014 – a $24 million project that increased Rwanda's total energy generation capacity by 6%.[113] The solar field was built in partnership with, and on lands owned by, the Agazoho-Shalom Youth Village for orphans – an educational institution that was founded in 2007 by American Jewish philanthropists and was modelled on the Israeli youth villages established during the 1950s for Holocaust orphans.[114] The government-owned Rwanda Energy Group (REG), the national energy generation and distribution company, signed a cooperation agreement with the Israel Electric Corporation (IEC) in 2015 for technical support and capacity building.[115] Two years later, the former vice-president of IEC, Ron Weiss, was hired by Rwanda to run REG.[116] Meanwhile, the chair of the Rwanda Development Board since late 2017 has been Israeli businessman and high-tech entrepreneur Itzhak Fisher, who also worked with Netanyahu's campaign in the 1990s.[117]

The Israeli media, fascinated by their extraordinary wealth and their mysterious access to lucrative opportunities in Africa, often misrepresents people like Stibbe, Bezalel and Ovadia, portraying them as 'puppeteers' of African leaders, as if they are the ones who secretly call the shots in Angola, Rwanda or Equatorial Guinea. But while the personal ties they have with leaders of the countries in which they work are clearly a key asset, it is equally true that their business opportunities and activities were shaped by the ambitions and needs of African leaders who explicitly sought foreign capital and expertise in specific areas to advance their domestic political, developmental and financial agendas. Rather than puppeteers, these individuals and the small Israeli communities in Angola, Equatorial Guinea or Rwanda should primarily be viewed as reliable and disciplined providers of services.[118]

Evidently, not all countries in which there is significant involvement of Israeli private actors are equally supportive of Israel at the formal diplomatic level. There is no formal Israeli policy that governs the relationship between Israeli officials and private actors and the specific dynamics between diplomats, politicians and entrepreneurs vary greatly from case to case, depending on the individuals involved, the nature of their activities and their political agendas. If during the 1960s state-sponsored initiatives came with the expectation that Israeli investment, donations and support would buy African political support, in the contemporary environment of neoliberal capitalism the ties between flows of capital and political leverage are much more evasive, as private actors enjoy limited formal Israeli institutional support and are rewarded financially by their African clients. African leaders, in other words, can tap into Israeli investments, technologies and expertise without having to pay it back directly in political support. For example, despite deep involvement of Israeli companies and despite the fact that on several occasions President José Eduardo dos Santos publicly described Angola's relations with Israel as warm, in 2016, as a non-permanent member of the Security Council, it did vote in favour of the resolution that declared Israeli settlements in the Palestinian Territories illegal.

Africa's Israels

No typology will do justice to the nuances of Israel's presence and role in different African countries and among different constituencies, but the four patterns of interactions presented above do indicate under what circumstances African leaders are most likely to support Israel: when they need its security assistance, when they want to improve their relationship with Washington, when local evangelical constituencies have significant political weight and, to a lesser extent, when they want to attract Israeli investment, expertise and entrepreneurs. These factors take various forms and converge (or not) in different ways in different countries, depending on the actors and interests involved. They are also very often entangled in one another in various ways, as the involvement of some Israeli firms and entrepreneurs in both security and infrastructure projects (or, in the case of the Mer Group in the DRC, in lobbying in the US) and the ties between businesses and religious organisations demonstrate. All four, together and apart, define Israel's hard and soft power in Africa today.

Clearly, however, from the perspective of African leaders, Israel's appeals for diplomatic support always have to be balanced with local and regional commitments to (largely but not only Muslim and Arab) populations and donor states that are more critical of Israel. Israel's ability to mobilise African political support therefore depends not only on its reputation in Africa and on what it can offer African leaders, but also on the 'penalties' its adversaries are willing and able to impose on those leaders who choose to publicly stand with Israel. In an increasingly monetised African political arena,[119] Israel often appears to be underestimating the price it has to pay in order to buy the full diplomatic support of African leaders. But its own efforts – benefiting from a wider range of political, religious and economic trends that are beyond its immediate control – have guaranteed valuable gestures of support, which it hopes, will only increase with time.

Chapter 5

MANAGING THE FRONTIER

If Israel's international strategy over the past decade has been primarily preoccupied with Iran and the Palestinians, at the domestic level successive governments under Netanyahu's leadership had another raison d'être with direct African implications: expelling the tens of thousands of refugees from the Horn of Africa that entered Israel starting from the mid-2000s and stopping others from following in their footsteps.[1] These efforts, however, were only the latest episode within a longer history of population movements between Africa and Israel and Israeli attempts to engineer or control them – efforts that repeatedly intertwined with Israel's other objectives in Africa and, much like its broader engagement with the continent, were characterised by a recurring resort to personal bargains with African leaders, the deployment of security apparatuses and the use of clandestine arrangements.

Managing Israel's frontiers and its demographic landscape was always seen as a matter of great strategic importance but was also the subject of intense debates. On the one hand, a Jewish majority was always perceived by the Israeli public and the country's leaders as crucial for the very survival of the Jewish state and the Jewish people. In order to consolidate it – to guarantee that a Jewish majority is maintained and to counter the Palestinian 'demographic threat' – Jewish diaspora communities were encouraged to settle in their 'ancestral homeland', while the immigration of non-Jewish populations was discouraged or prevented, and Palestinians in the Occupied Territories were blocked from accessing Israeli citizenship or encouraged to move elsewhere. Central to the Zionist ideology was therefore a powerful narrative of *Kibbutz Galuyot* – the 'ingathering of the exiles' in the Land of Israel. Accordingly, the Law of Return (enacted in 1950) provides for the automatic naturalisation of Jews in Israel, making every Jewish man and woman in the world eligible for Israeli citizenship.

On the other hand, what often goes unnoticed is that efforts to gather Jewish communities in Israel also evoked difficult questions about kinship, belonging, ethnic purity, race, genealogical roots and the manner in which one becomes, or qualifies as, a member of the Jewish people. These questions have, to a certain extent, preoccupied Jewish thinkers and communities for centuries. But since a Jewish state was established in 1948, they have also been linked to questions of access to citizenship. Consequently, while encouraging Jews to immigrate to Israel was always viewed as a priority in Israel's strategy against its adversaries and an important part of the Zionist national ethos, there was never a consensus between different constituencies within Israel and the wider Jewish world around how one defines a 'real' or 'genuine' Jew, and to what extent and under what circumstances the Jewish state should open its borders to non-Jewish populations. And Israel's relationships with African peoples have led to some of the most heated debates around these questions.

Israel and Africa's Jews

Jewish interactions with Africa date back to ancient times. According to the biblical narrative, Israelites first fled to Egypt to escape famine, and ultimately returned to the Middle East in a great exodus. In the Hellenistic and Roman periods, Egypt was a major centre of the Jewish diaspora and Jewish communities lived throughout the coastal towns of North Africa.[2] Ali Mazrui famously argued that Jewish and Hebraic cultures should be viewed as part of what he called Africa's 'ancient Triple Heritage' – the legacies of indigenous, Semitic and Greco-Roman influences that shaped the continent's history. Judaism had a direct impact on societies in the Horn of Africa, and an indirect impact on the rest of the continent through Christianity and Islam: 'Monotheism has been conquering Africa under the banner of either the cross or the crescent – but behind both banners is the shadow of Moses and the commandments he conveyed.'[3]

Examining Israel's relationship with Africa's Jewish communities in more recent history, however, one can distinguish between two broad groups of African Jews. The first group comprises Jewish communities that immigrated to Africa starting from the early modern period, fleeing persecution and following the expansion of European trade networks. Sephardi Jews from the Iberian Peninsula fled the Spanish Inquisition, from the end of the fifteenth century, and settled in North Africa and in the territories of the Ottoman Empire, joining pre-existing Jewish communities in these areas. Some also migrated further south along the West African coast, all the way to the Gulf of Guinea, where they were not forced to convert or hide their religion.[4]

Small numbers of European Jews migrated from Europe to South Africa before the nineteenth century, and were joined later by large numbers of refugees escaping persecution in czarist Russia and, during the 1930s, Nazi Germany.[5] Some of them migrated further north to Mozambique and Southern and Northern Rhodesia (today's Zimbabwe and Zambia), and small numbers of Jewish families settled in British East Africa, mainly but not only in Nairobi.[6] Arriving from other cities across the Ottoman Empire, Sephardi and other Middle Eastern Jews also settled in Sudan starting from the late nineteenth century,[7] while a small community of Jewish merchants from Aden and Yemen settled in Eritrea and Ethiopia.[8] In various colonial urban centres, Jews came to form part of a small class of foreign traders and businessmen, usually together with other migrants from the Middle East and Asia.

The Jewish identity of the descendants of Jewish migrants who settled in Africa was hardly ever questioned, and they were generally encouraged to immigrate to Israel in order to populate the new Jewish state after independence. Between 1948 and 1967, more than 370,000 Jews from Africa immigrated to Israel and, apart from a few thousand from South Africa, they all came from North African countries, primarily from Morocco (238,378).[9] The rise of Zionism and Arab nationalism and, more crucially, the war of 1948, complicated the position of Jewish communities in Arab countries, and many were uprooted from their homes and lost much of their property. Even though they were formally granted equal citizenship in Israel under the Law of Return, in a country that primarily saw itself as part of the West, North Africans were often viewed as 'uncivilised' and 'backward', were systemically marginalised and discriminated against and were intentionally settled in peripheral areas. Many understood their maltreatment as a direct consequence of the orientalist tendencies of Zionism and Israeli society.[10]

Immigration from Morocco deserves a brief mention, not least because some of the practices employed by Israel to manage it would later be redeployed in order to deal with other groups of migrants. It began when the country was still under French rule, through legal channels, but became a highly controversial issue as independence approached. Moroccan leaders argued that mass immigration would be viewed as indirect assistance to Israel in its war against other Arab countries. They also believed that it would damage Morocco's image as an independent sovereign country, and its economy. From 1956 Jewish immigration was officially restricted, and later Morocco joined the Arab League. The Israeli response was to deploy the Mossad and set up an elaborate covert mechanism that encouraged and facilitated the clandestine migration of thousands of Moroccan Jews by land and sea to Spain and France, and from there to Israel.

Shrouded in secrecy, this operation relied on the use of forged passports, the bribing of Moroccan officials and the services of Spanish and Moroccan smugglers.[11] Bin-Nun described how it created an 'emigration psychosis' among the Jewish population of Morocco, which was previously rather reluctant to leave the country.[12] In January 1961, more than 40 Moroccan Jews and one Israeli official died when the vessel the Mossad arranged to smuggle them to Gibraltar sank.[13] Israel utilised the tragedy to launch a propaganda campaign against Morocco and publicly criticised it for not allowing Jews to leave,[14] and later that year, official diplomatic understandings were reached which allowed for mass immigration to Israel – a project titled 'Operation Yachin' – in exchange for 'indemnities' to Moroccan leaders.[15]

Alongside the Jewish immigrants who settled in Africa and the Jewish communities of North Africa, there are numerous African communities who claim Jewish identity but whose diverse cultural and liturgical traditions, religious doctrines and often opaque histories place them outside mainstream taxonomies of Jewish identity. Some of these communities do not claim to have any 'blood' links to the ancient Israelites and have adopted Judaism in recent history under various circumstances. The Abayudaya of Uganda, for example, one of the most famous and widely studied African Jewish groups, adopted Judaism in the early twentieth century.[16] Many other communities, however, do claim a genealogical connection to the ancient People of Israel and therefore view themselves as ethnically Jewish or Jewish 'by blood'. As Edith Bruder writes, such groups 'carry with them the dream of a genesis outside Africa'.[17]

Communities that view themselves as descendants of ancient Israelites can be found across the African continent. The Lemba in Zimbabwe and South Africa, for example, claim to be connected to an ancient Jewish community that migrated from the Middle East, as do the Beta Israel of Ethiopia, whose relationship with Israel is further discussed in the following section. In south-eastern Nigeria, there are numerous Igbo groups that claim Jewish ancestry and practise different forms of Judaism. Igbo researcher and activist Remy Ilona has described the Igbos, who number in the tens of millions, as the 'largest Jewish diaspora', though in practice not all Igbos claim Jewish identity or origins.[18] Much smaller communities in other African countries – including Somalia, Kenya, Madagascar, Cameroon, Mali and Ghana – also claim to have 'Hebrew blood'. The list appears to be growing steadily. In recent years, members of some of these groups have sought to 'prove' their Jewish credentials through DNA tests.[19]

The histories of these communities are controversial, and the contexts in which they came to regard themselves as Jewish are diverse. African Judaism remains an understudied field, but thanks to the innovative work of several scholars over the past two decades there is now a small body of literature that shows how Israelite and Judaic identities were constructed across Africa, often as a result of encounters between Europeans and Africans. As Tudor Parfitt shows, in the West, myths about the presence of 'lost' Jewish communities in Africa have informed speculation about their whereabouts for centuries. With the advent of colonialism, Europeans began to project their ideas on specific African societies they came across, and some groups consequently internalised these ideas or drew on them to develop their own historical narratives that associate them with the People of Israel, often as part of an attempt 'to counter oppression, gain approval, re-create lost history, revolt against white authority, and forge new, more-useful identities'.[20] The Judaic identities that were created through these processes represented a fusion of pre-existing African oral traditions and European narratives and prejudices.

Most members of groups that view themselves as Jewish 'by blood' therefore adhere to Christian and in some cases even Islamic theological doctrines and practices today and not to mainstream Rabbinic Judaism, and usually see no contradiction between their faith and their claims of Jewish ancestry. Most Lemba and Igbo practise Christianity, for example, and the Zakhor Jews of Timbuktu, who claim to be the descendants of Saharan Jews, are Muslim. Various Messianic Jewish movements that fuse Jewish traditions and practices with belief in Jesus as the Messiah also gained popularity in Africa among such groups. But while

Messianic Jews understand their faith as the most authentic expression of Judaism and naturally promote it in such terms, Rabbinic Judaism, most Israeli Jews and the country's authorities view it as a form of Christianity.[21] In Africa as elsewhere, Messianic Jewish missionaries are usually primarily interested in groups that are considered to be Jewish 'by blood'. Interestingly, however, such movements have also generated Judaic identities and genealogical claims among people who did not previously see themselves as descendants of the ancient Israelites.

Among the Nuer in Ethiopia and South Sudan, for example, multiple messianic congregations have sprung up over the past decade, initially under the influence of members of the Jerusalem Church of God (Seventh Day) from Kenya. The members of at least one of these Nuer groups – the Congregation of Yahweh, which is part of an international messianic movement bearing the same name and with congregations in more than ten other African countries – have recently reached the conclusion that the Nuer are one of the Lost Tribes of Israel as well. This claim is primarily based on the comparison of 'traditional' Nuer norms with some of the Jewish practices and laws described in the Old Testament but is sometimes also justified as based on several biblical texts, which are interpreted as referring to the Nuer. The Congregation maintains its headquarters in western Ethiopia, where hundreds of its members live in a 'kibbutz' they founded in 2015. And although Israeli officials seem to be entirely unaware of the existence of this group, its members do aspire to 'return' to Israel and hope to have their DNA tested.[22]

Crucially, as the case of the Nuer Congregation of Yahweh indicates, the formation of Judaic identities in Africa is not a distant historical process but rather an ongoing one. The Kenyan Jews of Kasuku, to cite another example, are said to have left the Church of God in favour of Judaism around 2000, while the members of the Jewish Beth Yeshourun community in Cameroon claim to have 'discovered' Judaism through the internet in the late 1990s, and neither of the groups is messianic.[23] Indeed, social media platforms and the internet are playing an increasingly influential role in this global spiritual landscape, facilitating encounters and interconnections that were previously much more unlikely, slow or expensive. While Rabbinic Judaism is not a proselytising religion, the impact of the internet has been evident in the case of the success of Messianic Jewish doctrines in Africa, whose spread has been encouraged by international groups such as the Messianic Jewish Bible Institute (MJBI) and Jewish Voice Ministries. Such organisations have significant online presence as well as an evident interest in identifying (and evangelising) 'lost' Jewish communities around the world. The leaders of the Nuer Congregation of Yahweh in Ethiopia also claim that before joining the movement they first reached out to its leaders through the internet.

Despite their best efforts and the sympathy of some private Israeli individuals, however, the official Israeli reaction to the religious or ethnic claims of these African communities – and, by implication, their potential claims for Israeli citizenship – has varied between indifference and outright rejection. With the exception of the Beta Israel of Ethiopia, Israel has not formally recognised the Jewish identity of any of these communities, including those that follow Rabbinic Judaism.[24] And though some Africans and Messianic Jews may wish otherwise, it is also not trying to identify and reunite with any Lost Tribes in Africa or elsewhere. As opposed to the Israeli state, some Jewish diaspora groups have shown more interest in both recognising and actively supporting African Jewish communities. The most influential of these has been Kulanu ('all of us') – a US-based organisation that documents, assists and promotes 'isolated, emerging, and returning Jewish communities' across the globe and in several African countries.[25] Through their interactions with such organisations, African Jewish groups were able to achieve the recognition and support of at least some sections of the Jewish world, even though they remain formally excluded from the Jewish state.

The Beta Israel

The Beta Israel – better known previously as the Falasha, and now as Ethiopian Jews – are by far the most famous African Jewish community and the only one to be recognised as such by the Israeli state. Besides the fact that their fate dominated Israel's strategy in the Horn of Africa for many years and continues to influence its relationship with Ethiopia until today, the Beta Israel community is of contemporary relevance and is discussed here for two main reasons. First, because the (unfinished) story of its identification, recognition and immigration to Israel continues to serve today as an inspiration and an important point of reference for African Judaising groups – from the Lemba, through the Igbo, to the Nuer. Second, because as in the case of the Jews of Morocco, there are parallels between the practices used by Israel to bring the Jews of Ethiopia to Israel and the practices used more recently to get Sudanese and Eritreans out of Israel.

Since coming to the world's attention in the 1980s the Beta Israel have been the subject of an extensive body of literature, though scholarly interest in their identity and history dates much further back. Their origins remain controversial, not least because they stood at the heart of the discussions about the validity of their Jewish claims. According to the popular narrative, the Beta Israel are the descendants of migrants from biblical Israel – one of the Lost Tribes of Israel or descendants of ancient Jewish communities that immigrated to Africa via Egypt or the Arabian Peninsula – that settled in northern Ethiopia and maintained their ancient Jewish identity. Their formal recognition as Jews by the Israeli Chief Sephardic Rabbi in 1973 was based on a sixteenth century Jewish ruling according to which the Jews of Ethiopia are descendants of the Lost Tribe of Dan. This is largely the narrative perpetuated today by Israeli state institutions.

The consensus among historians and Ethiopianists, as it emerged in recent decades, maintains that there is no evidence

that the Beta Israel are descendants of an ancient Jewish community. Instead, they are believed to be an autochthonous Ethiopian
group that adopted Judaism sometime between the fourteenth and
sixteenth centuries.[26] From the late nineteenth century, Western
Jews became interested in this 'unknown' African Jewish group and
slowly began to promote its recognition by the Jewish world. The
most famous of these Jewish emissaries has been Jacques Faitlo-
vitch, who devoted his life to promoting the Beta Israel cause and
educating members of the community. A century of interactions
between European and American Jews and the Beta Israel slowly
led to the formation of a new African Jewish identity. 'Through a
process of events', Summerfield argued, 'they were gradually transformed from an existence as Falasha, whose history lay within
Ethiopia, into Ethiopian Jews, whose culture, religion, history and
identity became increasingly connected with that of the Jews in
[the] Diaspora and the State of Israel'.[27]

Throughout the 1960s, the Beta Israel issue hardly had any
impact on Israel's activities in Africa for two reasons. First,
despite the advocacy efforts of some Beta Israel elites and the vocal
American and European Jewish groups that supported them, they
were not formally recognised as Jewish by Israeli authorities and
were not eligible for Israeli citizenship. Even by the early 1970s,
Israeli officials still assumed that the 'Falasha problem' would be
solved through their local assimilation in Ethiopia rather than mass
immigration to Israel.[28] Second, Israel wanted to maintain its good
relationship with Emperor Haile Selassie, who was committed to
the unity and sovereignty of Ethiopia. Advocating for the right of
one ethnic group to leave the country while helping Ethiopia quell
separatist insurgencies in both the northern and the southern
regions of the country would have been untenable. Small numbers
of Ethiopians managed to get to Israel, often independently, but
overall Jewish immigration was discouraged.

By the time Israeli authorities formally recognised the Beta
Israel as Jews, ties with Ethiopia were severed and Haile Selassie

was deposed. After Israel's cooperation with the Derg ceased in 1978 (an episode discussed in Chapter 2), Israeli authorities turned to clandestine arrangements to facilitate the immigration of the Beta Israel. At the time, hundreds of thousands of Ethiopian refugees were seeking shelter in Sudan due to fighting and famine in Ethiopia. With the involvement of – though not always in full coordination with – American Jewish groups, attempts were made in the early 1980s to smuggle Beta Israel via Sudan, Kenya or through the UNHCR's resettlement programmes.[29] One of the Mossad's more audacious initiatives was establishing a beach resort in Sudan, on the coast of the Red Sea, under fake identities. The fully functional resort – 'Arous Village' – secretly doubled as a base for smuggling small groups of Ethiopian Beta Israel refugees out of the country.[30]

Overall these clandestine operations facilitated the movement of relatively small numbers of people, but they created a momentum that drove others to leave Ethiopia and travel to Sudan in the midst of war and famine, hoping to find a way to get to Israel as well. Refugees trekked for weeks, sometimes months, and then had to wait in the camps in Sudan where Ethiopians who worked with Mossad secretly registered them for evacuation. It has been estimated that out of 20,000 Beta Israel who left Ethiopia for Sudan between the late 1970s and 1985, a fifth lost their lives due to hunger, disease and violence. As the numbers of refugees in Sudan grew and the humanitarian situation deteriorated, pressure from American Jewish lobby groups and activists was mounting. With American intervention, and in return for its financial support, Sudanese President Jaafar Nimeiri agreed to a discreet airlift of the Beta Israel.

Between November 1984 and January 1985, a Belgian company was chartered to transfer more than 6,000 people from Khartoum to Tel Aviv via Europe. Operation Moses, as it was named, was halted only after it became public and was formally acknowledged by Israel. This resulted in Sudan being condemned by Arab countries and the Ethiopian government and withdrawing its consent to the operation.[31] Later that year, the clandestine Operation Sheba brought to Israel some of those who remained stuck in Sudan after Operation Moses was halted. Until today, the memories of suffering and determination associated with the treacherous journey from Ethiopia through Sudan remain central to the collective identity of those Ethiopian Jews that came to Israel during the 1980s, and in some respects sets them apart from other Beta Israel who immigrated later, directly from Ethiopia.[32]

In 1989 the Derg renewed ties with Israel and tried to exchange the remaining Beta Israel population in return for military aid or cash. The amounts and types of weapons that were supplied by Israel remain disputed. The US government estimated that Israel provided Mengistu with cluster bombs, possibly via another country.[33] Following debates within the Israeli foreign affairs and security circles and under US pressure, Israel claimed that the transfer of arms ceased during 1990.[34] As the rebel forces were approaching Addis Ababa in early 1991, it became clear that Mengistu's regime and the understandings Israel had with it might not survive much longer. Israel negotiated the mass evacuation of the remaining Beta Israel in return for a payment of $35 million to the Ethiopian government.[35] Between 24 and 25 May, more than 14,000 Beta Israel were airlifted from Addis Ababa as part of Operation Solomon. The operation ended just before the Ethiopian People's Revolutionary Democratic Front (EPRDF) captured the city.

As soon as the operation was completed, however, a new issue emerged. The 'Falash Mura' (or 'Feres Mura') – a group of an unknown size whose members were previously part of the Beta Israel community but converted to Christianity under disputed circumstances and were now interested in coming back into the Jewish fold – were also claiming the right to immigrate to Israel.[36] Some of them already had family members in Israel and sought to reunite with them. As Don Seeman describes in his nuanced ethnography of this group, immediately a new set of questions was raised, not so much with regard to their blood ties to other Jews but with regard to the authenticity of their religious claims: were they forced to convert to Christianity, or did they choose to do so? And why do they aspire to 'return' to Judaism now? Are they *really* driven by a commitment to Judaism, or opportunistically trying to find a way to immigrate to the wealthy Jewish state, where better living standards and opportunities supposedly await? Most Israeli officials subscribed to the latter view and until today view the claims of the 'Falash Mura' with great suspicion.[37]

It is not entirely surprising, therefore, that almost 30 years after it first emerged, the 'Falash Mura' issue is yet to be fully resolved. Thousands were allowed to migrate to Israel under special ad hoc arrangements from the 1990s and were required to convert to Judaism after their resettlement. But more remain in Ethiopia, and their relatives in Israel continue to fight for their right to immigrate as well. Israeli officials on their side have complained that whenever a group of 'Falash Mura' is allowed to immigrate, more show up, claiming Jewish origins and making similar demands for repatriation. While the official Israeli position in recent years has been that resettlement programmes are delayed because of financial constraints, the underlying concern appears to be that Israel has created a 'breach' in its immigration policy that allows Africans who are not 'really' Jewish to immigrate to Israel. Meanwhile, Messianic Jewish missionaries have made considerable efforts to win the hearts of 'Falash Mura' communities in both Israel and Ethiopia, and their achievements have further eroded the already limited patience and trust of Israeli institutions.

But suspicion and ambivalence also characterised Israel's treatment of those Beta Israel who immigrated to Israel earlier. Operations Moses and Solomon were celebrated and mythologised in Israeli popular culture as daring and heroic interventions, and Israel's image as the 'saviour' of a Jewish-African community was viewed by many as the ultimate refutation of the accusation that Zionism is a racist ideology. In Israel, however, Ethiopians were met with discrimination and marginalisation and soon found themselves locked at the bottom of Israel's stratified society – just 'below' the North African and Middle Eastern Jews who had immigrated to Israel a few decades earlier. They were concentrated in poor neighbourhoods that turned into Ethiopian 'enclaves', and maintained cultural, political and social links to the African spaces they had left behind.[38] If in Ethiopia they were differentiated from other communities because of their religious practices,[39] in Israel Ethiopians were primarily distinguished from wider Israeli society by the colour of their skin – a barrier that appeared painfully difficult to break.[40]

Long-simmering grievances exploded on several occasions over the years. In the spring of 2015, a widely circulated video of two policemen beating Demas Fikadey, an Israeli soldier of Ethiopian origin, with no apparent provocation, sparked a wave of protests by Israeli Ethiopians. The event was in fact only the latest in a series of cases of police violence against Israeli Ethiopians, and it triggered a debate about the systemic racism and discrimination against Ethiopians across government institutions and policies. The indifference of the Israeli government and public to the fate of Avera Mengistu, a mentally unstable young Israeli Ethiopian who crossed into Gaza in 2014 and has been held by Hamas since then, was another cause for rage and sentiments of disenfranchisement, and the Black Lives Matter protests in the US provided additional discursive inspiration. Another wave of protests broke out in July 2019, following the killing of a young Israeli Ethiopian by a policeman. Experiences of marginalisation and discrimination remain central in the lives and collective identity of Israel's 140,000 Ethiopian Jews, half of whom were born in Israel.[41]

Uninvited guests

From the 1990s, groups of non-Jewish Africans began to arrive in the Jewish state in significant numbers. In response to the Palestinian uprising that began in 1987, restrictions were placed on the movement of Palestinian workers from the Occupied Territories, creating a need for workers in Israel's agriculture and construction sectors.[42] The government reacted by issuing permits to tens of thousands of migrant workers, mainly from the Philippines, Thailand and Romania. Many others, however, also entered the country independently in search of work, among them a considerable number of West Africans. They usually travelled to Israel as tourists, for pilgrimage, and then stayed in the country with no legal status. By the mid-1990s, it was estimated that some 15,000 African migrants were living in Israel, most of them undocumented and working as cleaners in hotels, private homes and restaurants.[43]

In Hebrew, these Africans (like the Asians and Eastern Europeans who arrived in Israel at the same time) came to be known as 'foreign workers'. Israeli Africanist Galia Sabar has shown how members of this new community formed various social, political and religious networks of support that helped them cope with their precarious status in Israel. They lived, she argues, 'between two plains of existence'. The first was 'the Israeli reality, in which they were strangers in every way, black labourers exposed to exploitation, living in constant fear and lacking rights'. The second was a vibrant network of community organisations – clubs, churches and associations that were 'islands of Africanness' in the middle of the excluding Israeli reality.[44] Notably, there was hardly any overlap between the Jewish-Ethiopian communities of the Beta Israel and the new (non-Jewish) African ones that emerged primarily in southern Tel Aviv.

In the late 1990s, during Netanyahu's first term as prime minister, Israeli authorities began arresting and deporting foreigners who had no legal status. By 2003, the government announced a 'voluntary departure' operation, which encouraged foreigners to leave with the support of the government instead of being deported. Soon not much was left of these African communities. By then, however, a new group of non-Jewish Africans appeared in Israel, as refugees from the Horn of Africa started to cross the border from Egypt into Israel. First, Sudanese from southern Sudan and Darfur, and later also Eritreans. The small numbers of West Africans who had managed to stay in Israel despite the deportation campaigns of the early 2000s were soon overshadowed by a new African population from the other side of the continent, whose presence in Israel had a much greater impact on Israel's bilateral relations with African countries and on its domestic politics.

Most South Sudanese came to Israel after spending years – sometimes even decades – in northern Sudan or Egypt. As civil war raged in southern Sudan throughout the 1980s and 1990s, South Sudanese migrated to all neighbouring countries in East Africa, but also north, to Khartoum and Cairo. Many of those who ultimately arrived in Israel already knew each other from these two cities, and like the South Sudanese communities in Khartoum and Cairo, the community in Israel was a diverse one. It included considerable Dinka and Nuer populations from different parts of southern Sudan, as well as individuals and families from various other southern groups. Refugees from Darfur, as opposed to South Sudanese, were usually more recently displaced. The majority of them were Fur, Masalit and Zaghawa – Darfur's 'African' groups – who fled the fighting that broke out in 2003.

In the collective memory of the Sudanese community in Israel, it was the events of 'Mustapha Mahmoud' that triggered their decision to leave Egypt. In late September 2005, a small group of Sudanese in Cairo started a sit-in at the Mustapha Mahmoud Square, not far from UNHCR's offices. They gathered in protest at UNHCR's decision to stop processing asylum claims of Sudanese nationals and more broadly against their precarious status and harsh living conditions in Egypt. Within a month, some 2,000 people were camping in the square, including whole families with young children. Negotiations between the protestors, UNHCR and the Egyptian authorities led nowhere, and in the early hours of 30 December, 4,000 riot police raided the camp, beating the protestors and forcing them onto buses. Dozens were killed, including many women and children.[45]

While a small number of Sudanese had already entered Israel before the violent events in Cairo, the raid enhanced the sense of insecurity Sudanese felt in Egypt and their lack of trust in local UNHCR representatives. In the following years, the numbers of Sudanese entering Israel steadily increased: 271 crossed in 2006, and 1,688 in 2007.[46] At the time, the Israeli–Egyptian border was not entirely fenced. Smugglers dropped their clients near it, and they were able to cross by foot. First to receive them on the other side were Israeli soldiers. By 2008, the number of Eritreans crossing the border daily surpassed that of Sudanese. Migration out of Eritrea into Sudan and Ethiopia slowly increased after the end of the border war with Ethiopia (1998–2000) due to the expansion of compulsory national service in the country,[47] and for a short period in the late 2000s Israel was one of the main destinations for Eritreans leaving the Horn of Africa.

Just when travelling via the Sinai Peninsula into Israel became common, however, it also became deadly. While some Sudanese who crossed Sinai into Israel in the mid-2000s paid their smugglers as little as a few hundred US dollars for their services, around 2010, NGOs began to receive reports of smugglers who turned against their clients, kidnapping and torturing them in Sinai and demanding tens of thousands of US dollars from their relatives for their release. Some were held captive for months – beaten, raped, starved, burned, electrocuted, chained and enslaved. One study estimated that up to 10,000 people lost their lives between 2009 and 2013 as a result of these atrocities, out of a total of 25,000–30,000 trafficked through Sinai.[48] The precise number of victims will remain unknown. In some cases, Eritreans did not even attempt to travel to Israel but were kidnapped in eastern Sudan and taken by force to Sinai. This brutal but lucrative industry was largely operated by Rashaida nomads from Eritrea, Sudan and Egypt, with the authorities in these countries often actively participating and benefiting from it.[49]

By the end of 2012, more than 64,000 'infiltrators' had entered Israel, primarily Eritreans (36,101) and Sudanese (14,512).[50] While small communities of refugees settled in cities across Israel, it was Tel Aviv's southern neighbourhoods that became a cosmopolitan

hub, 'connected yet disconnected' from the wider city and maintaining cultural, political and economic links to other cities and
refugee camps across East Africa and the Horn.[51] Sudanese and
Eritrean restaurants, barbershops, photo studios and internet cafes
quickly emerged in between the older Romanian and Filipino bars
and grocery stores on Neve Sha'anan Street – the cramped and
neglected promenade leading towards Tel Aviv's massive central bus
station. Eritrean and Sudanese community organisations, political
associations and churches were also established, with some of the
southern Sudanese churches building on the remnants of the West
African religious institutions that had flourished in Tel Aviv in the
late 1990s. These became important social arenas for the emerging
African communities.[52]

The arrival of refugees also led to the emergence of a small
but tight cluster of Israeli NGOs, mostly based in southern Tel
Aviv and the surrounding neighbourhoods, that came to serve as
intermediaries between African refugees and Israeli policymakers,
journalists and the UN. Some of these organisations were previously concerned with the rights of migrant workers or Palestinians
but slowly shifted their focus as the number of refugees grew (the
Hotline for Migrant Workers, for instance, eventually changed its
name to Hotline for Refugees and Migrants). Others were new initiatives that emerged as a direct response to the challenges faced by
African refugees in Israel. 'The organisations' – as they came to be
known collectively in Israeli popular discourse – were soon seen as
the main actors obstructing the government's plans to 'solve' the
'infiltrators problem', not least because they repeatedly launched
legal battles challenging government measures.

'A cancer in our body'

Refugees who are neither Jewish nor Palestinian were largely a new
phenomenon for Israeli bureaucracy. Israel had an asylum system,
but it was previously in the hands of UNHCR and dealt with a tiny

number of cases.[53] In practice, if protection was granted it was usually through ad hoc decisions and based on government discretion rather than on a formal policy.[54] In this manner, in the 1970s, a small group of Vietnamese refugees were granted asylum in Israel, and small numbers of Bosnians and Albanians were granted asylum in the 1990s. Refugees from Sierra Leone, Liberia, Côte d'Ivoire and the DRC who came to Israel from the 1990s were granted legal status under a regime of collective temporary protection – a vaguely defined policy that accords refugees few rights and grants the state the power to terminate it at any time. Indeed, by 2007 protection was already withdrawn from citizens of Sierra Leone and Liberia, and they were required to leave or were deported, as were Ivorian nationals by 2011.[55]

If state institutions were unprepared to deal with large numbers of uninvited non-Jewish African refugees, it was also because at the very early stages of this phenomenon there seemed to be no national consensus about how such individuals should be treated and to what extent Israeli or Jewish solidarity should be extended to them. The realities Sudanese and Eritreans came from – Cairo, Khartoum, Asmara, the refugee camps of eastern Sudan, villages in Darfur and southern Sudan – were entirely unknown to the Israeli public, and the narratives that soon began to emerge about the causes for their plight and the possible implications of their presence in the country had less to do with the refugees themselves or their circumstances and more to do with Israeli demographic anxieties, national identity, historical memory and sense of security.

In public discourse, many of those advocating for the rights of refugees invoked Israel's Jewish character to argue that it has a special obligation to support those fleeing violence and abuse. Most commonly, this was justified by the Jewish history of persecution and genocide and the fact that Israel was established as a shelter for refugees. As former refugees, some Israelis have argued, the Jews had an obligation to assist today's refugees. In this context, refugees from southern Sudan and even more so from Darfur often benefited from more sympathy, as they fled an ethnic conflict that has already attracted great interest in the West and was labelled by many as a genocide.[56] In contrast, that refugees from Eritrea usually fled coercive military service worked against them, as military service is also compulsory in Israel. Therefore, and despite the obvious differences between forced and indefinite conscription in Eritrea and two to three years of service in Israel, it seemed that it was much more difficult for Eritreans to justify their need for asylum in Israeli eyes.

But solidarity, of any kind, was not the position taken by the Israeli government or the majority of the public. While government officials often stated that they agreed that Israel has to respect the rights of refugees, they argued that those people arriving in Israel were not refugees at all but opportunistic migrants looking for wealth and work, representing a great danger to the Israeli state. Since many of them came from a hostile state (Sudan), and through a porous border where trafficking in arms and drugs was not uncommon, their seemingly free movement into Israel was immediately associated with the threat of violence, terror and destabilisation. Some politicians warned that Africans would bring diseases and crime, and as their numbers grew, they were framed as a security concern for another reason: they were not Jewish. Opportunistic scaremongering about 'the infiltrators' soon became a common activity of Israeli politicians.

The Israeli media and right-wing anti-refugee activists began to speak of southern Tel Aviv as an 'African colony' that was threatening to draw the entire continent into Israel and swallow the Jewish state. While many local residents got along with their new African neighbours just fine, some began to complain of the worsening conditions in their overcrowded neighbourhoods and of southern Tel Aviv's cultural transformation due to the influx of refugees. Politicians capitalised on these resentments and encouraged a violent anti-refugee rhetoric that soon dominated the national discourse on the issue. The sense of pollution and threat associated with the presence of non-Jewish Africans in Israel was chillingly expressed by Miri Regev – a Knesset member from Netanyahu's Likud party – when she stated during a rally in southern Tel Aviv in 2012 that 'the Sudanese are a cancer in our body'. A consequent poll suggested that 52% of Jewish Israelis agreed.[57]

But Regev was far from the only Israeli policymaker or public figure to refer to Africans in such terms. 'In ten years, an official commission of inquiry will have to investigate how we lost the Jewish majority in Israel', Minister of Interior Eli Yishai predicted in 2010. 'Today it is tens of thousands, in growing numbers, that will reach a million. They will change the face of the state as a Jewish state. These are not refugees.'[58] By then, the main objectives of Israel's policy were already clear: prevent other Africans from entering the country and remove those in it. Earlier that year Israel had already started constructing a fence along its border with Egypt. While the fence was also meant to stop arms and drug trafficking, it was the 'infiltrators' that were the main impetus for its urgent construction. Its objective, Netanyahu stated, was to 'guarantee the Jewish and democratic character of the State of Israel'.[59]

The making of a predatory non-policy

Already before the fence, one of the first steps taken by the Israeli government as a response to the arrival of Africans at its southern border was to develop a procedure, known as 'Hot Return', that allowed soldiers to send refugees back to Egypt as soon as they arrived at the border, in violation of international law and despite evidence that Egyptian troops in Sinai were abusing refugees if not executing them.[60] From the beginning, there was great ambiguity with regard to the precise nature of the procedure and its implementation. In 2007, Israeli Prime Minister Ehud Olmert stated that 'understandings' were reached with Egyptian President Hosni Mubarak on the matter, but this was publicly denied by Egypt.[61] The Israeli army nonetheless sent hundreds of refugees back to Egypt in the following years.[62] When a legal petition that challenged this opaque procedure was filed by human rights organisations, Israeli officials claimed that Israel had stopped carrying out returns in 2011. In practice, occasional returns quietly continued, but the matter became less urgent when the border fence was completed and the numbers of refugees arriving at the border dropped.[63]

While the border was virtually sealed by the fence (Figure 5.1), something still had to be done with those refugees who had managed to enter Israel earlier. In 2009, the responsibility for assessing asylum claims was transferred from UNHCR to the Israeli government, ostensibly as part of Israel's commitment to implement a rights-based asylum policy in line with its international obligations. From the beginning, however, all Sudanese and Eritreans were barred from applying for asylum and were instead protected from deportation under a 'group protection' policy that was never fully articulated in any formal way and whose precise scope and rationale remained vague. In essence, it protected them from being deported but accorded them few other rights in Israel. Acknowledging that they would need to work in order to survive without humanitarian assistance, Israel did not enforce the *de jure* prohibition on the employment of Eritreans and Sudanese, and many of them found work at minimum wage jobs, usually as cleaners in restaurants and hotels.

Figure 5.1 Entry of 'infiltrators' to Israel, 2007–18[64]

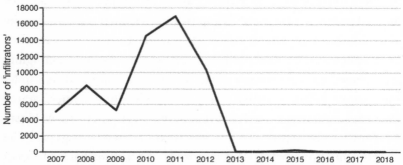

Meanwhile, the Refugee Status Determination (RSD) mechanism the Ministry of Interior established was as partisan as it was
dysfunctional – two characteristics that complemented each other.
Rather than fairly assessing refugee claims and granting protection
based on clear legal principles, its main objective appeared to be to
reject as many applications as possible. Even after Sudanese and
Eritreans were finally allowed to apply for asylum (from 2013), their
applications were either rejected or simply remained pending for
years. The overall recognition rate for Eritreans and Sudanese was
less than 1% – far below the global average for these groups. Israel's
asylum system, in other words, has not regulated refugees' access
to protection but blocked them from it, thereby also allowing the
government to perpetuate the claim that they are not refugees at all.

With Sudanese and Eritreans unable to access permanent
refugee status but also not deportable, Israeli governments repeatedly sought to use the threat of indefinite or prolonged detention
to persuade them to leave the country voluntarily. The weapon of
choice, somewhat symbolically, was the Prevention of Infiltration
Law, which was originally enacted to stop Palestinian refugees from
crossing back into Israel in the 1950s. At the time, some Palestinians
crossed the new border to carry out attacks against Jewish settlers,
while many others were trying to access their properties, cultivate
their lands, visit or unite with relatives, or smuggle goods.[65] The
law enabled their prosecution, imprisonment and deportation. In
2012, after years of discussions, the old legislation was resurrected:
the Knesset amended it to allow the authorities to hold Sudanese
and Eritreans in administrative detention for three years upon their
'illegal' entry to Israel. A controversial complementary regulation
also allowed for administrative detention – without indictment or a
trial – of any 'infiltrator' already in the country who was suspected
of involvement in criminal activity. This led to a wave of arbitrary
arrests, often based on groundless accusations.[66]

The Prevention of Infiltration Law became the main front in the
war between 'the organisations' and the state over the treatment of

refugees. A petition was filed by human rights organisations against the legislation, and in September 2013 the Supreme Court declared it void, as it violated the right to liberty enshrined in Israel's Basic Law: Human Dignity and Liberty. The legal victory turned out to be a mixed blessing, however, as the government's response was to enact a new amendment to the law, this time allowing for the detention of new arrivals for a period of one year (instead of three), and for the establishment of a new 'open facility', operated by the Israeli Prison Services, where 'infiltrators' were to be held for an indefinite period of time or until they agreed to leave the country. The facility, named 'Holot' (dunes), was built in the middle of the desert and right next to the prison that was already used to detain refugees. Refugees were allowed to leave it during the day, as long as they did not work and reported back at designated times.

From the perspective of most refugees, Holot's establishment only made things much worse than they previously were. Even though the facility itself was not big enough to host the entire refugee population, the summoning of thousands for detention spread confusion and fear. With no access to refugee status, changing detention policies, ambiguous labour rights and constant anti-refugee rhetoric, state power appeared arbitrary, violent and unpredictable. For some, this was an incentive to leave Israel. Others decided to protest. Days after Holot was opened in December 2013, dozens of its Eritrean and Sudanese 'residents' deserted it and embarked on a spontaneous march to Jerusalem. After reaching the capital and protesting in front of the Israeli Knesset, they were violently loaded onto buses and taken to prison. These events ignited a wave of demonstrations, strikes and sit-ins against the government's detention policies, in which tens of thousands of refugees participated.

The government easily ignored the demands of the protesting refugees, but the Supreme Court continued to be a thorn in its side. In September 2014, it declared the 2013 amendment of the Prevention of Infiltration Law void as well. Again, the government responded by passing another amendment, which limited the time 'infiltrators' are held in the 'open facility' to 20 months. This time the Supreme Court did not declare the law void but instructed the state to reduce the period of detention in Holot to one year. With this decision, the Prevention of Infiltration Law lost much of its effectiveness as a tool for pressuring refugees to leave: after spending a year in the desert, they had to be released. By then, however, thousands of refugees had already decided to leave Israel, and the government was planning to use the clandestine agreements it reached with African states in order to promote the forced removal of many more.

Deportations and informal transfer schemes

Following South Sudan's independence in July 2011, Israeli politicians started calling for the deportation of Sudanese of southern origin to the new state. It did not take long for these calls to translate into actions. In January 2012, the Ministry of Interior issued a 'Call for the People of South Sudan', announcing that 'it is time for you to return to your homeland'.[67] Those who agreed to leave were promised a grant of a €1,000. Those who did not agree could be arrested and deported without receiving the grant. Estimations of the size of the South Sudanese community in Israel at the time varied from 700 to more than 2,000 people, many of whom were young children who had never been to South Sudan. This was a fraction of the entire refugee population in Israel but nonetheless an easy target for a government keen to show the public that the 'infiltration problem' was being addressed.

Israeli authorities were in fact already working, from 2009, with two pro-Israel Christian NGOs – the evangelical ICEJ (see Chapter 4) and Operation Blessing International – to promote the voluntary repatriation of South Sudanese to the then semi-autonomous region of southern Sudan.[68] Hundreds agreed to leave before 2012; many of them were misinformed about the conditions in South Sudan due to the negligence and ignorance of the organisations involved.[69] Most South Sudanese, however, were reluctant to go back before the threats of imprisonment and deportation were invoked in 2012, and even then, many tried to reach out to the Israeli authorities and UNHCR and ask them to reverse their decision. Israeli human rights organisations also filed a petition against the scheme and tried to convince the government to postpone it. Their efforts were not successful, but the legal proceedings did delay the deportation for a few months.

Some tensions also emerged between Israeli government institutions over the scheme's implementation. While they did not object to the overall aim of returning South Sudanese to their new country, actors in the Israeli Ministry of Foreign Affairs were concerned about the Ministry of Interior's evident urge to carry out an aggressive and highly publicised operation that, they believed, could damage Israel's international image and relations with Juba and sour its highly positive reputation among ordinary South Sudanese citizens and elites. Israeli immigration officials and Minister of Interior Eli Yishai, primarily interested in removing as many 'infiltrators' from Israel as possible, were largely ignorant of the fact that many South Sudanese viewed Israel with great admiration and celebrated it as a close ally. Even if they did know this, they simply did not care.

The Ministry of Foreign Affairs therefore sought to convince other Israeli government agencies 'that it is not only the issue of returning people [to South Sudan] that is at stake but rather the entirety of building positive bilateral relations with a country that was only recently born', Haim Koren, Israel's ambassador to South Sudan at the time, explained. 'My priorities as an ambassador ... collided more than once with [the priorities of] those who believed that first of all, all South Sudanese must be returned to their country.'[70] Such concerns, however, may have overestimated the extent to which the government in Juba was actually concerned with how its citizens are treated. Keen to maintain good relations with Jerusalem, it did not object to the Israeli plan. The operation was publicly narrated as a peaceful repatriation scheme that would bring South Sudanese back to their homeland to help build it. Several delegations of officials from Juba travelled to Israel to coordinate the implementation.

Meanwhile, South Sudanese in Israel found themselves in an awkward position, as their attempts to delay their own return to the newly independent country, internationally celebrated at the time as a beacon of hope, were portrayed as not only unwarranted but also unpatriotic. Given the lack of support they received from both UNHCR and Juba, their efforts also seemed increasingly futile. Israeli immigration officials convinced several refugees to help them gather the names and addresses of the South Sudanese in Israel, so these could be easily identified and urged to sign up for 'voluntary' repatriation and as arrests began and the threat of imprisonment materialised, almost the entire community decided to accept the government's offer and leave. Between June and August 2012, seven flights transferred more than 1,000 South Sudanese from Tel Aviv to Juba. The Ministry of Interior titled the project 'Operation Returning Home'.

As South Sudanese were leaving the country, the Israeli government was already working on more ambitious transfer schemes. Hagai Hadas, an ex-Mossad official, was tasked by Netanyahu to negotiate the repatriation of Sudanese and Eritreans to either their home countries or any other country willing to accept them.[71] The Ministry of Foreign Affairs was deliberately less involved, and negotiations with African governments on this matter were reportedly led by the prime minister's special envoy. Later that year, Israel began sending Sudanese and Eritreans back to their countries under a clandestine arrangement and through a third country.[72] Very little formal information was ever revealed about this scheme, which was pursued without the knowledge of UNHCR even after its existence was exposed. In theory, unlike the South Sudanese, Sudanese and Eritreans were still protected from forced deportation under Israel's 'group protection' policy. In practice, they faced a similar choice: stay in detention or leave Israel. They also received a departure grant, but a higher one: $3,500.

The clandestine nature of the scheme created room for corruption and for a great degree of informality. Some Sudanese reported that Israeli immigration officials offered them what appeared to be forged Sudanese passports, which they could use to return to Khartoum.[73] In several cases Sudanese and Eritreans who agreed to be transferred to Uganda were sent instead to Sudan or Eritrea. One Sudanese man from Darfur who claimed to have understood that he was being sent to a 'third country' but later discovered that Israel had arranged him a flight back to Sudan, ended up spending nine days stranded at the airport in Addis Ababa because he refused to board his connection flight to Khartoum. The incident only exploded after an Israeli woman he knew met him by coincidence at the terminal and shared his story and image on social media. He was sent back to Israel, where he was subsequently detained.[74]

The vast majority of those returning to their home countries in 2013–14 were Sudanese. This was alarming not only because their decision to leave Israel was taken under the threat of detention – either in prison or in Holot facility – but because Sudan formally considers Israel an enemy state and Sudanese law criminalises visits to Israel. This means that any Sudanese who sought asylum in Israel was at risk of persecution upon returning to Sudan. With Israel being accused of bombing military facilities and arms smugglers inside Sudan, Sudanese authorities also suspected that refugees returning from Israel were serving as spies. In 2014 a Sudanese pro-government newspaper reported that the authorities 'carefully monitor Israel's espionage activities for a long time, particularly among Sudanese citizens who fled to Israel'.[75] International and Israeli human rights organisations documented cases of interrogation and torture of Sudanese who returned from Israel.[76]

By April 2014, the number of 'voluntary departures' back to Sudan dropped, possibly as a result of the exposure of the scheme and the reports of persecution and torture of returnees that began to circulate, but also because the initial panic that the opening of Holot facility caused had calmed down. By then, however, another scheme was in operation: transfers to Rwanda and Uganda. According to Israeli officials, in late 2013 and early 2014 two confidential transfer agreements (occasionally referred to as mere 'understandings') were concluded with the two African countries. The Israeli government explained that neither the names of these countries nor the agreements themselves could be made public because the two 'third countries' requested that their identities remain unknown to the public.[77] 'Neither Museveni nor Kagame wanted to come out of the closet', a former Israeli official said later.[78]

Some clues about these deals were exposed – perhaps accidentally – before the agreements were finalised. In July 2013, for instance, an Israeli official told the press that the country was in the final stages of negotiating a deal to send African refugees to 'third countries' in Africa in return for funds and assistance in the fields of defence and agriculture. 'Arms for Infiltrators', the Israeli daily *Yedioth Ahronoth* announced.[79] In August 2013, Israeli officials claimed that one of these countries was indeed Uganda, but the Ugandan government denied it.[80] In fact, the idea of paying African governments to take African refugees from Israel had been floating around since the late 2000s,[81] and multiple countries were approached by Israeli officials over the years on this issue. Whether or not Rwanda and Uganda received any direct payment for taking Sudanese and Eritreans from Israel is not known with certainty at this point, but both, as previous chapters suggested, have a close relationship with Israel.

Again, the confidentiality of the arrangements allowed them to operate outside the realms of the law and primarily by relying on a range of informal practices. Sudanese and Eritreans left Israel in small groups on regular commercial flights. Israeli officials provided them with letters that promised that they would receive a visa once they arrive in Kigali or Entebbe. Upon arrival, a Ugandan or Rwandan individual waited for them and allowed them out of the airport but did not grant them any legal status. 'It seemed like something [was] not entirely right. As if they are doing some kind of a shady business', one Sudanese man interviewed in Kampala in 2015 commented.[82] As part of the arrangement, Israel provided those transferred with accommodation for their first three nights at their destination. Once in the hotel, some were offered or even pressured to leave Uganda and Rwanda. The level of pressure changed between cases and seemed to decrease with time as criticisms of the scheme began to emerge.

Most of the refugees who travelled to Rwanda seem to have left the country almost immediately for Uganda by paying local smugglers, either because they had no intention of staying in Kigali in the first place, or because once there, they understood that staying was not really an option. Many of those leaving for Uganda were also persuaded to leave for other countries in the region or Europe – the prime destination for many Eritreans. Dozens of Eritreans who left Israel later re-emerged in France, Switzerland, Germany or the UK. Sudanese who were sent to Uganda, particularly in the earlier period of the scheme's operation, were often encouraged by various informal intermediaries who waited for them in Kampala to return home, to Sudan, via South Sudan. Entering Sudan through its porous and partly rebel-held southern border was considered safer than travelling by air to Khartoum, where security was tighter. In short, once in East Africa, Sudanese and Eritreans often used the departure grants of $3,500 to pay all sorts of smugglers and informal brokers.[83]

Uganda and Rwanda did not formally admit that they had signed an agreement with Israel, though Paul Kagame did indicate several times that negotiations between the countries were taking place.[84] When asked about the matter, Ugandan officials repeatedly claimed that they knew nothing about it, a stance that became pathetically unconvincing as the years passed and transfers continued. A senior immigration official in Entebbe airport once argued that the document Israel gave Sudanese and Eritreans – which promised that they would be legally admitted in Uganda – was 'completely fake'.[85] But in practice, thousands of individuals are known to have entered the country with it. These official denials inevitably left those trans-ferred in an ambiguous position vis-á-vis the local authorities, and they usually decided to conceal the fact that they came from Israel. In most cases those who did not leave Uganda tried to apply for asylum and lied, stating that they arrived in the country directly from Eritrea or Sudan.

In March 2015, after the Israeli Supreme Court reduced the period of detention in Holot to one year, the Israeli government responded by announcing a new plan to imprison indefinitely any 'infiltrator' whose asylum application was rejected or who did not apply for asylum and refused to leave Israel. Again, a petition was filed by several NGOs against this policy. But turning to the Israeli judiciary to challenge a transfer scheme whose details were confidential and only known to the state seemed to be an exercise in futility. To begin with, discussion before the court took place without acknowledging the identities of the countries involved. The court referred to Uganda and Rwanda as 'U' and 'R'. More problem-atically, no matter what data NGOs brought before the court that showed that refugees were not receiving legal status in Uganda and Rwanda and that Israel was not monitoring their situation following their transfer, the government presented behind closed doors its own confidential information that supposedly proved otherwise.

The limits of clandestine operations

In August 2017, the Supreme Court in Jerusalem accepted the state's position and approved the transfer schemes. It also ruled, however, that for Israel to be able to indefinitely detain individuals who refuse to leave, the 'third countries' involved first have to agree to receive people who are deported by force (and not only those whose departure is nominally voluntary). Israel quickly announced that at least one African country had agreed to this condition. Months later Netanyahu revealed that this country was Rwanda, though it remains unclear to what extent the Rwandan officials had been consulted on the matter. Some Israeli officials told the media that the government intended to pay Rwanda $5,000 for every 'infiltrator' it accepted.[86] In January 2018 a new plan was therefore announced: Holot facility would be closed and the government would embark on a mass deportation operation. Anyone refusing to leave Israel would be sent to jail.

One thing that undermines informal and clandestine arrangements is public attention, and the new deportation plan drew a great deal of it. The Israeli government is used to being condemned by the UN, the international media and human rights organisations, but this time Netanyahu's announcement of imminent deportation was also met with unprecedented levels of opposition from wide sections of the Israeli public and the Jewish diaspora, including from ardent supporters of Israel in the US who argued that it is at odds with their Jewish values and were concerned about its damaging reputational fallout for Israel. In Israel, a demonstration against the deportation drew more than 20,000 people, and petitions were brought before the Supreme Court challenging the plan. International attention also turned to Rwanda and Uganda: demonstrations were held in front of their embassies in Israel and across the world, and the topic repeatedly made headlines internationally and in Africa.

Within weeks, a campaign that was supposed to boost Netanyahu's popularity inside Israel was turning into a diplomatic and legal headache. Jewish diaspora groups were publicly criticising Netanyahu, but his supporters in Israel were insisting that the deportation must go ahead at all costs. Israeli diplomats were warning that the whole affair was damaging Israel's international image, while Rwanda and Uganda, eager to dispel reports and rumours that they were being paid for taking Israel's unwanted Africans, continued to publicly deny being party to any transfer agreements. In response to protests and media inquiries, Rwanda announced that its policy was to accept anyone arriving at its borders 'voluntarily and without any constraint', but this was still at odds with Israel's stated aim to expel all refugees by force.[87]

Seeking a way out of the muddled mess, in early April Netanyahu announced that instead of the initial deportation plan, Israel had reached an agreement with UNHCR according to which 16,000 Sudanese and Eritreans would be resettled from Israel to Western countries and the rest would remain in Israel and be granted protection.[88] The deal was proudly presented as the best possible option given the circumstances, but it did not go down well among Netanyahu's supporters and other right-wing politicians who immediately criticised him for surrendering to the demands of 'the organisations' and the Supreme Court and for cooperating with the UN. Hours after making the announcement, Netanyahu cancelled the agreement. In a Facebook post, he outed Rwanda, claimed that it had previously agreed to accept 'infiltrators' deported from Israel, and blamed it for withdrawing from the agreement due to 'great pressure' from Israeli NGOs and the European Union.[89] Israel sent an envoy to Uganda to try to renegotiate a deal, but eventually had to admit that its deportation plan had fallen apart and there was no agreement with either country that allowed for forced deportations.

Ultimately it was narrow electoral interests that dictated Netanyahu's decisions – interests that trumped not only the basic rights of the refugees but also Israel's bilateral relations and standing in Africa. To the relief of both the refugees and Netanyahu himself, soon after the deportation plan collapsed public attention shifted back to Iran and Gaza. By 2019, there were fewer than 34,000 'infiltrators' in Israel.[90] A growing number of them were already independently seeking avenues to migrate to Western countries under different family unification and sponsorship programmes, and meanwhile developed their own strategies to cope with the uncertainty of Israel's migration regime. Israeli officials promised that they would continue to pursue transfer agreements with other African countries, but the small Sudanese and Eritrean 'enclaves' in southern Tel Aviv – though becoming less and less dominant – are not likely to disappear from the city's landscape any time soon.

Managing the frontier

Mossad veteran Gad Shimron, who took part in the operations that brought the Beta Israel to Israel, recounts that members of the agency take pride in being 'the most professional smugglers in the world'.[91] Indeed, one important consequence of the securitisation of immigration to and from Israel has been an ongoing Israeli reliance on security agencies, special operations,[92] informal and clandestine arrangements and transactional elite bargains (populations in exchange for money or other support) rather than consistent and rule-bound policies as a means for managing migration. While in the cases of the Jews of Morocco and Ethiopia, special operations were used to evacuate populations from foreign lands, in the cases of Sudanese and Eritrean refugees they were deployed to remove them from Israel. As such, Israel's immigration practices were often at odds with civilian values of transparency and the rule of law or with basic norms of international human rights or refugee law, but they were consistent with its broader foreign and defence strategy in Africa, which has long been characterised by secrecy and informality.

Israel's latest clandestine cooperation with African governments on the transfer of refugees, however, should also be understood as part of a wider trend of externalisation and monetisation of Western migration management regimes, in which wealthy countries pay poorer governments to implement certain policies or measures with the ultimate aim of reducing the number of people migrating into their territories. Some have argued that from a legal perspective, the extent to which Israel's confidential transfer agreements with Uganda and Rwanda violated the rights of refugees was unprecedented, partly because under these agreements, refugees were sent to countries they did not previously travel through.[93] It is also clear that compared to Israel, European countries have engaged African governments and multilateral organisations in a more institutionalised manner, with more generous funds, and at least some rhetorical commitment to human rights and the rule of law.[94] Their underlying rationales and ultimate goals, however, were very similar.

But as much as Israel has sought to manage and reinforce its African border, the movement of people and ideas across it has created personal and cultural links that are slowly reshaping Israel's relationship with Africa from below – far away from high-level politics of arms deals, security cooperation or UN votes. In recent years, for example, growing numbers of Israelis of Ethiopian origin have been returning to Ethiopia for family visits, business and travel, proudly reasserting their *Avesha* (the Hebrewised version of Habesha) identity, not instead of their Israeli one but in addition to it – devising new ways of being Israelis of Ethiopian origin in opposition to the mainstream discourse that pressures them to 'assimilate' in Israel.[95] Underrepresented in mainstream Israeli popular culture, young Israeli Ethiopians also developed their own musical interests and trends, fusing Ethiopian and Middle Eastern influences with hip-hop and Jamaican reggae and dancehall, thereby linking themselves not only with Ethiopian narratives and discourses but with the wider African diaspora.[96]

Meanwhile, in capitals across East Africa, it is not uncommon today to run into Africans who previously spent time in Israel – people like Yohanes and his friends, the young Eritreans mentioned in the introduction of this book. Most South Sudanese who were deported to Juba in 2012 fled to Uganda, Kenya and Ethiopia after civil war broke out in December 2013. Some have returned to Sudan and Egypt – back to where they sought asylum before migrating to Israel more than a decade ago.[97] In the daily lives of many of these individuals, Hebrew words and slang now blend with Arabic or Tigre.[98] In their life histories, photo albums and social media profiles, cities like Tel Aviv, Haifa or Eilat often feature next to Cairo, Addis Ababa or Kampala – part of the landscape of the wider region, representing small episodes in much longer journeys shaped by many unexpected hurdles, attractive opportunities and consequential decisions.

CONCLUSION

This book has sought to explain Israel's renewed interest in the African continent and situate it in historical perspective. From the formal Israeli institutions that deal with African states, leaders and peoples to the networks of business and political entrepreneurs, diaspora groups, refugees and religious figures that shape Israel's presence and standing in the continent. From the memories that are proudly invoked by Israeli actors with a hint of nostalgia, to the skeletons in Israel's African closets that official rhetoric prefers to skip over. The aim was to pick out strands from the past and to weave them together with the multiple interests and actors that make up Israel in Africa today. The knit that emerged is wide-ranging, uneven and diverse. But when critically observed as a whole, several overarching arguments stand out.

The first is that Israel's interest in Africa was consistently driven by its local security concerns and was part of its effort to undermine and overpower its adversaries, militarily and diplomatically, in order to promote its objectives and guarantee its survival as a Jewish (and, since 1967, an 'expanded' or an occupying) state in the Middle East. The precise nature of these objectives and the ways in which they were pursued transformed throughout the decades – from countering Arab military and ideological influence, through feeding Israel's exports-dependent arms industry, to curbing Iranian influence and circumventing Palestinian legal and diplomatic efforts. Today the Palestinians do not represent a military threat to Israel, but their struggle for self-determination and an independent state does challenge Israel's ongoing control over the entire territory of

Israel/Palestine (without which, Israelis claim, their security will be compromised). And support from the global South and the Arab world allows them to continue to make their claims present in the international sphere, albeit with limited implications on the ground. At this level, the Israeli–Palestinian conflict is a diplomatic war of attrition, and Israel wants Africa on its side in this war.

The second argument, directly linked to the first, is that Israel's involvement in Africa, particularly since the late 1960s, was securitised. 'Securitisation' in this context is comprised of three processes. First, Israel's objectives in Africa were framed as directly linked to its stability and often its very survival. Second, the most dominant Israeli actors in Africa were consistently members of what Sheffer and Barak described as Israel's 'security network', namely, serving or former security officials, arms merchants or civilian actors with close ties with the latter two groups.[1] Third, the workings of Israeli state institutions in Africa were very often characterised by a great degree of informality, opacity and extra-legality – all values that characterise the 'national security' sector rather than civilian institutions. In recent years, securitisation in this sense has arguably reached its most striking level with Israel's treatment of refugees from the Horn of Africa: their presence in Israel was framed as an existential threat, their repatriation or transfer to other African countries was shrouded in secrecy and managed through special 'operations' or informal practices akin to smuggling, and civilian institutions that were supposed to protect them (the RSD bureaucracy, the judiciary, civil society organisations) were deliberately undermined.

Thirdly, I have tried to show how African leaders on their side were able to utilise Israel's geostrategic needs for their own ends. Their engagement with Israel therefore had less to do with their concern with Israel/Palestine than with their local political objectives. This argument may sound mundane or obvious, but it helps us think critically about Israel's accomplishments and challenges in Africa and analyse African responses to Israel's appeals beyond the narrow prism of solidarity with Zionism or the Palestinian cause. First, it highlights how Israel, despite its small size, limited resources and many opponents, was able to exploit a combination of factors – its sophisticated arms industry, its religious importance for evangelical groups, its influence in Washington and its techno-logical or development achievements – to try to advance its interests in Africa. Second, it explains why Israel always found it challenging to translate the positive bilateral relations it was able to develop with a considerable number of African states into African support in multilateral forums: for most leaders, forging relations with Israel but balancing them with support of its adversaries usually allowed for the optimal utilisation of international alliances.

Israelis often highlight the extent to which Israel's standing in Africa has been characterised by many twists, turns, breaks and 'radical changes',[2] most commonly represented by the formal diplomatic rupture of 1973. The analysis offered here, however, also identified significant continuities in the objectives Israel pursued in Africa, the ways in which it sought to achieve them, the rhetoric it deployed, and the ways in which African leaders responded to its forays. Binyamin Netanyahu and Golda Meir may represent very different political traditions in Zionist history, but they went to Africa for similar reasons and faced similar challenges in achieving their goals. More broadly, what these continuities also highlight is the longstanding links and interdependency between Israel/Pales-tine, the wider Middle East and Africa. They demonstrate how political and military rivalries and experiences of state forma-tion, violence, insecurity and displacement in these regions have constantly interacted with one another, and how leaders in both regions repeatedly sought each other's help in managing their own position within the international system.

Within this history of long-standing cross-regional inter-connectedness, it is not African views of Israel or Israeli views of Africa that have changed radically over the years so much as the actors and institutions that make up Israel in Africa and how they relate to each other – the ways in which different networks of power operate, interact and shape Israel's relationships with African countries and peoples. To study Israeli–African engagements during the 1960s, one can comfortably focus on the elites: diplomats, politicians and military leaders. But who shapes inter-state politics in an era of borderless and deregulated markets, enhanced international migration, mass religious movements, telecommunication and electronic media? African mega-pastors, Israeli generals-turned-arms traders, Eritrean and Sudanese exiles, American-Zionist advocacy organisations and Israeli humanitarians and entrepreneurs are all part of the story now. Influence and power are much more diffused and decentralised – determined by various cross-regional connections, encounters and the 'friction' they create.[3]

Israel's future in Africa

Although much of Israel's efforts in Africa from 2009 focused on high-level diplomacy and publicity, by the time Netanyahu's fourth term as prime minster was coming to an end in 2019 it was clear that the promise that 'Israel is coming back to Africa' was not mere rhetoric. Guinea and Chad have re-established ties with Israel, and there were signs that other African countries may follow. Despite significant cuts in the budget of the Ministry of Foreign Affairs, new Israeli embassies have opened in Ghana and Rwanda, while economic and trade missions have been opened in Kenya and Ghana. Numerous African leaders have visited Israel, particularly during 2016–18, demonstrating their interests in benefiting from the investments and political support which Israel seemed to promise. Israel's interest in Africa has assumed a new visibility and attracted renewed attention on the continent, and a notable buzz was generated at least among some circles of entrepreneurs in Israel with regard to the opportunities Africa may offer. Meanwhile, Israel's controversial treatment of African refugees has hardly damaged its relationship with its African allies.

Whether these achievements will be leveraged to further consolidate Israel's position on the continent is yet to be seen. Building stable and long-lasting partnerships with countries beyond Israel's traditional African allies will require greater Israeli investment in institutionalised engagements and less reliance on the often arbitrary opportunities opened up by private business interests or immediate, short-term diplomatic or security objectives. Even if Israel's overall strategy remains committed to the idea that ties with African countries must be consolidated and maintained through private sector and civil society engagements, much more can be done to encourage and facilitate their activities. Unlike some other Middle Eastern actors, Israel does not tend to make grand financial pledges which it has no intention of following up on. But its rhetoric does generate expectations, and without a realistic strategy for their fulfilment, its political influence will remain limited and largely dependent on factors that are beyond its immediate control.

And yet another key question remains open: How far can Israel's relations with African countries go without a just peace in Israel/Palestine? Some observers claim that without progress on the Palestinian issue, Israel will not be able to significantly improve its international standing or realise its economic potential.[4] Clearly, a peace agreement with the Palestinians could benefit Israel's position in Africa on multiple levels. The Arab nations of North Africa as well as neighbouring Sudan and Mauritania would probably normalise their relations with Israel, and Israel's 'cold peace' with Egypt would defrost. Most, if not all, North African and Middle Eastern countries would cease their efforts to curb Israel's influence in Africa, allowing Israel to be openly welcomed at African multilateral institutions, including the AU. Israeli businesses would be able to operate more freely across the continent. Trade and tourism would increase, in both directions. Israeli airlines would be able to fly over the Sahel to Latin America. New opportunities for cultural and academic cooperation would emerge.

This is certainly a hopeful scenario. But what if all, or at least some, of these developments can be achieved even without peace in Israel/Palestine? What if Israel can improve its international status despite its ongoing military control over millions of Palestinian non-citizens? The main problem with the suggestion that Israel must pursue peace at home in order to improve its international standing is that it ignores the fact that the main objective of Israel's international efforts since the late 2000s has been to allow it to maintain the status quo in Israel/Palestine while also eliminating international support for the Palestinians. The logic underlying this strategy is simple: the better Israel's international standing is, the less likely it is to be pressured into a peace agreement it does not like, and the weaker the Palestinians are, the more likely they are to be forced into an agreement on Israel's terms or simply accept that the occupation is there to stay. Netanyahu has always seemed to believe that the occupation is a non-issue – that Israel's challenge is not to bring it to an end, but to convince the world to accept it. This was also the rationale that guided his foreign policy strategy.

And much to the dismay of his critics, it seemed to be working. 'In Africa, things are changing. In China, India, Russia, Japan, attitudes towards Israel have changed as well', Netanyahu declared before the UN General Assembly in September 2016, three months after his first African tour. 'Israel's diplomatic relations are undergoing nothing less than a revolution.'[5] And in the subsequent years it only got better. Under Donald Trump, the risk that the US will apply any pressure on Israel to end the occupation has practically vanished. European countries, while supposedly still supporting the two-state solution, were hardly showing any interest in the issue. The leaders of China, Japan, India, Brazil, as well as a host of smaller nations across the world, were openly celebrating their relationships with Israel. And at every possible opportunity, Netanyahu has boasted about Israel's improving ties with Arab countries. Occasional condemnations from international organisations, which have never had much impact anyway, have continued, but felt increasingly like harmless slaps on the wrist.

Israel's advances in Africa were therefore part of a wider trend. 'Undoubtedly, when African countries see the improvement in the relationships between Israel and various Arab countries, they understand that there is no reason not to get closer to Israel as well', the Ministry of Foreign Affairs' Gideon Behar noted, shortly after reading to me the long list of African leaders that visited Jerusalem during 2017–18. 'It is true that the fact there are many Arab countries in the continent and that the continent is united under one large political body makes it difficult for Israel', he admitted. 'But this is not a barrier. We are past that.'[6] And while many African countries continued to vote 'against' Israel at multilateral fora even after widely publicised diplomatic visits and press conferences, diplomats often cited the favourable voting patterns of Togo, Rwanda, South Sudan and Cameroon as well as smaller gestures of support from other African countries as indications that the wind was blowing in the right direction.

Looking ahead, however, this game is far from over. As long as the occupation continues and Israel and the Palestinians remain locked in conflict – and it seems that this will be the case for the foreseeable future – African countries will continue to balance their support for Israel with their support for countries that seek to curb its influence and aspirations. They have neither the leverage nor the shared interest to dictate the international stance towards Israel, but their political support can nonetheless help accelerate any existing trends. The less interest Arab countries and the international community demonstrate in the Palestinian issue, the greater the manoeuvring space African leaders will have when determining their position on the matter, and Israel will certainly seek to take advantage of this. Regardless of its own policies in the continent, then, Israel's position in Africa will continue to be shaped by the nature and evolution of its Middle Eastern relationships.

NOTES

Prelims

1   Julius Nyerere to David Ben-Gurion, 22 June 1963, Israel State Archives (ISA), 4315/16.

Introduction

1   'PM Netanyahu's remarks upon leaving for Nairobi', 28 November 2017, available at: www.mfa.gov.il/MFA/PressRoom/2017/Pages/PM-Netanyahu %27s-remarks-upon-leaving-for-Nairobi-.aspx (all links were accessed in September 2019).

2   'PM Netanyahu's Remarks at Inauguration of Kenyan President', available at: www.youtube.com/watch?v=KIjK_m7--go&t=5s&frags=pl%2Cwn

3   Not his real name. These paragraphs are based on interviews conducted in December 2017 in Kampala.

4   *Mizrahi* music is an Israeli genre that combines pop with North African and Middle Eastern influences. It is usually performed by (and enjoys greater popularity among) Jews of North African and Middle Eastern origins.

5   'Israel/Palestine' is used here to refer to the territories of historic Palestine, from the Mediterranean Sea to the Jordan River, which today comprise of Israel and the Occupied Palestinian Territories (the West Bank and Gaza). 'Israel' is used to refer to the Israeli state and its institutions, which exercise different degrees and forms of control over the territories of Israel/Palestine.

6   For a recent critique of this division in the context of the relationship between the Horn of Africa and Gulf countries, see Verhoeven, 2018.

7   Kreinin, 1964; Reich, 1964; Heymont, 1967; Jacob, 1971; Curtis and Gitelson, 1976.

8   Ben-David, 1967; Aynor, 1969; Ruppin, 1986.

9   The two seminal books on Israel–Africa relations, by Ojo (1988) and Peters (1992) end in the late 1980s. Decalo (1998) continues until the mid-1990s, though his book is a collection of papers published earlier. See additional references to journal articles and book chapters in the first and second chapters of this book.

10   Erlich (2013) explored Israel's relationship with Imperial Ethiopia, and Levey
      (2012) wrote a detailed account of Israeli diplomacy in Ghana, Ethiopia, the
      DRC, Nigeria and Uganda up until the 1970s. Levey's study stands out in the
      detailed use he makes of Israeli archival materials, primarily of the Ministry
      of Foreign Affairs. Oded (2011), who worked at the Israeli Ministry of Foreign
      Affairs for many years, wrote an informative but also highly selective overview
      of Israel's relationship with the continent. His book seems to be particularly
      popular among Israeli officials, who view it as the most authoritative source
      on the history of Israel's diplomacy on the African continent. Heimann (2016)
      wrote about Israel's relationship with the former French colonies before 1962,
      focusing on the dynamics between Israel and France with regard to Israel's
      involvement in Francophone Africa. Mooreville (2016) wrote about Israeli
      medical aid projects in Africa (in the field of ophthalmology), and Levin (2015),
      on the involvement of Israeli architects and construction companies in Ethiopia,
      Sierra Leone and Nigeria. Both deal with the 1960s. Schler and Gez (2018)
      and Schler (2018) examined the rise, fall and 'afterlife' of Israeli agricultural
      cooperatives that were established in the Zambian Copperbelt in the 1960s. I
      (Gidron, 2018) wrote on the Mossad's involvement in Sudan's first civil war,
      which ended in 1972. Yacobi (2015) and Bar-Yosef (2014) both recently explored
      Israeli perceptions of 'Africa' and the ways in which engagement with Africa
      influenced Israeli identity, particularly during the 1960s. As such, their focus is
      not so much on Israeli–African relations as it is on the Israeli 'idea of Africa'.
11   Abulof, 2009; Maoz, 2009.
12   Shlaim, 2014a.
13   Sheffer and Barak, 2013.
14   On Israel's 'clandestine diplomacies', see also Jones and Petersen, 2013.
15   Chazan, 2006: 12.
16   Clapham, 1996. See also Bayart, 2009.
17   Meir, 1975: 264.

Chapter 1

1   Morris, 1994: 291.
2   Quoted in Brand, 1988: 44.
3   Shlaim, 2014a: 56.
4   Warburg, 1992.
5   Ronen, 2013: 156–60.
6   Final communiqué of the Asian–African Conference Held at Bandung, 18–24
     April 1955.
7   Ojo, 1988: 7.
8   Bergman, 2008: 14–15; Parsi, 2008: 19–28; Alpher, 2015.
9   Meir, 1975: 263.
10   Medzini, 2017: 309.

11 Shlaim, 2014a: 180–97.
12 When the UN General Assembly voted on the Partition Plan for Palestine in 1947 (Resolution 181), Ethiopia abstained while Liberia and South Africa supported the resolution.
13 Avriel, 1976: 71–2.
14 Levey, 2003: 158.
15 Levey, 2003.
16 Adekson, 1976: 260–61.
17 'MASHAV Overview no. 49–50', 25 October 1963, ISA 1421/11.
18 Thompson, 1969: 46–8.
19 Levey, 2012: 20–22.
20 Heimann, 2016.
21 Levey, 2012: 92.
22 Ruppin, 1986: 98–121.
23 Naim, 2005.
24 Israel never had ties with all 33 of these countries at the same time during the 1960s, because by the time Swaziland, Mauritius and Equatorial Guinea gained independence in 1968, Guinea had already severed its ties with Israel (in 1967).
25 Meir, 1975: 267–73; Oded, 2011: 9–11, 18–19.
26 Alpher, 2015.
27 Quoted in Erlich, 2002: 160–61.
28 MASHAV Personnel in Ethiopia, 1963, ISA 4311/4.
29 Israeli Police Mission to Abyssinia, 1963 ISA 4311/4.
30 IDF Delegation in Ethiopia, An Overview of the Delegation's Work for the Minister of Foreign Affairs, 2, ISA 4311/4.
31 Erlich, 2013: 133–4.
32 Middle East Department, Untitled overview of relations with Middle East and periphery countries, 15 August 1962, p. 23, ISA 4906/13.
33 Michael, 2018: 80–99.
34 Erlich, 1983: 55–9. See also Erlich, 1994: 130–57; Markakis, 2011: 123–5.
35 Levey, 2012: 131. See also SIPRI Arms Transfers Database.
36 Jacob, 1971: 179.
37 Quoted in Reich, 1964: 19.
38 See also Jacob, 1971.
39 Mboya, 1963: 93.
40 Israel did extend a few loans to African countries. See the list in Ojo, 1988: 22.
41 Oded, 2009: 93.
42 Ojo, 1988: 18.
43 Kreinin, 1964. See also MASHAV's reports from 1962–63, compiled in ISA-1421/11.
44 See, for example, Mooreville, 2016.

45 Kreinin, 1964: 133–46; Eger, 1976; Decalo, 1998.
46 Migdal, 2001.
47 Herbst, 2000.
48 Heymont, 1967.
49 Z. Zellner, 'Project for the Establishment of an Ethiopian National Youth Organization', Ministry of Foreign Affairs, Department of International Cooperation, 1963, available at the library of the Institute of Ethiopian Studies, Addis Ababa University. See also Silverburg, 1968; Decalo, 1998: 74–7.
50 Decalo, 1998: 80, 113; Yacobi, 2010; Bar-Yosef, 2014: 123–84.
51 MASHAV Personnel in Ethiopia, 1963, 8, ISA 4311/4.
52 Brennan, 2010.
53 Ruppin, 1986: 123–4.
54 Ruppin, 1986: 124–5.
55 Summary of the African Committee's Meeting, 4 February 1966, ISA 4329/10.
56 Kreinin, 1964: 77; Decalo, 1998: 80, 85.
57 Levey, 2004: 80–84.
58 Consultations at the CEO on Africa, 7 July 1966, ISA 3158/1; Surveys before visits, ca. 1966, ISA 4906/13.
59 Ismael, 1971: 116–17.
60 The First Conference of Independent African States, 'Resolution no. 10: Consideration of the Problem of International Peace and Conformity with the Charter of the United Nations and the Re-affirmation of the Principles of the Bandung Conference', April 1958, available in Legum, 1965: 166.
61 Ojo, 1988: 14.
62 The Second Conference of Independent African States, 'Resolution no. 1: The Strengthening of International Peace and Security in Conformity with the Charter of the United Nations and the Bandung and Accra Resolutions,' June 1960, available in Legum, 1965: 167.
63 The Casablanca Conference, 'Resolution on Palestine,' January 1961, available in Legum, 1965: 206. See also pp. 50–52 on the conference itself.
64 Peters, 1992: 25–6.
65 In the early 1960s, Israel sought African support to promote a UN resolution that called for direct negotiations between Israel and the Arabs, in order to circumvent the Arab insistence on the Palestinian right of return. The resolution was eventually never adopted, but Israel was only able to promote it due to the support of African states. See Ministry of Foreign Affairs, Summary of the discussion on the issue of the Palestinian refugees at the UN eighteenth session, 29 November 1963, ISA-4315/12; Ministry of Foreign Affairs, Instructions ahead of the discussion on the problem of Arab refugees at the seventeenth session of the UN General Assembly, 27 July 1962, ISA-4315/10; Decalo, 1998: 39.
66 Decalo, 1998: 53.

67 'Question of French Nuclear Tests in the Sahara', A/RES/1379(XIV).

68 Levey, 2012: 72.

69 Mazrui, 1977: 136.

70 Israel's links with such liberation movements are an understudied topic. These links seem to have been coordinated mostly via the Israeli embassy in Dar es Salaam. See, for example, Dar es Salaam to Jerusalem (letter titled 'Our assistance to liberation movements'), 28 July 1967, ISA-4092/6; Conclusion of the Africa Committee's Meeting, 6 February 1966, ISA 4329/10.

71 Bar-Yosef, 2014; Yacobi, 2015.

72 See also: Likhovski, 2009; Yacobi, 2010.

73 Quoted in Levey, 2004: 82.

Chapter 2

1 Links with Southern Sudan (unsigned memorandum), [July 1963?], ISA-3779/14.

2 Shlaim, 2014a: 232–67. On the American position, see Segev, 2007: 326–35.

3 On the impact of Israel's expansion on its foreign strategy see also Barak, 2017.

4 Leading the operation in southern Sudan was David Ben-Uziel, a military advisor who had previously spent two years in Ethiopia training military forces in the Ogaden. Some southern Sudanese rebels complained that Israel did not provide them with enough weapons and that the ones it did provide were of poor quality (see for example, Poggo, 2009: 161). The Israeli position, as it was described to me by Ben-Uziel, was that Israel did not provide the rebels with weapons the Mossad assessed they had no capacity to use. Interview with David Ben-Uziel, Netanya, March 2017.

5 The episode of support to the Anya-Nya is described in greater detail in Gidron, 2018.

6 Erlich, 1994: 169–72. See also, Levey, 2012: 56–65.

7 The extent to which Israel enabled or encouraged the 1971 coup has been debated over the years. Given the deep Israeli involvement in military affairs and Israel's deteriorating relationship with Obote, it was widely assumed that Israelis were somehow involved. Publicly, the Israeli government denied allegations that Israel supported the coup, but as Levey shows, archival documents of the Ministry of Foreign Affairs indicate that Colonel Bar-Lev, head of the IDF mission in Uganda, knew about Amin's plans in advance and guided him during the coup. See Mazrui, 1977: 143; Levey, 2012: 133; Bergman, 2018: 203.

8 Decalo, 1998: 54.

9 Shlaim, 2014a: 277–8.

10 'Declaration', AHG/ST.2.

11 'Resolution on the Aggression Against the UAR', AHG/Res. 53 (V). The OAU Resolution referred to the UN Resolution 242, but was in fact harsher towards

Israel, as the UN Resolution intentionally required Israel to withdraw from 'territories', and not from 'all Arab territories', which left Israel some room to argue that its withdrawal did not necessarily have to be to the pre-war boundaries.

12 Peters, 1992: 28–9.
13 Nyerere, 1968: 371; Ojo, 1988: 47.
14 Shlaim, 2014a: 303–5.
15 'Resolution on the Continuing Aggression Against AUR', AHG/Res. 66 (VIII).
16 Touval, 1982: 210; Oded, 2011: 81.
17 Kochan, 1973: 193–4.
18 Zevi, 1972: 12.
19 'The situation in the Middle East', A/RES/2799(XXVI).
20 Akinsanya, 1976: 522.
21 'Resolution on the Continued Aggression against the Arab Republic of Egypt', AHG/Res. 67 (IX).
22 Oded, 2002: 69–103.
23 'Resolution on the Continued Occupation by Israel of Part of the Territory of the Arab Republic of Egypt', AHG/Res. 70(X).
24 Levey describes how in August 1973 foreign minister Abba Eban summoned all Israeli ambassadors in Africa to a meeting in Jerusalem in order to discuss Israel's reaction to the events in Africa. See Levey, 2012: 165.
25 'Resolution on the Middle East Situation and the Palestine Issue', NAC/ALG/CONF.4/P/Res.2.
26 Levey, 2012: 170–71.
27 Clapham, 1996: 128.
28 Levey, 2012: 178–9.
29 Peters, 1992: 63–7.
30 Levey, 2012: 185.
31 Ojo, 1988: 55–80.
32 Ojo provides a detailed list of resolutions from 1975 to 1977: Ojo, 1988: 64, 70–71.
33 'Elimination of all forms of racial discrimination', A/RES/3379(XXX).
34 Oded, 1990.
35 Sheffer and Barak, 2013: 40.
36 Klieman, 1985: 23–6.
37 Klieman, 1985: 21–3; Reiser, 1989: 111–14, 204.
38 Steinberg and Marks, 2013. As Steinberg and Marks show, this tradition and the knowledge and experience volunteers gained in Israel later had an important impact on the development of the Community Security Organisation which was established by and for the Jewish community in South Africa in the 1990s.
39 Polakow-Suransky, 2011: 80–84.

40 Bunce, 1984: 44.

41 For a comprehensive overview, based on files declassified in 2016, see William Burr and Avner Cohen, 'The Vela Incident: South Atlantic Mystery Flash in September 1979 Raised Questions about Nuclear Test', National Security Archive (The George Washington University), 6 December 2017, available at: https://nsarchive.gwu.edu/briefing-book/nuclear-vault/2016-12-06/vela-incident-south-atlantic-mystery-flash-september-1979. See also Polakow-Suransky, 2011: 136–42.

42 Erlich, 1994: 175–8.

43 Erlich, 1983: 102–4.

44 Teshome, 1991: 565.

45 Alpher, 2015.

46 Ojo, 1988: 75.

47 Alpher was personally dispatched to Mogadishu in 1980 to meet Barre. See Alpher, 2015.

48 On both operations and Kenya's role, see Bergman, 2018: 195–207.

49 The Golan Heights were unilaterally annexed by Israel in 1981.

50 Shlaim, 2014a: 386–406.

51 Raviv and Melman, 1991: 154–5.

52 Van de Walle, 2001.

53 On 'coup proofing' and the debt crisis, see de Waal, 2015: 45.

54 Peters, 1992: 115.

55 Sharon and Chanoff, 1989: 410–11.

56 Quoted in Kitchen, 1983: 3.

57 Crawford and Turner, 1985: 46.

58 Hakim and Stevens, 1983.

59 Kitchen, 1983.

60 Africa Department to Washington, Kinshasa and Brussels, 27 November 1983, ISA-8735/4.

61 'Mobutu Wants and Expects Increased Israeli Investment, Trade with Zaire', *Jewish Telegraphic Agency*, 20 May 1985, available at: www.jta.org/1985/05/20/archive/mobutu-wants-and-expects-increased-israeli-investment-trade-with-zaire

62 'Mobutu and Israel', *Journal of Palestine Studies*, Autumn 1985: 171–5.

63 Barak, 2017.

64 Shlaim, 2014a: 406–31.

65 Human Rights Watch, 2016: 19.

66 According to Raviv and Melman, the advisors returned within a short period of time due to disagreements in Jerusalem over their mission. See Raviv and Melman, 1991: 273–5.

67 Ellis, 2006: 54–6.

68 Kieh, 1989. See also Peters, 1992: 128–30; Ellis, 2006: 158.

69   Ellis, 2006: 62–3.

70   Peters, 1992: 135.

71   Liba, 2013: 71–2. On Meyouhas in Zaire, see also Beit-Hallahmi, 1987: 60–61.

72   Chazan, 1983.

73   'Cameroonians Greet Israelis in Exuberant Hebrew', *New York Times*, 26 August 1986, available at: https://www.nytimes.com/1986/08/26/world/cameroonians-greet-israelis-in-exuberant-hebrew.html. See also Polakow-Suransky, 2011: 188. Polakow-Suransky quotes a slightly different version of this statement but provides a detailed account of Israel's *hasbara* efforts and strategy around its relationship with South Africa.

74   See the list at Oded, 2011: 261.

75   Alpher, 2015; Abadi, 2017.

76   Neuberger, 2009: 22.

77   'The Development of Israel's Foreign Relations, 1948 to 2003', 7 April 2003 [Hebrew; all Hebrew titles in the Notes are translated by the author], http://www.mfa.gov.il/mfaheb/aboutus/pages/foreign_relation.aspx

78   Belman Inbal and Zahavi, 2009.

79   Decalo, 1998: 151; Bayart et al., 1999: 7; Chazan, 2006: 8-12.

80   International Crisis Group, 2010a: 9.

81   Ariela Ringel Hoffman, 'The bullet that will kill me was not yet invented', *Yediot Aharonot*, 26 November 2010 [Hebrew].

82   Hagai Amit, 'The man who lost to Michael Golan wants to start the new Golan Telecom', *The Marker*, 15 July 2016 [Hebrew], available at: https://www.themarker.com/markerweek/1.3007437; Guy Leshem, 'Hezi's tales in the Black continent', *Haaretz*, 16 June 2006 [Hebrew], available at: https://www.haaretz.co.il/misc/1.1112987

83   Oded, 2002: 205–6.

84   Tangri and Mwenda, 2003.

85   Golan also facilitated Netanyahu's trip to Uganda in 2005, then as finance minister. Yossi Melman, 'Ugandan president in Israel for arms shopping', *Haaretz*, 15 January 2003, available at: https://www.haaretz.com/1.4823113; 'Netanyahu mourns brother at Entebbe', *New Vision*, 5 July 2005, available at: https://www.newvision.co.ug/new_vision/news/1121910/netanyahu-mourns-brother-entebbe

86   American Embassy (Tel Aviv), 'Response to Blue Lantern Level 3 post-shipment', Wikileaks Cable: 09TELAVIV729_a, 27 March 2009, https://wikileaks.org/plusd/cables/09TELAVIV729_a.html

87   On Angola and Equatorial Guinea, see Chapter 4.

88   Sheffer and Barak, 2013.

89   Yossi Melman and Asaf Carmel, 'Diamond in the rough', *Haaretz*, 24 March 2005, available at: https://www.haaretz.com/1.4777668 and https://www.haaretz.com/1.4777697; UN Security Council, 2001.

90 'United States sanctions human rights abusers and corrupt actors across the globe', 21 December 2017, available at: https://home.treasury.gov/news/press-releases/sm0243

91 See also Klieman, 1985; Halper, 2015.

Chapter 3

1 Del Sarto, 2017.

2 Marzano, 2013.

3 As Nathan Thrall argues, the political and financial costs of maintaining the occupation were always lower than the costs associated with bringing it to an end. Thrall, 2017: 5–74.

4 The shifts and battles that brought about this rivalry, and the extent to which it revolved around access to American support, are described in detail in Parsi, 2008.

5 See, for example, Guzansky, 2014; Alpher, 2015.

6 Al Kurwy and Abbas, 2011.

7 'Foreign Minister Liberman to visit Africa', 1 September 2009, available at: http://mfa.gov.il/MFA/PressRoom/2009/Pages/FM_Liberman_visit_Africa_1-Sep-2009.aspx

8 'FM Liberman signs first agreement between Israel and ECOWAS', 9 September 2009, available at: http://mfa.gov.il/MFA/PressRoom/2009/Pages/FM-Liberman-signs-first-agreement-between-Israel-and-ECOWAS-9-Sep-2009.aspx. Guinea restored ties with Israel in 2016.

9 According to Israeli journalist Ronen Bergman, the Mossad even attempted to assassinate bin Laden in Sudan at the time. See Bergman, 2008: 217–26.

10 Watts et al., 2007.

11 'Eastern Africa: a battleground for Israel and Iran', Stratfor, 29 October 2012, available at: https://worldview.stratfor.com/article/eastern-africa-battleground-israel-and-iran. Media reports associated two other similar incidents in 2014 and 2015 with Israel. See Joshua Davidovich, 'Sudan denies attack after "foreign" planes said to hit military site', The Times of Israel, 6 May 2015, available at: https://www.timesofisrael.com/witnesses-claim-israeli-jets-strike-sudanese-city-report/. Israel also intercepted vessels with arms that were on their way to Gaza in the Red Sea. In January 2002, Israel intercepted a vessel, Karin A, loaded with 50 tons of weapons off the coast of the Sudan–Eritrea border. The ship was on its way to Port Sudan, where the weapons were supposed to be unloaded and smuggled via Egypt into Gaza. Another vessel carrying weapons from Iran, the Klos C, was intercepted in the Red Sea in March 2014 on its way to Sudan.

12 Small Arms Survey, 'The Military Industry Corporation (MIC)', 2 July 2014, available at: www.smallarmssurveysudan.org/fileadmin/docs/facts-figures/sudan/HSBA-MIC-Open-Source-Review-2014.pdf

13 On Israel's view of the Arab Spring in Egypt, see: Shlaim, 2014b. On the Arab Spring, Egypt and Israel's 'new periphery' thinking, see Alpher, 2015.

14 Kenya sought Israeli assistance in public defence and counterterrorism from at least 2010, but Odinga's 2011 visit turned into a diplomatic blunder. It was widely covered in the press, and al-Shabaab seized the opportunity and issued a statement describing the Israeli–Kenyan partnership as an anti-Muslim plot. The Kenyan Ministry of Defence was quick to publicly distance itself from Odinga's actions and to clarify that despite his statements about Israeli security support to Kenya, Israeli aid would only concern internal security and not Kenya's activities in southern Somalia. The whole affair was particularly embarrassing for President Mwai Kibaki, as it took place days before his trip to the Gulf to obtain support from the United Arab Emirates (UAE). See International Crisis Group, 2012; Gil Ronen, 'Kenya wants Israel's help against jihadists', *Arutz Sheva*, 11 February 2010, available at: www.israelnationalnews.com/News/News.aspx/135978; 'President Museveni meets Mossad discreetly', *Africa Intelligence*, 17 November 2011, available at: https://www.africaintelligence.com/ion/alert-ion/2011/11/17/president-museveni-meets-mossad-discreetly,94562867-art; Mugumo Munene, 'Israeli offer causes cracks in Kenya's diplomatic offensive', *Daily Nation*, 19 November 2011, available at: https://www.nation.co.ke/news/politics/Israeli-offer-causes-cracks-in-Kenyas-diplomatic-offensive/1064-1276046-157afeoz/index.html

15 Barak Ravid, 'Israel: Sudan violates human rights, but has distanced itself from Iran', *Haaretz*, 14 September 2016, available at: https://www.haaretz.com/israel-news/.premium-officials-israel-objects-to-sudans-human-rights-record-1.5434000

16 Ethiopian Airlines stopped travelling over Sudan in 2018 following the peace between Ethiopia and Eritrea, which opened a shorter route between Tel Aviv and Addis Ababa over the Red Sea and Asmara.

17 Saeb Erekat, 'Response to Jason Greenblatt: the Trump administration, peddling Israeli extremism, is killing the peace process, not me', *Haaretz*, 10 June 2018, available at: https://www.haaretz.com/middle-east-news/.premium-trump-envoys-peddling-israeli-extremism-are-killing-peace-not-me-1.6159732; Adam Entous, 'Donald Trump's new world order', *The New Yorker*, 18 June 2018, available at: https://www.newyorker.com/magazine/2018/06/18/donald-trumps-new-world-order

18 Interview with Avi Granot, former ambassador to Ethiopia and former head of the Africa Division at the Ministry of Foreign Affairs, October 2018, Tel Aviv. On Gaddafi and the founding of the AU, see also Tieku, 2004; Solomon and Swart, 2005.

19 'Declaration on the Arab Peace Initiative', Assembly/AU/Decl.1(IX).

20 For further analysis see International Crisis Group, 2010b, 2011.

21 Barak Ravid, 'Lieberman to Haaretz: Israel must launch concerted campaign

to delegitimize Abbas', *Haaretz*, 26 August 2012, available at: https://www.haaretz.com/fm-israel-must-delegitimize-abbas-1.5290985

22 'Decision on the Situation in Palestine and the Middle East', Assembly/AU/Dec.396(XVIII).

23 Tabu Butagira, 'Uganda sides with Palestine in UN vote', *Daily Monitor*, 30 November 2012, available at: www.monitor.co.ug/News/National/Uganda-sides-with-Palestine-in-UN-vote/688334-1633032-8ujk07z/index.html

24 'FM Liberman promotes strengthening Israel–Africa ties', 19 May 2014, available at: http://mfa.gov.il/MFA/PressRoom/2014/Pages/FM-Liberman-promotes-Israel-Africa-ties-19-May-2014.aspx

25 It should be emphasised that the AU call for boycott refers solely to products produced in the settlements and not all Israeli exports. Israeli politicians deliberately conflate boycotts of settlement good with boycotts of Israel as a whole, and view both as illegitimate attacks against the Israeli state. But legally, there is a fundamental difference between the two, as boycotts of the settlements only delegitimise Israel's activities in the Occupied Territories, which are widely recognised as illegal under international law.

26 According to Granot, who was the head of the Africa Division in the Ministry of Foreign Affairs at the time, there was a disagreement over whether or not Israel's membership has to be approved by the AU Assembly or can be granted by the chairperson (interview with Avi Granot, October 2018, Tel Aviv).

27 For an engaging recent biography, see Pfeffer, 2018.

28 'PM Netanyahu attends launch of Knesset caucus for Israel–Africa relations', 29 February 2016, available at: http://mfa.gov.il/MFA/PressRoom/2016/Pages/PM-Netanyahu-attends-launch-of-Knesset-caucus-for-Israel-Africa-relations-29-Feb-2016.aspx

29 Naomi Chazan, 'What is Israel doing in Africa?', *The Times of Israel*, 4 December 2017, available at: https://blogs.timesofisrael.com/what-is-israel-doing-in-africa/

30 Amir Oren, 'Netanyahu's wasteful journey in Africa brought Israel benefit – on condition', *Haaretz*, 8 July 2016 [Hebrew], available at: https://www.haaretz.co.il/news/politics/.premium-1.3000736

31 'FM Liberman proposes Middle Eastern–African joint anti-terrorism mechanism', 18 June 2014, available at: http://mfa.gov.il/MFA/PressRoom/2014/Pages/FM-Liberman-proposes-joint-anti-terrorism-mechanism-18-June-2014.aspx

32 'Joint Declaration of the Regional Summit on Counter-terrorism', 4 July 2016, available at: http://mfa.gov.il/MFA/PressRoom/2016/Pages/Uganda-regional-counterterrorism-summit-joint-declaration-4-July-2016.aspx. At the centre of the trip to East Africa was also a big ceremony in Entebbe International Airport marking 40 years since Israel's Entebbe Operation during which Netanyahu's brother, Yoni, was killed. Beyond the personal significance for Netanyahu in

commemorating the event, the Israeli operation has been mythologised as a daring Israeli victory against the forces of terror, a theme that was highlighted during the event.

33 Van de Walle, 2016.

34 See, for example, Jones et al., 2013; Fisher and Anderson, 2015.

35 The data for 2009–17 is from the UN Comtrade Database (https://comtrade. un.org). Data for 2018 is from 'Trade countries – imports and exports', Israel Central Bureau of Statistics, available at: www.cbs.gov.il/he/mediarelease/ doclib/2019/021/16_19_021t1.pdf

36 UN Comtrade Database (https://comtrade.un.org).

37 Ibid.

38 'Foreign Minister Liberman to visit Africa', 1 September 2009, available at: http://mfa.gov.il/MFA/PressRoom/2009Pages/FM_Liberman_visit_Africa_1-Sep-2009.aspx

39 'FM Liberman on official visit to Africa', 9 July 2014, available at: http://mfa. gov.il/MFA/PressRoom/2014/Pages/FM-Liberman-to-leave-on-state-visit-to-Africa-9-June-2014.aspx

40 Shuki Sadeh, 'From homeland security to water, with Netanyahu's visit, Israeli businesses rediscover Africa', *Haaretz*, 21 July 2016, available at: https://www. haaretz.com/israel-news/business/.premium-with-netanyahu-s-visit-israeli-businessmen-rediscover-africa-1.5414276

41 'ECOWAS, Israel sign $1 bn solar energy for member states', *Vanguard*, 3 June 2017, available at: https://www.vanguardngr.com/2017/06/ecowas-israel-sign-1-bn-solar-energy-member-states/

42 The BDS movement is an international campaign, launched in 2005, that calls for the political, economic and cultural isolation of Israel until it meets three demands: end the military occupation of Gaza and the West Bank, respect the rights of Palestinian refugees to return to their homes and property, and guarantee the full equality of Palestinian citizens of Israel.

43 'Strengthening economic ties and cooperation with the countries of the continent of Africa', Government decision 1585, 26 June 2016 [Hebrew], available at: https://www.gov.il/he/Departments/policies/2016_dec1585

44 'PM Netanyahu to submit plan to strengthen economic ties and cooperation with Africa', 24 June 2016, available at: http://mfa.gov.il/MFA/PressRoom/2016/Pages/PM-Netanyahu-to-submit-plan-to-strengthen-economic-ties-and-cooperation-with-Africa-24-June-2016.aspx

45 ASHRA, Annual report 2017 [Hebrew], available at: https://www.ashra.gov. il/_Uploads/dbsAttachedFiles/SCRHZ417.pdf

46 'The promotion of Israeli activity in the field of international development', Government decision 4021, 23 June 2018 [Hebrew], available at: https:// www.gov.il/he/Departments/policies/dec4021_2018. The quote is from the explanatory text to the decision (on file with author).

47 Hagai Amit, "'Act fast": Netanyahu is advancing bank for private investments in developing countries', *The Marker*, 20 January 2019 [Hebrew], available at: https://www.themarker.com/allnews/.premium-1.6852301

48 The figure for 2018 is an estimate based on official data from the Ministry of Defense according to which sales to Africa represented 2% of a total of $7.5 billion. See 'Concluding 2018 at SIBAT: exports in more than 7.5 milliard dollars,' 17 April 2019 [Hebrew], available at: www.mod.gov.il/Defence-and-Security/articles/Pages/17.4.19.aspx. The figure for 2017 is similarly an estimate based on official data from the Ministry of Defense according to which sales to Africa represented 5 percent of a total of $9.2 billion that year. See: 'SIBAT concludes a year: a rise of 40 percent in defence exports,' 2 May 2018 [Hebrew], available at: www.mod.gov.il/Defence-and-Security/articles/Pages/2.5.18.aspx. Data for 2009–16 is based on: 'Israel's defence exports: a rise in Africa, a record in Europe', *Haaretz*, 29 March 2017 [Hebrew], available at: www.haaretz.co.il/news/politics/.premium-1.3957524

49 These reports can be consulted at: https://www.unroca.org. On Israel's transparency with regard to exports of small arms, see also Holtom and Pavesi, 2017: 41.

50 Yossi Melman, 'Free trade: this is how the security sector defends exports to shady countries', *Forbes Israel*, 7 October 2017 [Hebrew], available at: www.forbes.co.il/news/new.aspx?Pn6VQ=EG&or9VQ=EJEKE

51 'Israel strengthens the battle against bribery and corruption', Ministry of Justice, available at: www.justice.gov.il/En/about/mankal/BattleBriberyCorruption/Pages/InIsrael.aspx. Several Israeli mining and construction firms were accused of bribing officials in Africa in recent years.

52 Defense Export Controls Bill (Amendment – Restrictions on Exports to Security Forces Involved in Gross Human Rights Violations), 2016 [Hebrew], available at: http://m.knesset.gov.il/Activity/Legislation/Laws/Pages/LawBill.aspx?t=lawsuggestionssearch&lawitemid=2003958

53 Israeli lawyer-activist Itay Mack, in particular, filed multiple petitions in recent years demanding that the Israeli authorities reveal files concerning the involvement of Israeli arms in past atrocities (such as in Rwanda) or stop military deliveries to countries in which human rights violations occur today (such as South Sudan, Cameroon and Burundi).

54 'Foreign minister inaugurates agricultural center in Rwanda', 11 June 2014, available at: http://mfa.gov.il/MFA/mashav/Latest_News/Pages/Foreign-Minister-Inaugurates-Agricultural-Center-in-Rwanda.aspx

55 Barak and Cohen, 2006: 24.

56 Seth J. Frantzman, 'Jerusalem orders to cancel all aid programs to resolution co-sponsor Senegal', *The Jerusalem Post*, 24 December 2016, available at: www.jpost.com/Israel-News/Politics-And-Diplomacy/Jerusalem-orders-to-cancel-all-aid-programs-to-resolution-co-sponsor-Senegal-476421

57 Knesset announcement, 16 December 2015 [Hebrew], available at: http://m.
    knesset.gov.il/News/PressReleases/pages/press161215b-b.aspx

58 Neta Akhitov, 'Israel calculates budgets for absorption basket and Holot facility
    as foreign aid, and is still ranked in the last place', *Haaretz*, 14 April 2016 [Hebrew],
    available at: www.haaretz.co.il/magazine/tozeret/.premium-1.2914750

59 OECD, 2017: 289–90.

60 David Shamah, 'Lighting up Africa with Israeli technology', *Times of Israel*, 2
    December 2018, available at: www.timesofisrael.com/lighting-up-africa-with-
    israeli-technology/

61 The quote is from Sivan Ya'ari's talk at the American Israel Public Affairs
    Committee (AIPAC) conference, 4 March 2018, available at: www.
    policyconference.org/article/transcripts/2018/yaari.asp

62 'Ministry of Foreign Affairs initiates cooperation with Israeli organisations
    operating in Africa', 12 February 2017 [Hebrew], available at: http://mfa.gov.
    il/MFAHEB/PressRoom/Pages/MFA-initiates-collaboration-with-Israeli-
    organizations-active-in-Africa-120217.aspx

63 'President Reuven Rivlin participates in the "Impact for Good" conference in
    Ethiopia', 3 May 2018, available at: http://mfa.gov.il/MFA/PressRoom/2018/
    Pages/President-Reuven-Rivlin-participates-in-the-Impact-for-Good-
    conference-in-Ethiopia-3-May-2018.aspx

64 Interview with Gideon Behar, Head of the Africa Bureau at the Ministry of
    Foreign Affairs, Jerusalem, May 2019.

65 See, for example: 'The collapse of the Israeli Foreign Service: summary of a
    Knesset conference held on 15 January 2018', Mitvim: The Israeli Institute for
    Regional Foreign Policies, January 2018 [Hebrew], available at: www.mitvim.
    org.il/images/Hebrew_-_The_Collapse_of_the_Israeli_Foreign_Service_-_
    Knesset_event_summary_-_15_January_2018.pdf

Chapter 4

1   US Embassy Addis Ababa, 'Ethiopia: broken promises, unmet expectations–fixing
    mil-to-mil relations', 21 May 2007, WikiLeaks Cable 07ADDISABABA1535_a,
    available at: https://wikileaks.org/plusd/cables/07ADDISABABA1535_a.html.
    See also US Embassy Addis Ababa, 'Ethiopia's broken promises', 9 June 2008,
    WikiLeaks Cable 08ADDISABABA1571_a, available at: https://wikileaks.
    org/plusd/cables/08ADDISABABA1571_a.html; US Embassy Addis Ababa,
    'Ethiopia: prime minister weighed down by Somali and Ogaden operations',
    25 July 2007, WikiLeaks Cable 07ADDISABABA2361_a, available at: https://
    wikileaks.org/plusd/cables/07ADDISABABA2361_a.html

2   De Waal, 2015: 182–5.

3   'Israel–Ghana strengthen military cooperation', *GhanaWeb*, 6 September 2018,
    available at: www.ghanaweb.com/GhanaHomePage/NewsArchive/Israel-
    Ghana-strengthen-military-cooperation-682875; 'Diary of RDF Command

and Staff Course international study tour 2018 to Israel and Czech Republic from 20–29 April 2018', Rwanda Defence Force Command and Staff College, 24 May 2018.

4   Branu Tegene, 'The Israelis who are training forces in Africa', *Mako*, 9 April 2017 [Hebrew], available at: www.mako.co.il/news-channel2/Channel-2-Newscast-q2_2017/Article-38639f37ad35b51004.htm

5   'Magal wins $5.5 million in new projects for integrated security systems', 12 January 2017, available at: www.prnewswire.com/news-releases/magal-wins-55-million-in-new-projects-for-integrated-security-systems-610502095.html

6   See https://magalsecurity.com/markets/seaports.

7   'Magal awarded a $6.4 million contract to secure Nairobi international airport', 7 May 2014, available at: www.prnewswire.com/news-releases/magal-awarded-a-64-million-contract-to-secure-nairobi-international-airport-258259501.html

8   'The Israeli company that wants to build Trump's wall at the US–Mexico border', *The Marker*, 2 August 2016 [Hebrew], available at: www.themarker.com/wallstreet/1.3026928

9   'Keter seals a pipeline security alliance with Israel', *Africa Intelligence*, 28 February 2017, available at: www.africaintelligence.com/aem/oil/2017/02/28/keter-seals-a-pipeline-security-alliance-with-israel,108213892-art

10   Isaac Khisa, 'Anti-terror squad passed out in time for al Shabaab', *Daily Monitor*, 19 July 2010, available at: www.monitor.co.ug/News/National/688334-960314-bpdutpz/index.html; US Embassy Kampala, 'State of counterterrorism in Uganda', 11 March 2009, WikiLeaks Cable 09KAMPALA271_a, available at: https://wikileaks.org/plusd/cables/09KAMPALA271_a.html; Human Rights Watch, 2009.

11   'Faure Gnassingbe's high-risk Israeli gamble', *Africa Intelligence*, 12 July 2017, available at: www.africaintelligence.com/lce/corridors-of-power/2017/07/12/faure-gnassingbe-s-high-risk-israeli-gamble,108254161-eve; 'M.E. Roy welcomes the presidential guard of the Republic of the Congo upon arrival to its facilities for a one month security training', 25 November 2015, available at: www.facebook.com/735682936447762/photos/pppbo.735682936447762/1203400133009371/?type=3

12   According to Amnesty International the grenades and vehicles were sold by two private Israeli companies specialising in 'riot control' gear, both of which also supply equipment to Israeli security forces. Amnesty International, 2015.

13   'Inside Kenya's death squads', *Al Jazeera*, 7 December 2014, available at: https://interactive.aljazeera.com/aje/KenyaDeathSquads/

14   Ami Rojkes Dombe, 'Israeli experts help the Nigerian air force to establish first commando unit', *Israel Defense*, 27 February 2018, available at: www.israeldefense.co.il/en/node/33230

15 'Touadera deploys his military diplomacy', *Africa Intelligence*, 8 November 2017, available at: www.africaintelligence.com/lce/corridors-of-power/2017/11/08/touadera-deploys-his-military-diplomacy,108279854-art

16 Wezeman, 2009: 7, 9. Transfers of additional armoured vehicles from 2015 are also listed at on the Stockholm International Peace Research Institute (SIPRI) database.

17 International Crisis Group, 2010a: 9.

18 Georges Dougueli, 'Cameroun: Paul Biya sous protection israélienne', *Jeune Afrique*, 19 November 2015, available at: www.jeuneafrique.com/mag/276021/politique/cameroun-paul-biya-sous-protection-israelienne/

19 Guy Elster, 'Under the training of Duvdevan commander: the "Israeli unit" that protects the autocrat at any price', *Walla!*, 1 March 2018 [Hebrew], available at: https://news.walla.co.il/item/3136810; 'Cameroon operating Musketeer armoured vehicles', *defenceWeb*, 23 March 2016, available at: www.defenceweb.co.za/index.php?option=com_content&view=article&id=42839:cameroon-operating-musketeer-armoured-vehicles. For more images of BIR troops with Israeli rifles from 2014, see 'Obangame Express 2014', Commander, US Naval Forces Europe-Africa/US 6th Fleet (Flickr gallery), available at: www.flickr.com/photos/cne-cna-c6f/sets/72157644086189844/page1

20 'Rapid intervention military unit strays from its mission', *IRIN*, 29 August 2008, available at: www.irinnews.org/report/80065/cameroon-rapid-intervention-military-unit-strays-its-mission

21 Amnesty International, 2017a, 2017b; Human Rights Watch, 2018.

22 I am referring here to the song 'Jesh SPLA' (SPLA army), sung by Nyajuok Keat, in the Nuer language.

23 UN Security Council, 2016: 26. In July 2012, South Sudan's minister of water and irrigation, Paul Mayom Akec, also signed an opaque agreement with the then-government-owned arms manufacturer Israel Military Industries (IMI). The agreement was signed under the auspices of the Israeli Energy and Water Ministry as a plan for cooperation on 'water infrastructure and technology development'. See Sharon Udasin, 'Israel signs 1st agreement, on water, with S. Sudan', *Jerusalem Post*, 24 July 2012, available at: www.jpost.com/Enviro-Tech/Israel-signs-1st-agreement-on-water-with-S-Sudan

24 UN Security Council, 2016: 26.

25 UN Security Council, 2008: 61–2.

26 Barak Ravid, 'Israel told UN it was not selling lethal weapons to South Sudan', *Haaretz*, 14 January 2016, available at: www.haaretz.com/israel-news/.premium-israel-told-un-it-was-not-selling-lethal-weapons-to-south-sudan-1.5390399

27 Wezeman, 2011: 7.

28 Department of the Treasury, 'Treasury sanctions three individuals for their roles in the conflict in South Sudan', 14 December 2018, available at: https://home.treasury.gov/news/press-releases/sm574

29 I approached Israel's ambassador to South Sudan on the matter by email in May 2019 but was told that the Ministry of Foreign Affairs could not comment on it as it was still being 'examined'.

30 UN Security Council, 2016: 45–6.

31 Privacy International, 2016: 4–6, 9.

32 'Israeli firms step in to tackle cybercrime', *Africa Intelligence*, 15 June 2018, available at: www.africaintelligence.com/ion/business-circles/2018/06/15/israeli-firms-step-in-to-tackle-cybercrime,108313829-art

33 Bill Marczak, Geoffrey Alexander, Sarah McKune, John Scott-Railton and Ron Deibert, 'Champing at the cyberbit: Ethiopian dissidents targeted with new commercial spyware', *The Citizen Lab*, 2 December 2017, available at: https://citizenlab.ca/2017/12/champing-cyberbit-ethiopian-dissidents-targeted-commercial-spyware/

34 Mearsheimer and Walt, 2008. Mearsheimer and Walt have been criticised for overestimating the influence of the 'Israel lobby', but their book nonetheless provides a comprehensive analysis of its role in US politics.

35 Department of State, 'Voting Practices in the United Nations 2017: Report to Congress Submitted Pursuant to Public Laws 101-246 and 108-447', March 2018, available at: www.state.gov/documents/organization/281458.pdf

36 'Press release: Ambassador Haley on the release of the U.S. report on UN voting practices', 26 April 2018, available at: https://usun.state.gov/remarks/8411

37 Peter Beaumont, 'US will "take names of those who vote to reject Jerusalem recognition"', *The Guardian*, 20 December 2017, available at: www.theguardian.com/us-news/2017/dec/20/us-take-names-united-nations-vote-to-reject-jerusalem-recognition

38 This comparison has been debated and problematised by scholars. See Miles, 2000; Lemarchand, 2002.

39 Gardiner Harris and Isabel Kershner, 'Hard-line supporter of Israel offers to pay for U.S. embassy in Jerusalem', *New York Times*, 23 February 2018, available at: www.nytimes.com/2018/02/23/world/middleeast/trump-embassy-jerusalem-.html

40 Nathan Guttman, 'Rwanda leader Paul Kagame gets Jewish embrace — but what about human rights?', *Forward*, 28 March 2014, available at: https://forward.com/news/israel/195368/rwanda-leader-paul-kagame-gets-jewish-embrace-bu/

41 'Jewish groups line up to denounce ad on Sudan Rice', *Jerusalem Post*, 1 March 2015, available at: www.jpost.com/Diaspora/Jewish-groups-line-up-to-denounce-Boteach-ad-on-Susan-Rice-392519

42 Shmuley Boteach, 'Hero of the Rwandan genocide emerges as Israel's African ally', *Jerusalem Post*, 20 March 2017, available at: www.jpost.com/Opinion/Hero-of-the-Rwandan-Genocide-emerges-as-Israels-African-ally-484712

43 Dave Clark, 'Kagame hails Rwanda–Israel bond at AIPAC', *Times of Israel*, 26 March 2017, available at: www.timesofisrael.com/kagame-hails-rwanda-israel-bond-at-aipac/

44 'Faure Gnassingbe's high-risk Israeli gamble', *Africa Intelligence*, 12 July 2017, available at: www.africaintelligence.com/lce/corridors-of-power/2017/07/12/faure-gnassingbe-s-high-risk-israeli-gamble,108254161-eve; 'Faure's soft spot for Rwanda', *Africa Intelligence*, 9 May 2018, available at: www.africa intelligence.com/lce/corridors-of-power/2018/05/09/faure-s-soft-spot-for-rwanda,108309797-bre

45 Domegni, 2017.

46 'Togo's president: we were impressed by your expertise in phosphate', *News1*, 28 November 2012, available at: www.news1.co.il/Archive/001-D-315396-00.html

47 'Yaakov Engel will establish a 1.4 USD billion phosphates and fertilisers project in Togo', *The Marker*, 8 September 2015, available at: www.themarker.com/markets/1.2726326

48 Farida Nabourema's remarks at a panel discussion hosted by the International Republican Institute and Vanguard Africa, 17 January 2018, available at: www.facebook.com/InternationalRepublicanInstitute/videos/1015 6000049709509/

49 'Building bridges towards greater shared prosperity: The Africa–Israel summit in Lome, Togo, October 23–27 2017', available at: https://docs.wixstatic.com/ugd/9fb845_30cbcdd7bd714ba49370b19c0eba470d.pdf

50 Azad Essa and Linah Alsaafin, 'Israel–Africa summit cancelled as Togo unrest continues', *Al Jazeera*, 13 September 2017, available at: www.aljazeera.com/news/2017/09/israel-africa-summit-cancelled-togo-unrest-continues-170912060426962.html

51 'Faure faced with the anger of the street … and the Arab world!', *Africa Intelligence*, 7 February 2018, available at: www.africaintelligence.com/lce/business-circles/2018/02/07/faure-faced-with-the-anger-of-the-street…and-the-arab-world,108293115-art

52 'Chad rejects U.S. bribery allegations against president', Reuters, 23 November 2017, available at: www.reuters.com/article/us-usa-china-corruption-chad/chad-rejects-u-s-bribery-allegations-against-president-idUSKBN1DN1BJ

53 Shuki Sadeh, 'Israeli lobbyists working for Congo in D.C. hire GOP insiders, including Bob Dole and Trump campaign liaisons', *Haaretz*, 31 October 2017, available at: www.haaretz.com/israel-news/business/the-strange-case-of-israeli-lobbyists-bob-dole-and-congo-1.5461704. Mer Group is a company specialising in interception equipment, cybersecurity, training of law enforcement and intelligence units as well as the supply, design and maintenance of communication infrastructure for mobile operators. See 'Mer Group markets low-cost SIGINT to Africa', *Intelligence Online*, 25 January 2017,

available at: www.intelligenceonline.com/corporate-intelligence/2017/01/25/mer-group-markets-low-cost-sigint-to-africa,108198610-art

54 US Embassy Ouagadougou, 'Burkina Faso: Compaore seeks to win favor with United States during visit to Israel', 22 May 2008, WikiLeaks Cable 08OUAGADOUGOU432_a, available at: https://wikileaks.org/plusd/cables/08OUAGADOUGOU432_a.html

55 'The vision of the Africa Israel Initiative', promotional video, available at: www.youtube.com/watch?v=_cne6ohWT2Q

56 Obong Akpaekong, 'Nigerian chapter of Africa–Israel Initiative (AII) strategising for impact', New Telegraph, 30 September 2017, available at: https://newtelegraphonline.com/2017/09/nigerian-chapter-africa-israel-initiative-aii-strategising-impact/

57 On CUFI's outreach efforts among Black communities in the US, see also Baumann, 2016.

58 Pro-Israel groups reject what is commonly known as 'replacement theology': the idea that the Jewish people have been 'replaced' by the Church (and the Christian community) as God's chosen due to their rejection of Jesus Christ.

59 For a detailed discussion of the reasoning and history of evangelical support of Israel, see Ariel, 2013. On the American context specifically, see Spector, 2009.

60 Gil Ronen, 'Nigerian pastor of millions visits Samaria', Arutz Sheva, 25 August 2011, available at: www.israelnationalnews.com/News/News.aspx/147219. On the demonisation of Islam in Pentecostal rhetoric, see Kalu, 2008: 243–6.

61 'Exclusive interview with Rev Gilbert Apreala, a prominent Ghana based Nigerian pastor: speaking on God, Mission, Africa-Israel Initiative and more', Pleasure Magazine, 1 August 2017, available at: http://pleasuresmagazine.com.ng/2017/08/exclusive-interview-with-rev-gilbert-apreala-a-prominent-ghana-based-nigerian-pastor-speaks-on-god-mission-africa-israel-initiative-and-more/

62 Ibid.

63 See, for example, Oge Okonkwo, 'RCCG leader donates ambulance to Israel', Pulse Nigeria, 14 May 2015, available at: www.pulse.ng/communities/religion/pastor-enoch-adeboye-rccg-leader-donates-ambulance-to-israel-id3758425.html

64 Yaakov Lappin, 'Christians offer "repentance"', Ynetnews, 3 March 2007, available at: www.ynetnews.com/articles/0,7340,L-3382412,00.html

65 'Tourists arrivals, by country of citizenship, 2009–2016', Israel Central Bureau of Statistics, available at: https://old.cbs.gov.il/publications18/1707/pdf/t04.pdf

66 Wale Odunsi, 'Why I'm relocating my ministry to Israel – TB Joshua', Daily Post, 2 May 2017, available at: http://dailypost.ng/2017/05/02/im-relocating-ministry-israel-tb-joshua/

67 Obadare, 2018.

68 Ibid.: 100.

69 'Nigerian President Jonathan visits Israel', 28 October 2013, available at: http://
    mfa.gov.il/MFA/PressRoom/2013/Pages/Nigerian-President-Jonathan-visits-
    Israel-28-Oct-2013.aspx

70 Oge Okonkwo, 'Jonathan and Oyedepo arrive Nigeria from Israel', *Pulse
    Nigeria*, 27 October 2014, available at: www.pulse.ng/communities/religion/
    pilgrimage-jonathan-and-oyedepo-arrive-nigeria-from-israel-id3227350.html

71 Itamar Eichner, 'Behind the UN vote: how the Palestinian bid was
    defeated', *Ynetnews*, 31 December 2014, available at: www.ynetnews.com/
    articles/0,7340,L-4609884,00.html

72 Herb Keinon, 'Nigeria putting brakes on Israeli participation in West African
    summit', *Jerusalem Post*, 23 August 2016, available at: www.jpost.com/
    Israel-News/Politics-And-Diplomacy/Nigeria-putting-brakes-on-Israeli-
    participation-in-West-African-summit-464856

73 See, for example: '"Ghanaians' love for Israel is amazing"– Ambassador',
    14 April 2016, available at: https://embassies.gov.il/accra/NewsAndEvents/
    Pages/'Ghanaians'-love-for-Israel-is-amazing'---Israeli-Ambassador.aspx

74 For example, 'Ghana, Israel strengthen bilateral relations through culture',
    Ghana Business News, 30 October 2017, available at: www.ghanabusinessnews.
    com/2017/10/30/ghana-israel-strengthen-bilateral-relations-through-culture/

75 Phone interview with Shani Cooper-Zubida, Ambassador of Israel to Ghana,
    Liberia and Sierra Leone, December 2018.

76 'Ghana–Israel toast to greater cooperation and benefits', *Business Ghana*, 22
    April 2018, available at: www.businessghana.com/site/news/politics/163605/
    Ghana-Israel-toast-to-greater-cooperation-and-benefits

77 Since then, the organisation has established a presence in a number of other
    African countries.

78 These paragraphs are based on an interview conducted (in English) with
    a volunteer and an employee of Christians for Israel – Uganda (Kampala,
    September 2019). See also the organisation's newsletter: *Israel & Christians
    Today: Africa Edition* (July 2016).

79 Agnes Kyotalengerire, 'Gov't of Israel donates hospital beds to Ralpha health
    center', *New Vision*, 16 May 2017, available at: www.newvision.co.ug/new_
    vision/news/1453404/gov-israel-donates-hospital-beds-ralpha-health-center

80 These are listed on SAFI's website, at: www.safisa.co.za/about-us/friendship-
    network/

81 The two organisations have cooperated to organise a number of events in
    South Africa in recent years. There is also a personal connection between key
    figures on both sides: DEISI's Olga Meshoe is married to Joshua Washington,
    the son of Dumisani Washington, who is the National Diversity Outreach
    Coordinator at CUFI in Africa and among Black communities in the US.
    See Howard Sackstein, 'A wedding conceived for the love of Zion', *South*

African Jewish Report, 25 January 2018, available at: www.sajr.co.za/news-and-articles/2018/01/25/a-wedding-conceived-for-the-love-of-zion

82 Noa Amouyal, 'Ministry of Strategic Affairs hosts series of South Africa anti-BDS events', *Jerusalem Post*, 11 June 2018, available at: www.jpost.com/Diaspora/Ministry-of-Strategic-Affairs-hosts-series-of-South-Africa-anti-BDS-events-559697

83 On Israel's strategy in combating BDS internationally, see Nathan Thrall, 'BDS: how a controversial non-violent movement has transformed the Israeli–Palestinian debate', *The Guardian*, 14 August 2018, available at: www.theguardian.com/news/2018/aug/14/bds-boycott-divestment-sanctions-movement-transformed-israeli-palestinian-debate

84 Ben Swartz, speech at the SAFI Annual Conference, Johannesburg 2018, available at: www.youtube.com/watch?v=Zizj5kGeyXI&frags=pl%2Cwn

85 Whether or not African initiated churches such as the ZCC should be included within the family of Pentecostal and charismatic Christianity has been debated. See Kalu, 2008: 65–84.

86 Müller, 2017.

87 Benji Shulman, 'Taking Zion to Zion', *South African Jewish Report*, 26 October 2017, available at: www.sajr.co.za/news-and-articles/2017/10/26/taking-zion-to-zion

88 Ben Swartz, speech at the SAFI Annual Conference, 2018.

89 Russian-Israeli businessmen Arkady Gaidamak was probably the most well-connected and became renowned for his involvement in the Angolagate scandal concerning illegal arms sales by France to Angola. See Global Witness, 2002.

90 Yossi Melman, 'Angling in on Angola', *Haaretz*, 4 January 2002, available at: www.haaretz.com/1.5475242

91 Guy Leshem, 'How did the pilots Eytan Stibbe, Roy Ben-Yami and Ami Lustig earn hundreds of millions of dollars in Africa', *The Marker*, 10 April 2008 [Hebrew], available at: www.themarker.com/markets/1.479217

92 Yossi Melman, 'A diamond in the rough', *Haaretz*, 15 July 2011, available at: www.haaretz.com/1.5028876

93 Kimhi, 2010.

94 Soares de Oliveira, 2015: 68–70.

95 On the split from LR, see Moshe Gorali, 'The man who sold helicopters to Angola battles for a place in the consensus', *Calcalist*, 13 February 2018 [Hebrew], available at: www.calcalist.co.il/local/articles/0,7340,L-3731736,00.html; on the fate of Aldeia Nova, see also: Yigal Mosko, 'The pilot that became a king in Africa', *Ulpan Shishi* (TV programme), 3 February 2012 [Hebrew], available at: www.mako.co.il/news-channel2/Friday-Newscast/Article-2da1527c6944531018.htm

96 These are listed on Mitrelli's website, at https://mitrelli.com. See also Croese, 2017.

97 Devin Thorpe, 'Does impact investing work? Vital Capital case study shows it does', *Forbes*, 26 June 2013, available at: www.forbes.com/sites/devinthorpe/2013/06/26/does-impact-investing-work-vital-capital-case-study-shows-it-does/#4de780972ce2

98 This is, at the time of writing, the only academic centre for African Studies in Israel. It offers an undergraduate programme in collaboration with Tel Aviv University and the Open University, which is in turn the only undergraduate programme in African Studies in Israel. See www.africacentre.co.il/about/team-steering-committee-and-donors/

99 Soares de Oliveira, 2015: 74. Soares de Oliveira's book offers a vivid and detailed account of Angola's reconstruction and domestic and international politics since the civil war and is recommended reading for anyone wishing to understand Israel's involvement in the country within the broader Angolan context.

100 Yossi Melman, 'Sources: Israeli businesswoman brokering E. Guinea arms sales', *Haaretz*, 12 November 2008, available at: www.haaretz.com/1.5057421. Ovadia later confirmed mediating missile boats deals in an interview: Chaim Etgar, 'Yardena Ovadia: I am nobody's CEO', *Mako*, 17 February 2013 [Hebrew], available at: www.mako.co.il/tv-people/list-index/category3/Article-a94e3eb0b87ec31006.htm

101 Appel, 2012: 452–60.

102 First, one hospital was established in the coastal city of Bata, in 2007, and later similarly lavish facilities were opened in the capital Malabo, and in Mongomo and Oyala. Mongomo is the president's hometown, and Oyala is the new capital being built from scratch in the middle of the jungle.

103 IMS International Medical Services GE S.A, 'Company profile', available at: www.imsge.com/Content.aspx?id=5

104 'lapaz hospital Guinea equatorial', promotional video, available at: www.youtube.com/watch?v=JkI537wmYYo&t=144s

105 'Madam Ovadia', *Uvda* (TV programme), 8 November 2008 [Hebrew], available at: www.mako.co.il/tv-ilana_dayan/2009-b5585054a908d110/Article-beaf4a1e14b7d11004.htm

106 Human Rights Watch, 2017: 3.

107 See for example, Friederici, 2016: 123–4.

108 Melanie Lidman, 'Rwanda hopes high-tech can replace genocide as its defining feature', *Times of Israel*, 7 April 2017, available at: www.timesofisrael.com/rwanda-hopes-high-tech-can-replace-genocide-as-its-defining-feature/

109 On the relationship between Rwanda's developmental vision and its leadership's political objectives, see: Mann and Berry, 2016.

110 Marathon Group company profile, in a brochure of the Israel Export and International Cooperation Institute, available at: www.export.gov.il/uploadfiles/06_2014/delegationtoafrica.pdf

111 Shterny Isseroff, 'From tragedy to tech: Israelis and Rwandans partner to build the "African Start-Up Nation"', *Jerusalem Post*, 18 March 2017, available at: www.jpost.com/Metro/From-tragedy-to-tech-481720

112 David Smith, 'Rwanda launches circumcision campaign to tackle HIV', *The Guardian*, 27 November 2013, available at: www.theguardian.com/world/2013/nov/27/rwanda-non-surgical-circumcision-hiv

113 David Smith, 'How Africa's fastest solar power project is lighting up Rwanda', *The Guardian*, 23 November 2015, available at: www.theguardian.com/environment/2015/nov/23/how-africas-fastest-solar-power-project-is-lighting-up-rwanda

114 Schimmel, 2011.

115 Similar consultancy services were provided by IEC to other African governments, including Angola. See 'Israel Electric Corporation is operating in Africa', 15 December 2015, available at: www.iec.co.il/spokesman/pages/ruanda.aspx

116 Avi Bar-Eli, 'A senior IEC official led a deal with Rwanda – and moves to work for it', *The Marker*, 13 April 2017, available at: www.themarker.com/dynamo/1.4022165

117 Jean dAmour Ahishakiye, 'RDB gets new chairperson', *KT Press Rwanda*, 9 November 2017, available at: http://ktpress.rw/2017/11/rdb-gets-new-chairperson/

118 This is an argument Soares de Oliveira makes with regard to foreign involvement in Angola more broadly. Soares de Oliveira, 2015.

119 De Waal, 2015.

Chapter 5

1 As discussed in this chapter, Israeli law does not refer to Sudanese and Eritreans as 'refugees' but as 'infiltrators'. Human rights organisations often refer to them as 'asylum-seekers', as they came to Israel in search of protection but were not formally recognised as refugees by the Israeli authorities. Given that Israel nominally adopted a policy of non-removal with regard to these populations, the United Nations High Commissioner for Refugees (UNHCR) considers them to be in a 'refugee-like situation'. I therefore refer to these populations here as 'refugees'. According to the 1951 Convention Relating to the Status of Refugees, the formal recognition of a person as a refugee is a declarative and not a constitutive act, meaning that one can be a refugee even if one is not formally recognised as such by the state in which one is hosted. See 'UNHCR's position on the status of Eritrean and Sudanese nationals defined as "infiltrators" by Israel', UNHCR, November 2017, available at: www.refworld.org/docid/5a5889584.html

2 Hull, 2009: 16–36.

3 Mazrui, 1984. See also Lis et al., 2016.

4   Mark and Horta, 2013.

5   Hull, 2009: 119–41.

6   Carlebach, 1962; Macmillan and Shapiro, 1999; Hull, 2009: 181–3.

7   Malka, 1997.

8   Klorman, 2009.

9   Cohen, 2002.

10   Until today Jews of North African and Middle Eastern origin (known as *Mizrachim*) remain underrepresented in positions of power and subject to racism. There is a considerable body of critical scholarship on their treatment in Israel, inspired by anti-colonial and postcolonial theories. See, for example, Shohat, 2017.

11   Knafo, 2011.

12   Bin-Nun, 2013.

13   Laskier, 1994: 222–37.

14   Bin-Nun, 2009.

15   Laskier, 2000.

16   Oded, 2003.

17   Bruder, 2008: 97.

18   Ilona, 2014. For a more detailed discussion of all of these communities and others, see Bruder, 2008; Miles, 2014; Lis et al., 2016. Igbo identification with Israel and the Jewish people was also reinforced by comparison between the war in Biafra and the Nazi holocaust. These comparisons were perpetuated by Igbo activists and Jewish diaspora groups and repeatedly complicated Israel's relations with Abuja. During the civil war in Nigeria in the late 1960s, Israel sold arms to the Nigerian government but also supported Biafrans (Levey, 2012: 91–112.). Igbo activists continue to associate their struggle with Israel and Jewish history today, and the separatist group Indigenous People of Biafra (IPOB) maintains a 'liaison office' in Israel, in southern Tel Aviv.

19   Parfitt (2013) discusses the case of the Lemba in detail. More recently Igbo activists made similar attempts whose results remain disputed. See Sam Kestenbaum, '"Irresponsible" Jewish DNA test sparks backlash in Nigeria', *Forward*, 20 August 2017, available at: https://forward.com/news/world/380398/ irresponsible-jewish-dna-test-sparks-backlash-in-nigeria/

20   Parfitt, 2013: 133. See also Bruder, 2008.

21   This fact does not seem to be well-known among followers of this faith in Africa, who often seem to hope that their religious devotion will ultimately also allow them to dwell in the Holy Land, regardless of their ethnic origin.

22   As in the case of several other African communities that claim Jewish origins, Nuer identification with Israel has also been fuelled by the sense that the Nuer have been dispersed, persecuted and marginalised. It should be noted that the theory that the Nuer are descendants of the People of Israel seems to be popular among Christian Nuer in general, far beyond the Congregation of

Yahweh. I draw here on interviews with the leaders of the Congregation of Yahweh community in Gambella, Ethiopia, as well as interviews with members and leaders of other Nuer messianic congregations and evangelical churches, conducted between November 2018 and June 2019.

23 On the Beth Yeshourun community, see Devir, 2016.
24 On Igbo attempts to be recognised as Jewish by Israel, see Lis, 2012.
25 See the description on Kulanu's website at: https://kulanu.org/about/
26 Kaplan, 1993. See also, Kaplan, 1992; Pankhurst, 1992; Quirin, 1992.
27 Summerfield, 2003: 129.
28 Erlich, 2013: 197–9.
29 Parfitt, 1985: 45–63; Karadawi, 1991.
30 Shimron, 2011: 206–33.
31 Parfitt, 1985: 102–7.
32 Ben-Ezer, 2002.
33 Spector, 2005: 70–72.
34 Human Rights Watch, 1991.
35 Spector, 2005.
36 Both names were imposed on this group by outsiders. I use the term 'Falash Mura' because this is how they came to be known and referred to in official and public discourse in Israel.
37 Seeman, 2010.
38 Shokeid, 2015.
39 On the relationship between Beta Israel and Christians in Ethiopia, see Salamon, 1999.
40 For a recent account, see also Engdau-Vanda, 2019.
41 The committee for the eradication of racism against Israelis of Ethiopian origin, Final Report, July 2016 [Hebrew], available at: www.justice.gov.il/Pubilcations/Articles/Documents/ReportEradicateRacism.pdf
42 Bartram, 1998.
43 Given the clandestine nature of their migration into Israel, there are no official numbers of migrant workers in Israel. Sabar, 2008: 16–18.
44 Sabar, 2008: 53.
45 Forced Migration and Refugee Studies Program, 2006.
46 UNHCR figures quoted in Human Rights Watch, 2008: 11.
47 Kibreab, 2013.
48 Van Reisen et al., 2012, 2014.
49 Human Rights Watch, 2014b.
50 Population and Immigration Authority, 'Statistics of Foreigners in Israel: 2013 summary', January 2014 [Hebrew], available at: www.gov.il/BlobFolder/generalpage/foreign_workers_stats/he/סוכיס%202013.pdf
51 Cf. Carrier, 2016: 24.
52 Sabar, 2010.

53 From the early 2000s the Israeli government had the authority to make the final decision with regard to asylum applications assessed by the UN. Nonetheless, few applications were processed through this mechanism, and even fewer were granted status.

54 Kagan, 2015: 443–4.

55 Harel, 2015.

56 For a critique of the labelling of the violence in Darfur as genocide, see de Waal, 2007.

57 '52% of Israeli Jews agree: African migrants are "a cancer"', *Times of Israel*, 7 June 2012, available at: www.timesofisrael.com/most-israeli-jews-agree-africans-are-a-cancer/

58 Ronen Medzini, 'Netanyahu against the refugees: threatening Israelis' jobs', *Ynet*, 28 November 2010 [Hebrew], available at: www.ynetnews.com/articles/0,7340,L-3990776,00.html

59 Barak Ravid and Dana Weiler-Polak, 'Netanyahu approved the building of a fence to block infiltration of migrant workers at the border with Egypt', *Haaretz*, 11 January 2010 [Hebrew], available at: www.haaretz.co.il/1.1183763

60 Human Rights Watch, 2008: 31–60.

61 Ibid.

62 During 2008–9, more than 500 Africans were reportedly returned from Israel to Egypt under 'Hot Returns'. See US Department of State, '2010 Human Rights Report: Israel and the occupied territories', 8 April 2011, p. 17, available at: www.state.gov/documents/organization/160463.pdf

63 See for example, the testimonies at: '*Non refoulement* – story untold', *Social TV*, 16 October 2017, available at: https://tv.social.org.il/en/non-refoulement-story-untold

64 Population and Immigration Authority, 'Statistics of Foreigners in Israel: concluding edition for 2018',' January 2019 [Hebrew], available at: www.gov.il/BlobFolder/generalpage/foreign_workers_stats/he/foreigners_summary_2018.pdf

65 Morris, 1993.

66 Hotline for Refugees and Migrants, 2017: 8–11.

67 Quoted in: African Refugee Development Center and Hotline for Migrant Workers, 2013: 6.

68 Southern Sudan became an autonomous region within Sudan following the 2005 Comprehensive Peace Agreement (CPA) that ended Sudan's Second Civil War. Independence was gained in July 2011, after a transition period of six years and following a referendum.

69 Gerver argued that the organisations' 'failure to adequately inform the refugees of their prospects looks like exploitation rather than negligence'. See Gerver, 2014.

70 Email from Haim Koren to author, April 2019.

71 Tal Shalev, 'Netanyahu appointed Hagai Hadas to take care of the infiltrators issue', *Walla!*, 30 August 2012 [Hebrew], available at: https://news.walla.co.il/item/2562836

72 'Israel: detained asylum seekers pressured to leave', Human Rights Watch, 13 March 2013, available at: www.hrw.org/news/2013/03/13/israel-detained-asylum-seekers-pressured-leave

73 Hotline for Refugees and Migrants and ASSAF, 2015: 10.

74 The story was first published by Dafna Lichtman on her Facebook profile and consequently covered by various newspapers. See, for example, Ilan lior, 'Asylum seeker finds himself rerouted from safety back to Sudan', *Haaretz*, 7 May 2014, available at: www.haaretz.com/.premium-asylum-seeker-rerouted-to-where-he-fled-1.5247439

75 'Sudanese security capture key member of Israeli spy network: report', *Sudan Tribune*, 22 March 2014, available at: www.sudantribune.com/spip.php?article50390

76 Human Rights Watch, 2014a.

77 The Supreme Court, sitting as High Court of Administrative Affairs, Tsegeta vs. Minister of the Interior and others (Administrative Appeal 8101/15), ruling, August 28, 2017 [Hebrew], available at: https://supremedecisions.court.gov.il/Home/Download?path=HebrewVerdicts\15\010\081\c29&fileName=15081010.C29&type=4. Quoted in paragraph 3 in the ruling of Chief Justice Naor.

78 Interview with a former Ministry of Foreign Affairs official, October 2018, Tel Aviv.

79 Itamar Eichner, 'Arms for infiltrators', *Yedioth Ahronoth*, 9 July 2013 [Hebrew].

80 Anshel Pfeffer and Ilan Lior, 'Gag order lifted Uganda will take in thousands of Israel's African migrants', *Haaretz*, 29 August 2013, available at: www.haaretz.com/.premium-uganda-to-take-in-israel-s-migrants-1.5326957

81 'Olmert and Livni approved: the Israeli government will offer African states payment by head for 10,000 Sudanese refugees', *Globes*, 12 June 2008 [Hebrew], available at: www.globes.co.il/news/article.aspx?did=1000350888

82 Interview with a Sudanese man, Kampala, May 2015. For more details, see International Refugee Rights Initiative, 2015: 13.

83 International Refugee Rights Initiative, 2015. On attempts to persuade Sudanese to travel back to Sudan from Uganda, see also Andrew Green, 'Inside Israel's secret program to get rid of African refugees', *Foreign Policy*, 27 June 2017, available at: https://foreignpolicy.com/2017/06/27/inside-israels-secret-program-to-get-rid-of-african_refugees_uganda_rwanda/

84 For example, Amir Tibon, 'Rwanda's president to "Haaretz": we do not need assistance from the West with human rights', *Haaretz*, 1 April 2017 [Hebrew], available at: www.haaretz.co.il/news/world/africa/.premium-1.3974010

85 Phone conversations (in English) with a senior official in the Directorate of Citizenship and Immigration Control office at Entebbe International Airport,

January 2018. For more details, see Hotline for Refugees and Migrants and ASSAF, 2018. Israeli journalist Lee Yaron later followed up on the issue and was given a similar reply by an official in the Ugandan president's office. See Lee Yaron, 'Uganda says Israel gives deported asylum seekers fake visas', *Haaretz*, 13 April 2018, available at: www.haaretz.com/israel-news/.premium-uganda-says-israel-gives-deported-asylum-seekers-fake-visas-1.5994836

86 Ilan lior, 'Israel to pay Rwanda $5,000 for every deported asylum seeker it takes in', *Haaretz*, 20 November 2017, available at: www.haaretz.com/israel-news/israel-to-pay-rwanda-5-000-for-every-asylum-seeker-deported-there-1.5466805

87 Government of Rwanda on Twitter, 22 January 2018, available at: https://twitter.com/RwandaGov/status/955532915940700162

88 'UNHCR and Israel sign agreement to find solutions for Eritreans and Sudanese', UNHCR press release, 2 April 2018, available at: www.unhcr.org/uk/news/press/2018/4/5ac261bd4/unhcr-israel-sign-agreement-find-solutions-eritreans-sudanese.html

89 Facebook post from 2 April 2018 [Hebrew], available at: www.facebook.com/Netanyahu/posts/10155499430642076

90 Population and Immigration Authority, 'Statistics of Foreigners in Israel: concluding edition for 2018', January 2019 [Hebrew], available at: www.gov.il/BlobFolder/generalpage/foreign_workers_stats/he/foreigners_summary_2018.pdf

91 Shimron, 2011: 206.

92 On 'operations' as a style of governance, see also Fontein, 2009; Alexander, 2013.

93 Bar-Tuvia, 2018.

94 On the European approach, see, for example, Oette and Babiker, 2017.

95 Lyons, 2016. This is also based on informal conversations and observations in Addis Ababa, where there is a small community of Israeli Ethiopians.

96 On the listening habits of young Israeli Ethiopians, see also Ratner, 2015.

97 Dozens of South Sudanese children who grew up in Israel are now studying together in boarding schools in Uganda under a private initiative run by Israeli activists who sought to help their friends after they were deported. It is worth noting that in addition to the difficult humanitarian conditions deportees faced after their removal from Israel, they were also often seen by their fellow South Sudanese back at home as criminals who were deported because they all misbehaved in Israel. This narrative was partly fuelled by the Israeli government's own discourse about these populations.

98 Tigre is the language spoken in Eritrea.

Conclusion

1 Sheffer and Barak, 2013: 46–75.

2 Oded, 2011.

3   Tsing, 2005.
4   For example, see Oded, 2011: 396.
5   'PM Netanyahu addresses the United Nations General Assembly', 22
    September 2016, available at: https://mfa.gov.il/MFA/PressRoom/2016/
    Pages/PM-Netanyahu-addresses-the-United-Nations-General-Assembly-22-
    September-2016.aspx
6   Interview with Gideon Behar, Head of Africa Bureau at the Ministry of Foreign
    Affairs, Jerusalem, May 2019.

REFERENCES

Abadi, Jacob (2017), 'Tunisia and Israel: relations under stress', *Middle Eastern Studies*, 53 (4), 507–32.

Abulof, Uriel (2009), '"Small peoples": the existential uncertainty of ethnonational communities', *International Studies Quarterly*, 53 (1), 227–48.

Adekson, J. 'Bayo (1976), 'Army in a multi-ethnic society: the case of Nkrumah's Ghana, 1957–1966', *Armed Forces & Society*, 2, 251–2.

African Refugee Development Center, and Hotline for Migrant Workers (2013), *'Do Not Send Us So We Can Become Refugees Again': From 'nationals of a hostile state' to deportees: South Sudanese in Israel* (Tel Aviv: ARDC and HMW).

Akinsanya, Adeoye (1976), 'The Afro-Arab alliance: dream or reality', *African Affairs*, 75 (301), 511–29.

al-Kurwy, Mahmood and Faysal Shalal Abbas (2011), 'Mauritanian–Israeli relations: from normalization to freeze to suspension', *Contemporary Arab Affairs*, 4 (1), 30–50.

Alexander, Jocelyn (2013), 'Militarisation and state institutions: "professionals" and "soldiers" inside the Zimbabwe prison service', *Journal of Southern African Studies*, 39 (4), 807–28.

Alpher, Yossi (2015), *Periphery: Israel's Search for Middle East Allies* (Lanham, MD: Rowman & Littlefield).

Amnesty International (2015), *Braving Bullets: Excessive Force in Policing Demonstrations in Burundi* (London: Amnesty International).

Amnesty International (2017a), *Cameroon's Secret Torture Chambers: Human Rights Violations and War Crimes in the Fight Against Boko Haram* (London: Amnesty International).

Amnesty International (2017b), *A Turn for the Worse: Violence and Human Rights Violations in Anglophone Cameroon* (London: Amnesty International).

Appel, Hannah (2012), 'Walls and white elephants: oil extraction, responsibility, and infrastructural violence in Equatorial Guinea', *Ethnography*, 13 (4), 439–65.

Ariel, Yaakov (2013), *An Unusual Relationship: Evangelical Christians and Jews* (New York: New York University Press).

Avriel, Ehud (1976), 'Israel's beginnings in Africa', in Curtis, Michael and Susan Aurelia Gitelson (eds), *Israel in the Third World* (New Brunswick, NJ: Transaction Books), 69–74.

Aynor, Hanan S. (1969), *Notes from Africa* (New York : Frederick A. Praeger).

Bar-Tuvia, Shani (2018), 'Australian and Israeli agreements for the permanent transfer of refugees: stretching further the (il)legality and (im)morality of Western externalization policies', *International Journal of Refugee Law*, 30 (3), 474–511.

Bar-Yosef, Eitan (2014), *A Villa in the Jungle: Africa in Israeli Culture* (Jerusalem: The Van Leer Jerusalem Institute) [Hebrew].

Barak, Oren and Chanan Cohen (2006), *The Future of Israel's Ministry of Foreign Affairs* (Jerusalem: Leonard Davis Institute for International Relations, The Hebrew University of Jerusalem) [Hebrew].

Barak, Oren (2017), *State Expansion and Conflict: In and Between Israel/Palestine and Lebanon* (Cambridge: Cambridge University Press).

Bartram, David V. (1998), 'Foreign workers in Israel: history and theory', *International Migration Review*, 32 (2), 303–25.

Baumann, Roger (2016), 'Political engagement meets the prosperity gospel: African American Christian Zionism and Black church politics', *Sociology of Religion: A Quarterly Review*, 77 (4), 359–85.

Bayart, Jean-François, Stephen Ellis and Béatrice Hibou (1999), *The Criminalization of the State in Africa* (Oxford; Bloomington: The International African Institute; James Currey).

Bayart, Jean-François (2009), *The State in Africa: The Politics of the Belly* (2nd edn., Cambridge: Polity Press).

Beit-Hallahmi, Benjamin (1987), *The Israeli Connection: Who Israel Arms and Why* (New York: Pantheon Books).

Belman Inbal, Aliza and Shachar Zahavi (2009), *The Rise and Fall of Israel's Bilateral Aid Budget 1958–2008* (Tel Aviv: The Harold Hartog School of Government and Policy, Tel Aviv University).

Ben-David, Yehuda (1967), *A Seed of White Corn* (Tel Aviv: Ministry of Defense) [Hebrew].

Ben-Ezer, Gadi (2002), *The Ethiopian Jewish Exodus: Narratives of the Journey* (London: Routledge).

Bergman, Ronen (2008), *The Secret War with Iran: The 30-Year Clandestine Struggle against the World's Most Dangerous Terrorist Power* (New York: Free Press).

Bergman, Ronen (2018), *Rise and Kill First: The Secret History of Israel's Targeted Assassinations* (New York: Random House).

Bin-Nun, Yigal (2009), 'The Israeli press campaign against Morocco after the sinking of the "Pisces" in January 1961', *Kesher*, 38, 55–65 [Hebrew].

Bin-Nun, Yigal (2013), 'The disputes regarding the Jewish emigration from Morocco 1956–1961', in Cooperman, Bernard Dov and Tsevi Zohar (eds), *Jews and Muslims in the Islamic World* (Bethesda: University Press of Maryland), 51-99.

Brand, Laurie A. (1988), *Palestinians in the Arab World: Institution Building and the Search for State* (New York: Columbia University Press).

Brennan, James R. (2010), 'Radio Cairo and the decolonization of East Africa, 1953–1964', in Lee, Christopher J. (ed.), *Making a World after Empire: The Bandung Moment and Its Political Afterlives* (Athens: Ohio University Press), 173–95.

Bruder, Edith (2008), *The Black Jews of Africa: History, Religion, Identity* (Oxford: Oxford University Press).

Bunce, Peter L. (1984), 'The growth of South Africa's defence industry and its Israeli connection', *The RUSI Journal*, 129 (2), 42–9.

Carlebach, Julius (1962), *The Jews of Nairobi, 1903–1962* (Nairobi: The Nairobi Hebrew Congregation).

Carrier, Neil (2016), *Little Mogadishu: Eastleigh, Nairobi's Global Somali Hub* (London: Hurst).

Chazan, Naomi (1983), 'The fallacies of pragmatism: Israeli foreign policy towards South Africa', *African Affairs*, 82 (327), 169–99.

Chazan, Naomi (2006), 'Israel and Africa: challenges for a new era', in The Africa Institute of the American Jewish Committee and Harold Hartog School of Government and Policy (eds), *Israel and Africa: Assessing the Past, Envisioning the Future* (Tel Aviv: Tel Aviv University), 1–15.

Clapham, Christopher (1996), *Africa and the International System: The Politics of State Survival* (Cambridge: Cambridge University Press).

Cohen, Yinon (2002), 'From haven to heaven: changes in immigration patterns to Israel', *Israeli Sociology*, 1, 39–60 [Hebrew].

Crawford, Young and Thomas Turner (1985), *The Rise and Decline of the Zairian State* (Madison: The University of Wisconsin Press).

Croese, Sylvia (2017), 'State-led housing delivery as an instrument of developmental patrimonialism: the case of post-war Angola', *African Affairs*, 116 (462), 80–100.

Curtis, Michael and Susan Aurelia Gitelson (eds) (1976), *Israel in the Third World* (New Brunswick: Transaction Books).

De Waal, Alex (2007), 'Reflections on the difficulties of defining Darfur's crisis as genocide', *Harvard Human Rights Journal*, 20, 25–33.

De Waal, Alex (2015), *The Real Politics of the Horn of Africa: Money, War and the Business of Power* (Cambridge: Polity Press).

Decalo, Samuel (1998), *Israel and Africa: Forty Years, 1956–1996* (Gainesville: Florida Academic Press).

Del Sarto, Raffaella A. (2017), *Israel under Siege: The Politics of Insecurity and the Rise of the Israeli Neo-Revisionist Right* (Washington, DC: Georgetown University Press).

Devir, Nathan P. (2016), 'The "Internet Jews" of Cameroon: inside the digital matrix of globalized Judaism', in Lis, Daniel, William F. S. Miles and Tudor Parfitt (eds), *In the Shadow of Moses: New Jewish Movements in Africa and the Diaspora* (Los Angeles: Tsehai Publishers), 113–30.

Domegni, Maxime (2017), 'Togo: the president's friends handle the phosphates', *The Plunder Route to Panama: How African Oligarchs Steal from Their Countries* (Amsterdam: The African Investigative Publishing Collective, Africa Uncensored and ZAM), 4–7.

Eger, Akiva (1976), 'Histadrut: pioneer and pilot plant for Israel's international cooperation with the Third World', in Curtis, Michael and Susan Aurelia Gitelson (eds), *Israel in the Third World* (New Brunswick, NJ: Transaction Books), 75–80.

Ellis, Stephen (2006), *The Mask of Anarchy: The Destruction of Liberia and the Religious Dimension of an African Civil War* (New York: New York University Press).

Engdau-Vanda, Shelly (2019), *Resilience in Immigration: The Story of Ethiopian Jews in Israel from a Perspective of 30 Years* (Tel Aviv: Resling).

Erlich, Haggai (1983), *The Struggle over Eritrea, 1962–1978: War and Revolution in the Horn of Africa* (Stanford, CA: Hoover Institution Press).

Erlich, Haggai (1994), *Ethiopia and the Middle East* (London: Lynne Rienner Publishers).

Erlich, Haggai (2002), *The Cross and the River: Ethiopia, Egypt, and the Nile* (London: Lynne Rienner).

Erlich, Haggai (2013), *Alliance and Alienation: Ethiopia and Israel in the Days of Haile Selassie* (Tel Aviv: Moshe Dayan Center for Middle Eastern and African Studies, Tel Aviv University) [Hebrew].

Fisher, Jonathan and David M. Anderson (2015), 'Authoritarianism and the securitization of development in Africa', *International Affairs*, 91 (1), 131–51.

Fontein, Joost (2009), 'Anticipating the tsunami: rumours, planning and the arbitrary state in Zimbabwe', *Africa*, 79 (3), 369–98.

Forced Migration and Refugee Studies Program (2006), *A Tragedy of Failures and False Expectations: Report on the Events Surrounding the Three-Month Sit-In and Forced Removal of Sudanese Refugees in Cairo, September–December 2005* (Cairo: The American University in Cairo).

Friederici, Nicolas (2016), 'Innovation hubs in Africa: assemblers of technology entrepreneurs' (DPhil diss., University of Oxford).

Gerver, Mollie (2014), 'The role of non-governmental organizations in the repatriation of refugees', *Philosophy & Public Policy Quarterly*, 32 (1), 2–13.

Gidron, Yotam (2018), '"One people, one struggle": Anya-Nya propaganda and the Israeli Mossad in Southern Sudan, 1969–1971', *Journal of Eastern African Studies*, 12 (3), 428–53.

Global Witness (2002), *'All the Presidents' Men': The Devastating Story of Oil and Banking in Angola's Privatised War* (London: Global Witness).

Guzansky, Yoel (2014), 'Israel's periphery doctrine 2.0: the Mediterranean plus', *Mediterranean Politics*, 19 (1), 99–116.

Hakim, Najib J. and Richard P. Stevens (1983), 'Zaire and Israel: an American connection', *Journal of Palestine Studies*, 12 (3), 41–53.

Halper, Jeff (2015), *War against the People: Israel, the Palestinians and Global Pacification* (London: Pluto Press).

Harel, Sharon (2015), 'Israel's asylum system: the process of transferring the treatment of asylum applications from UNHCR to the Israeli state', in Kritzman-Amir, Tally (ed.), *Where Levinsky Meets Asmara: Social and Legal Aspects of Israeli Asylum Policy* (Jerusalem: The Van Leer Jerusalem Institute), 43–87 [Hebrew].

Heimann, Gadi (2016), 'A case of diplomatic symbiosis: France, Israel and the former French colonies in Africa, 1958–62', *Journal of Contemporary History*, 51 (1), 145–64.

Herbst, Jeffrey Ira (2000), *States and Power in Africa: Comparative Lessons in Authority and Control* (Princeton, NJ: Princeton University Press).

Heymont, Irving (1967), 'The Israeli nahal program', *The Middle East Journal*, 21 (3), 314–24.

Holtom, Paul and Irene Pavesi (2017), *Trade Update 2017: Out of the Shadows* (Geneva: Small Arms Survey).

Hotline for Refugees and Migrants (2017), *'Ye Shall Have One Law': Administrative Detention of Asylum Seekers Implicated in Criminal Activity* (Tel Aviv: HRM).

Hotline for Refugees and Migrants and ASSAF (2015), *Where There Is no Free Will: Israel's 'Voluntary Return' Procedure for Asylum-Seekers* (Tel Aviv: HRM and ASSAF).

Hotline for Refugees and Migrants and ASSAF (2018), *Departures of Asylum Seekers from Israel to Rwanda and Uganda: Main Findings* (Unpublished report) [Hebrew].

Hull, Richard (2009), *Jews and Judaism in African History* (Princeton, NJ: Markus Wiener Publishers).

Human Rights Watch (1991), *Evil Days: 30 Years of War and Famine in Ethiopia* (New York: Human Rights Watch).

Human Rights Watch (2008), *Sinai Perils: Risks to Migrants, Refugees, and Asylum Seekers in Egypt and Israel* (New York: Human Rights Watch).

Human Rights Watch (2009), *Open Secret: Illegal Detention and Torture by the Joint Anti-Terrorism Task Force in Uganda* (New York: Human Rights Watch).

Human Rights Watch (2014a), *Make Their Lives Miserable: Israel's Coercion of Eritrean and Sudanese Asylum Seekers to Leave Israel* (New York: Human Rights Watch).

Human Rights Watch (2014b), *'I Wanted to Lie Down and Die': Trafficking and Torture of Eritreans in Sudan and Egypt* (New York: Human Rights Watch).

Human Rights Watch (2016), *Enabling a Dictator: The United States and Chad's Hissène Habré 1982–1990* (New York: Human Rights Watch).

Human Rights Watch (2017), *'Manna From Heaven'? How Health and Education Pay the Price for Self-Dealing in Equatorial Guinea* (New York: Human Rights Watch).

Human Rights Watch (2018), 'These Killings Can Be Stopped': Government and Separatist Groups Abuses in Cameroon's Anglophone Regions (New York: Human Rights Watch).

Ilona, Remy (2014), The Igbos and Israel: An Inter-cultural Study of the Largest Jewish Diaspora (New York: Epicenter Stories).

International Crisis Group (2010a), Cameroon: The Dangers of a Fracturing Regime (Dakar: International Crisis Group).

International Crisis Group (2010b), Tipping Point? Palestinians and the Search for a New Strategy (Ramallah: International Crisis Group).

International Crisis Group (2011), Curb Your Enthusiasm: Israel and Palestine after the UN (Ramallah: International Crisis Group).

International Crisis Group (2012), The Kenyan Military Intervention in Somalia (Nairobi: International Crisis Group).

International Refugee Rights Initiative (2015), 'I Was Left with Nothing': 'Voluntary' Departures of Asylum Seekers from Israel to Rwanda and Uganda (Kampala: IRRI).

Ismael, Tareq Y. (1971), The UAR in Africa: Egypt's Policy under Nasser (Evanston, IL: Northwestern University Press).

Jacob, Abel (1971), 'Israel's military aid to Africa, 1960–66', The Journal of Modern African Studies, 9 (2), 165–87.

Jones, Clive and Tore T. Petersen (2013), Israel's Clandestine Diplomacies (London: Hurst).

Jones, Will, Ricardo Soares de Oliveira and Harry Verhoeven (2013), Africa's Illiberal State-Builders (Oxford: Refugee Studies Centre).

Kagan, Michael (2015), 'Refugees & Israel's shifting concept of the "enemy national"', in Kritzman-Amir, Tally (ed.), Where Levinsky Meets Asmara: Social and Legal Aspects of Israeli Asylum Policy (Jerusalem: The Van Leer Jerusalem Institute), 427–55 [Hebrew].

Kalu, Ogbu (2008), African Pentecostalism: An Introduction (Oxford: Oxford University Press).

Kaplan, Steven (1992), The Beta Israel (Falasha) in Ethiopia: From Earliest Times to the Twentieth Century (New York: New York University Press).

Kaplan, Steven (1993), 'The invention of Ethiopian Jews: three models', Cahiers d'études africaines, 132, 645–58.

Karadawi, Ahmed (1991), 'The smuggling of the Ethiopian Falasha to Israel through Sudan', African Affairs, 90 (358), 23–49.

Kibreab, Gaim (2013), 'The national service/Warsai-Yikealo Development Campaign and forced migration in post-independence Eritrea', Journal of Eastern African Studies, 7 (4), 630–49.

Kieh, George (1989), 'An analysis of Israeli repenetration of Liberia', Liberian Studies Journal, 14 (2), 117–29.

Kimhi, Ayal (2010), 'Revitalising and modernising smallholder agriculture: the Aldeia Nova project in Angola', Development Southern Africa, 27 (3), 381–95.

Kitchen, J. Coleman (1983), 'Zaire and Israel', *CSIS Africa Notes*, 1–8.

Klieman, Aaron S. (1985), *Israel's Global Reach: Arms Sales as Diplomacy* (Washington, DC: Pergamon-Brassey's International Defense Publishers).

Klorman, Bat-Zion Eraqi (2009), 'Yemen, Aden and Ethiopia: Jewish emigration and Italian colonialism', *Journal of the Royal Asiatic Society*, 19 (4), 415–26.

Knafo, Michel-Meir (2011), *Mossad and the Secret Jewish Network in Morocco: The 'Misggeret' and its Secret Operations (1955–1964)* (Dalia: Maarekhet).

Kochan, Ran (1973), 'An African peace mission in the Middle East: the one-man initiative of President Senghor', *African Affairs*, 72 (287), 186–96.

Kreinin, Mordechai (1964), *Israel and Africa: A Study in Technical Cooperation* (New York: Praeger).

Laskier, Michael M. (1994), *North African Jewry in the 20th Century* (New York: New York University Press).

Laskier, Michael M. (2000), 'Israel and the Maghreb at the height of the Arab–Israeli conflict: 1950s–1970s', *Middle East*, 4 (2), 96–108.

Legum, Colin (1965), *Pan-Africanism: A Short Political Guide* (revised edn.) (New York: Praeger).

Lemarchand, René (2002), 'Disconnecting the threads: Rwanda and the Holocaust reconsidered', *Journal of Genocide Research*, 4, 499–518.

Levey, Zach (2003), 'The rise and decline of a special relationship: Israel and Ghana, 1957–1966', *African Studies Review*, 46 (1), 155–77.

Levey, Zach (2004), 'Israel's strategy in Africa, 1961–67', *International Journal of Middle East Studies*, 36 (1), 71–87.

Levey, Zach (2012), *Israel in Africa: 1956–1976* (Dordrecht: Martinus Nijhoff Dordrecht).

Levin, Ayala (2015), 'Exporting Zionism: architectural modernism in Israeli–African technical cooperation, 1958-1973' (PhD diss., Columbia University).

Liba, Moshe (2013), *In the Foreign Service* (Jerusalem: Hamaatik) [Hebrew].

Likhovski, Assaf (2009), 'Argonauts of the Eastern Mediterranean: legal transplants and signaling', *Theoretical Inquiries in Law*, 10 (2), 619–51.

Lis, Daniel (2012), 'Israeli foreign policy towards the Igbo', in Bruder, Edith and Tudor Parfitt (eds), *African Zion: Studies in Black Judaism* (Newcastle upon Tyne: Cambridge Scholars Publishing), 87–16.

Lis, Daniel, William F. S. Miles and Tudor Parfitt (2016), *In the Shadow of Moses: New Jewish Movements in Africa and the Diaspora* (Los Angeles: Tsehai Publishers).

Lyons, Len (2016), 'Building bridges: Ethiopian Israelis take a second look at Ethiopia', in Lis, Daniel, William F. S. Miles and Tudor Parfitt (eds), *In the Shadow of Moses: New Jewish Movements in Africa and the Diaspora* (Los Angeles: Tsehai Publishers), 201–20.

Macmillan, Hugh and Frank Shapiro (1999), *Zion in Africa: The Jews of Zambia* (London: I. B. Tauris).

Malka, Eli S. (1997), *Jacob's Children in the Land of the Mahdi: Jews of the Sudan* (Syracuse, NY: Syracuse University Press).

Mann, Laura and Marie Berry (2016), 'Understanding the political motivations that shape Rwanda's emergent developmental state', *New Political Economy*, 21 (1), 119–44.

Maoz, Zeev (2009), *Defending the Holy Land: A Critical Analysis of Israel's Security and Foreign Policy* (Ann Arbor: University of Michigan Press).

Mark, Peter and José da Silva Horta (2013), *The Forgotten Diaspora: Jewish Communities in West Africa and the Making of the Atlantic World* (Cambridge: Cambridge University Press).

Markakis, John (2011), *Ethiopia: The Last Two Frontiers* (Woodbridge: James Currey).

Marzano, Arturo (2013), 'The loneliness of Israel: the Jewish state's status in international relations', *The International Spectator*, 48 (2), 96–113.

Mazrui, Ali A. (1977), *Africa's International Relations: The Diplomacy of Dependency and Change* (Boulder, CO: Westview Press).

Mazrui, Ali A. (1984), 'The Semitic impact on Black Africa: Arab and Jewish cultural influences', *Issue: A Journal of Opinion*, 13, 3–8.

Mboya, Tom (1963), *Freedom and After* (London: Andre Deutsch).

Mearsheimer, John J. and Stephen M. Walt (2008), *The Israel Lobby and U.S. Foreign Policy* (London: Penguin).

Medzini, Meron (2017), *Golda Meir: A Political Biography* (Berlin: De Gruyter Oldenbourg).

Meir, Golda (1975), *My Life* (London: Weidenfeld and Nicolson).

Michael, Woldemariam (2018), *Insurgent Fragmentation in the Horn of Africa: Rebellion and Its Discontents* (Cambridge: Cambridge University Press).

Migdal, Joel S. (2001), *Through the Lens of Israel: Explorations in State and Society* (Albany: State University of New York Press).

Miles, William F. S. (2000), 'Hamites and Hebrews: problems in "Judaizing" the Rwandan genocide', *Journal of Genocide Research*, 2 (1), 107–15.

Miles, William F. S. (2014), *Afro-Jewish Encounters: From Timbuktu to the Indian Ocean and Beyond* (Princeton, NJ: Markus Wiener Publishers).

Mooreville, Anat (2016), 'Eyeing Africa: the politics of Israeli ocular expertise and international aid, 1959–1973 , *Jewish Social Studies*, 21 (3), 31–71.

Morris, Benny (1993), *Israel's Border Wars, 1949–1956: Arab Infiltration, Israeli Retaliation, and the Countdown to the Suez War* (Oxford: Clarendon Press).

Morris, Benny (1994), *1948 and After: Israel and the Palestinians* (Oxford: Oxford University Press).

Müller, Retief (2017), 'Constructing separatism in South Africa's racially charged religiosity: 20th century Afrikaner discourses on African initiated Christianity', *Religion Compass*, 11 (1–2), e12231.

Naim, Asher (2005), 'Perspectives: Jomo Kenyatta and Israel', *Jewish Political Studies Review*, 17 (3–4), 75–80.

Neuberger, Benyamin (2009), *Israel's Relations with the Third World (1948–2008)* (Tel Aviv: S. Daniel Abraham Center for International and Regional Studies, Tel Aviv University).

Nyerere, Julius K. (1968), *Freedom and Socialism: A Selection from Writings and Speeches 1965–1967* (Dar es Salaam: Oxford University Press).

Obadare, Ebenezer (2018), *Pentecostal Republic: Religion and the Struggle for State Power in Nigeria* (London: Zed Books).

Oded, Arye (1990), *Africa, the PLO and Israel* (Jerusalem: Leonard Davis Institute, The Hebrew University of Jerusalem).

Oded, Arye (2002), *Uganda and Israel: The History of a Complex Relationship* (Jerusalem: The Israel–Africa Friendship Association) [Hebrew].

Oded, Arye (2003), *Judaism in Africa: The Abayudaya of Uganda* (Jerusalem: The Israel–Africa Friendship Association) [Hebrew].

Oded, Arye (2009), 'Fifty years of MASHAV activity', *Jewish Political Studies Review*, 21 (3–4), 87–107.

Oded, Arye (2011), *Africa and Israel: A Unique Case of Radical Changes in Israel's Foreign Relations* (Jerusalem: Magnes Press) [Hebrew].

OECD (2017), *Development Co-operation Report 2017: Data for Development* (Paris: OECD Publishing).

Oette, Lutz and Mohamed Abdelsalam Babiker (2017), 'Migration control á la Khartoum: EU external engagement and human rights protection in the Horn of Africa', *Refugee Survey Quarterly*, 36 (4), 64–89.

Ojo, Olusola (1988), *Africa and Israel: Relations in Perspective* (Boulder, CO: Westview).

Pankhurst, Richard (1992), 'The Falashas, or Judaic Ethiopians, in their Christian Ethiopian setting', *African Affairs*, 91 (365), 567–82.

Parfitt, Tudor (1985), *Operation Moses: The Untold Story of the Secret Exodus of the Falasha Jews from Ethiopia* (London: Weidenfeld and Nicolson).

Parfitt, Tudor (2013), *Black Jews in Africa and the Americas* (Cambridge, MA: Harvard University Press).

Parsi, Trita (2008), *Treacherous Alliance: The Secret Dealings of Israel, Iran, and the United States* (New Haven, CT: Yale University Press).

Peters, Joel (1992), *Israel and Africa: The Problematic Friendship* (London: British Academic Press).

Pfeffer, Anshel (2018), *Bibi: The Turbulent Life and Times of Benjamin Netanyahu* (London: Hurst).

Poggo, Scopas S. (2009), *The First Sudanese Civil War: Africans, Arabs, and Israelis in the Southern Sudan, 1955–1972* (New York: Palgrave Macmillan).

Polakow-Suransky, Sasha (2011), *The Unspoken Alliance: Israel's Secret Relationship with Apartheid South Africa* (New York: Vintage Books).

Privacy International (2016), 'Stakeholder Report Universal Periodic 26th Session: The Right to Privacy in Uganda', available at: https://cipesa.org/?wpfb_dl=217

Quirin, James (1992), *The Evolution of the Ethiopian Jews: A History of the Beta Israel (Falasha) to 1920* (Philadelphia: University of Pennsylvania Press).

Ratner, David (2015), *Black Sounds: Black Music and Identity among Young Israeli Ethiopians* (Tel Aviv: Resling) [Hebrew].

Raviv, Daniel and Yossi Melman (1991), *Every Spy a Prince: The Complete History of Israel's Intelligence Community* (Boston: Houghton Mifflin Company).

Reich, Bernard (1964), 'Israel's policy in Africa', *Middle East Journal*, 18 (1), 14–26.

Reiser, Stewart (1989), *The Israeli Arms Industry: Foreign Policy, Arms Transfers, and Military Doctrine of a Small State* (New York: Holmes & Meier).

Ronen, Yehudit (2013), 'Israel's clandestine diplomacy with Sudan: two rounds of extraordinary collaboration', *Israel's Clandestine Diplomacies* (London: Hurst), 153–68.

Ruppin, Rafael (1986), *Assignment – Tanganyika* (Tel Aviv: Ministry of Defense).

Sabar, Galia (2008), *'We're Not Here to Stay': African Migrant Workers in Israel and Back in Africa* (Tel Aviv: The Haim Rubin Tel Aviv University Press) [Hebrew].

Sabar, Galia (2010), 'Israel and the "Holy Land": the religio-political discourse of rights among African migrant labourers and African asylum seekers, 1990–2008', *African Diaspora*, 3 (1), 42–75.

Salamon, Hagar (1999), *The Hyena People: Ethiopian Jews in Christian Ethiopia* (Berkeley: University of California Press).

Schimmel, Noam (2011), 'The Agahozo-Shalom youth village: community development for Rwandan orphans and its impact on orphaned genocide survivors', *Progress in Development Studies*, 11 (3), 243–50.

Schler, Lynn (2018), 'Dilemmas of postcolonial diplomacy: Zambia, Kenneth Kaunda and the Middle East crisis, 1964–1973', *Journal of African History*, 59 (1), 97–119.

Schler, Lynn and Yonatan N. Gez (2018), 'Development shadows: the afterlife of collapsed development projects in the Zambian copperbelt', *Africa Spectrum*, 53 (3), 3–31.

Seeman, Don (2010), *One People, One Blood: Ethiopian-Israelis and the Return to Judaism* (New Brunswick, NJ: Rutgers University Press).

Segev, Tom (2007), *1967: Israel, the War, and the Year that Transformed the Middle East* (New York: Metropolitan Books).

Sharon, Ariel and David Chanoff (1989), *Warrior: The Autobiography of Ariel Sharon* (New York: Simon and Schuster).

Sheffer, Gabriel and Oren Barak (2013), *Israel's Security Networks: A Theoretical and Comparative Perspective* (Cambridge: Cambridge University Press).

Shimron, Gad (2011), *The Mossad and Its Myth* (Jerusalem: Keter Books) [Hebrew].

Shlaim, Avi (2014a), *The Iron Wall: Israel and the Arab World* (London: Penguin Books).

Shlaim, Avi (2014b), 'Israel, Palestine, and the Arab uprising', in Gerges, Fawaz A. (ed.), *The New Middle East: Protest and Revolution in the Arab World* (New York: Cambridge University Press), 380–401.

Shohat, Ella (2017), *On the Arab Jew, Palestine and Other Displacements* (London: Pluto Press).

Shokeid, Moshe (2015), 'Newcomers at the Israeli national table: transforming urban landscapes and the texture of citizenship', *City & Society*, 27 (2), 208–30.

Silverburg, Sanford Robert (1968), 'Israeli military and paramilitary assistance to Sub-Saharan Africa: a harbinger for the role of military in developing states' (Master's diss., The American University).

Soares de Oliveira, Ricardo (2015), *Magnificent and Beggar Land: Angola since the Civil War* (London: Hurst).

Solomon, Hussein and Gerrie Swart (2005), 'Libya's foreign policy in flux', *African Affairs*, 104 (416), 469–92.

Spector, Stephen (2005), *Operation Solomon: The Daring Rescue of the Ethiopian Jews* (Oxford: Oxford University Press).

Spector, Stephen (2009), *Evangelicals and Israel: The Story of American Christian Zionism* (New York: Oxford University Press).

Steinberg, Jonny and Monique Marks (2013), 'The labyrinth of Jewish security arrangements in Johannesburg: thinking through a paradox about security', *British Journal of Criminology*, 54 (2), 244–59.

Summerfield, Daniel (2003), *From Falashas to Ethiopian Jews: The External Influences for Change, c. 1860–1960* (London: RoutledgeCurzon).

Tangri, Roger and Andrew M. Mwenda (2003), 'Military corruption and Ugandan politics since the late 1990s', *Review of African Political Economy*, 30 (98), 539–52.

Teshome, Wagaw (1991), 'The international political ramifications of Falasha emigration', *Journal of Modern African Studies*, 29 (4), 557–81.

Thompson, W. Scott (1969), *Ghana's Foreign Policy, 1957–1966: Diplomacy Ideology, and the New State* (Princeton, NJ: Princeton University Press).

Thrall, Nathan (2017), *The Only Language They Understand: Forcing Compromise in Israel and Palestine* (New York: Metropolitan Books).

Tieku, Thomas Kwasi (2004), 'Explaining the clash and accommodation of interests of major actors in the creation of the African Union', *African Affairs*, 103 (411), 249–67.

Touval, Saadia (1982), *The Peace Brokers: Mediators in the Arab–Israeli Conflict, 1948–1979* (Princeton, NJ: Princeton University Press).

Tsing, Anna Lowenhaupt (2005), *Friction: An Ethnography of Global Connection* (Princeton, NJ: Princeton University Press).

UN Security Council (2001), Report of the Panel of Experts on the Illegal Exploitation of Natural Resources and Other Forms of Wealth of DR Congo (S/2001/357).

UN Security Council (2008), Letter dated 7 November 2008 from the Chairman of the Security Council Committee established pursuant to Resolution 1591 (2005) addressed to the President of the Security Council (S/2008/647).

UN Security Council (2016), Letter dated 22 January 2016 from the Panel of Experts on South Sudan established pursuant to Security Council Resolution 2206 (2015) addressed to the President of the Security Council (S/2016/70).

Van de Walle, Nicolas (2001), *African Economies and the Politics of Permanent Crisis, 1979–1999* (Cambridge: Cambridge University Press).

Van de Walle, Nicolas (2016), 'Conclusion: democracy fatigue and the ghost of modernization theory', in Hagmann, Tobias and Filip Reyntjens (eds), *Aid and Authoritarianism in Africa: Development without Democracy* (London: Zed Books), 161–78.

Van Reisen, Mirjam, Meron Estefanos and Conny Rijken (2012), *Human Trafficking in the Sinai: Refugees between Life and Death* (Oisterwijk: Wolf Legal Publishers).

Van Reisen, Mirjam, Meron Estefanos and Conny Rijken (2014), *The Human Trafficking Cycle: Sinai and Beyond* (Oisterwijk: Wolf Legal Publishers).

Verhoeven, Harry (2018), 'The Gulf and the Horn: changing geographies of security interdependence and competing visions of regional order', *Civil Wars*, 20 (3), 1–25.

Warburg, Gabriel R. (1992), 'The Sudan and Israel: an episode in bilateral relations', *Middle Eastern Studies*, 28 (2), 385–96.

Watts, Clint, Jacob Shapiro and Vahid Brown (2007), *Al-Qa'ida's (Mis) Adventures in the Horn of Africa* (West Point, NY: Harmony Project).

Wezeman, Pieter D. (2009), *Arms Flows to the Conflict in Chad* (Stockholm: SIPRI).

Wezeman, Siemon T. (2011), *Israeli Arms Transfers to Sub-Saharan Africa* (Stockholm: SIPRI).

Yacobi, Haim (2010), 'The moral geopolitics of exported spatial development: revisiting Israeli involvement in Africa', *Geopolitics*, 15 (3), 441–61.

Yacobi, Haim (2015), *This Is no Africa: Boundaries, Territory, Identity* (Jerusalem: The Van Leer Jerusalem Institute) [Hebrew].

Zevi, Tullia (1972), 'Interview with President Senghor of Senegal', *Africa Report*, 17 (7), 11–13.

INDEX

Note: Page numbers in italic indicate figures or tables; page numbers followed by *n* indicate an endnote with relevant number.

mediation efforts, 40; non-member observer status for Palestine, 68–9, *69*; Resolution 64/10 (war crimes allegations), 61, *61*; Resolution on Jerusalem, *96*; voting on Israel-related resolutions, 95; Zionism resolutions, 43, 53

United Nations Security Council: Resolution 242 (Israel), 38; resolutions on Israeli settlements, 82, 103, 114; South African arms embargo, 45

United States: Black Lives Matter, 130; human rights concerns, 89; Israel as intermediary for Africa, 48, 52, 94; and Israeli-Ethiopian cooperation, 46; Jerusalem embassy, 96, *96*; Jewish diaspora, 83; *Kulanu* ('all of us'), 124; and Middle East, 65–6; pro-Israel groups and patronage, 94–9, 101; sanctions against South Sudanese, 93; Yom Kippur war, 42; and Zaire, 49

USAID, Power Africa, 112–13

Vital Capital Fund, 110
Vorster, John, 45

war crimes allegations, 61, *61*
war on terror, 7, 59, 63–4, 88, 89
Weiss, Ron, 113
West Africa: intelligence agencies, 62; Pentecostal churches, 100

Ya'ari, Sivan, 83–4
Yacobi, Haim, 33
Yemen, civil war, 65
Yishai, Eli, 137, 142
Yom Kippur war (1973), 5, 41–2, 43–4
youth programmes, 24, 26, 28–9, 113

Zaire, 41, 48–50
Zakhor Jews, 122
Zambia, 119
ZCC (Zion Christian Church), 107–8
Zimbabwe, 119, 121
Zimbabwe African National Union (ZANU), 32
Zion Christian Church (ZCC), 107–8
Zionism, 23–4, 33, 41, 43, 53, 118
Ziv, Israel, 92–3